Bob Brooks

Yarmouth County

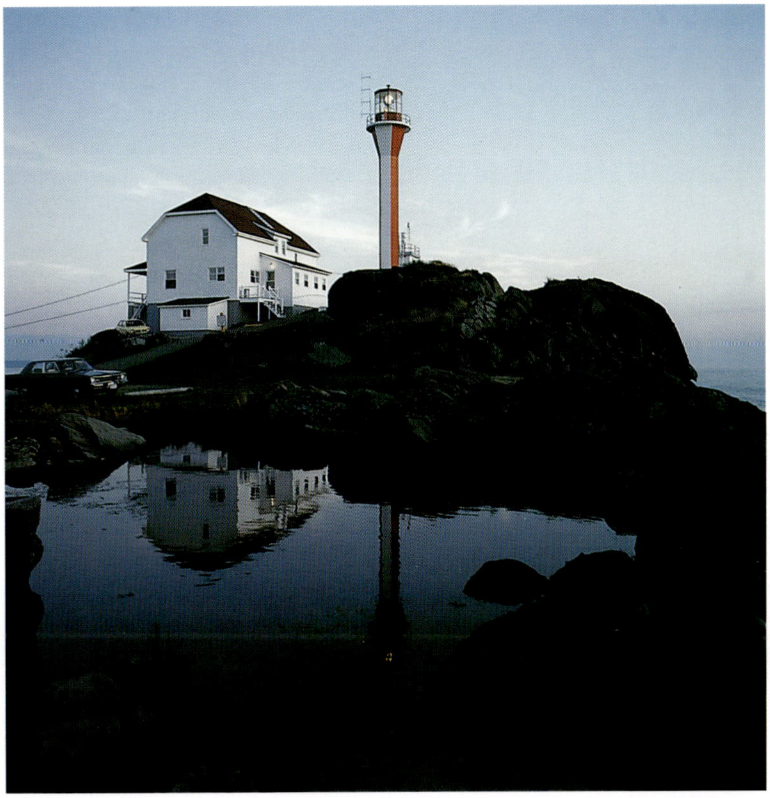

NIMBUS
PUBLISHING

Dedication

To Marion, Beth, Maureen, Randy, and to the people of Yarmouth County.

Nimbus Publishing Limited
PO Box 9301, Station A
Halifax, NS B3K 5N5
(902)455-4286

Design: Semaphor Design Co.
Cameras used: Hassablad system (lenses from 50mm–250mm)
Nikon system F-3 and F-4 (lenses from 18mm–600mm)
Film used: Kodak Ektachrome, Kodachrome

Front Cover: Yarmouth Lighthouse; the drawbridge at Sandford; catch of the day; lupins heralding summer.

Back Cover: North America's fastest car ferry, The Cat, breaks through the fog on the catamaran's exciting first appearance in Yarmouth Harbour, May, 1998.

Title page: Yarmouth Lighthouse at sundown is reflected in a tiny pond at Cape Forchu.

Printed and bound by Everbest Printing, Hong Kong

Canadian Cataloguing in Publication Data
Brooks, Bob.
Yarmouth County
ISBN 1-55109-264-6
1. Yarmouth (N.S. : County) — Pictorial works. I. Title
FC2345.Y3B75 1998 971.16'31 C98-950096-9
F1039.Y3B76 1998

Nimbus Publishing acknowledges the financial support of the Canada Council and the Department of Canadian Heritage.

Acknowledgements

While it is impossible to name everyone, and I apologize for that, I would like to express my sincere gratitude to the following for their assistance and support in making this book: Captain Victor LeBlanc, his crew and the folks on Harris Island, Captain Bob Rogers and crew; in the Pubnicos, Adeline and Arnold Muise, Father Gusto Oulet, the Pubnico Fire Department, the West Pubnico Acadian Festival Committee, Pubnico Historical Society, D'Arcy d'Eon, Jean d'Entremont, the more than four hundred d'Entremonts who sat for my "d'Entremont family portrait," Laurent d'Entremont, Acadian Museum, David Pothier and NSPC for providing the NSPC truck which allowed me my "aerial angle."

Also many thanks to George Cottreau, Hugh Cook, Randy Ritcey, Lloyd Churchill, Cliffy Gavel, Betty Cann, Michael and Frances Morris, Della Muise, Louise Vincelli, Garth Dalton and his reenactment regiment, *The Yarmouth Vanguard, Le Courrier,* Cyrille LeBlanc, the Wedgeport Tuna Museum, Andy Wallace, the Yarmouth Sea Fest Committee, Frank Anderson and Western Nova Scotia Exhibition staff, Barry MacGregor and Camp Wapomeo staff, Anne d'Entremont, Gerald Smith and staff, Brian Thompson, Billy Newell, Keith Condon and staff at Tri-Star Industries, Laura Bradley, Yarmouth County Museum and Archives staff and volunteers, staff at the Firefighters' Museum of Nova Scotia, Yarmouth County Tourist Association, John Clulee, Blaine Anthony and staff.

At Nimbus, thanks to publisher Dorothy Blythe who gave unlimited freedom and enthusiasm for this special project, Dan Soucoup, Helen Matheson and Paula Sarson.

My appreciation to Steven Slipp of Semaphor Design for his patience and creativity, Richard Jarry, François Pauzé, and KODAK CANADA, Inc. for their support. I am also indebted to Fred Hatfield for his inspiring introduction as well as his suggestions and enthusiasm for this book and for Yarmouth County.

Of course, I could not have done this book without the constant advice and support from my wife Marion, who continually makes sure the "circus" remains within three rings, and my daughter. Beth assisted me at every level from mapping out where to shoot—accompanying me on 90 per cent of the journey—to long hours over a light table selecting images while boosting my morale with her confidence, humour, and determination.

This book is about Yarmouth County. It could not have been accomplished without help and support of the people there. Countless individuals contributed directly and indirectly to the making of this book. From those who posed as one of my "victims," to those writing in suggestions, I thank you all.

Preface

THE CLEAREST CONNECTION I've ever had on a cell phone was when I phoned my daughter in Ottawa from Harris Island, one of the chain of Tusket Islands off the South-West coast of Yarmouth. I was there for three days trying to capture on film the wild and intense November opening of the lobster season, and I called Beth to say I had forgotten just how hard fishermen work and the extreme weather conditions they face. It was the end of a very long day of fishing, a day which began at three in the morning and included photographing Capt. Victor LeBlanc and his crew at sea, twelve miles off the island.

I tried to describe to Beth the eerie contrast between the peacefulness of the scene when we left the dock before dawn—the twinkling lights along wharves showing a dusting of snow—and the hectic flurry of activity along those same wharves during the day.

The Harris Island shoot was my "launching pad" for this book, a project I considered a privileged opportunity. Over the many years that I have been a professional photographer, I have shot Yarmouth from every angle, including hanging from a plane and burrowing in the mud at low tide, but it was usually on

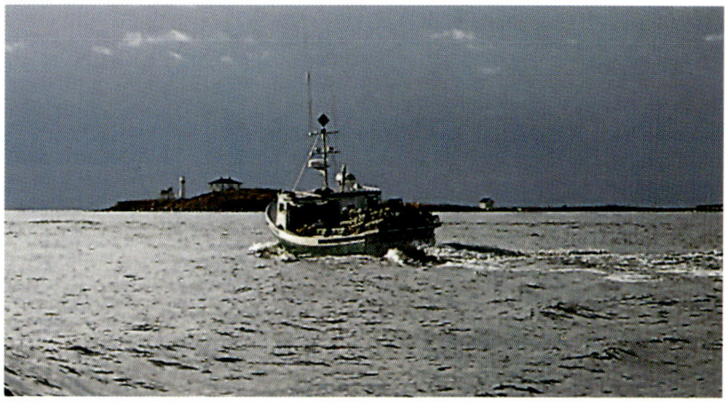

A heavily laden lobster boat passes by Pease Lighthouse as it hurries out from Wedgeport to Harris Island on opening day of lobster season.

assignments with specific topics. This book allowed me to revisit some people and places of the county on a much grander scale.

I decided that in order to do justice to the whole county as it is today, I would do new shooting for this book. So, with a few exceptions, the images you see have been taken within the last two years.

Yarmouth County covers a lot of territory and tackling it was a logistical challenge. Beth and I planned the shooting like a military operation, dividing the county into zones.

As we travelled around, it struck me again and again that no matter how often I photographed certain scenes I never tire of the beauty and variety of Yarmouth County. Sandford with its tiny drawbridge always attracts me, and mosquitoes swarming my lens will never drive me from attempting to capture

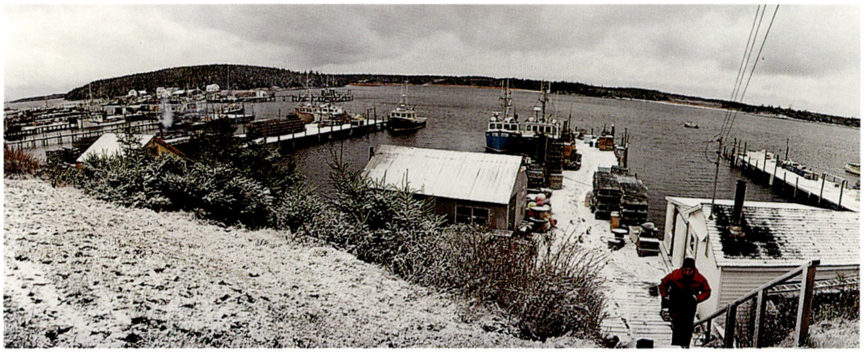

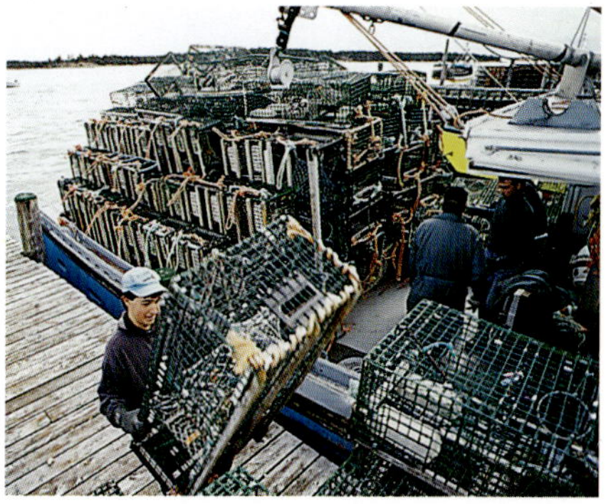

Above left: Evening falls on snow-dusted Harris Island a seasonal fishing community used by fishermen for 150 years as a safe winter shelter. Above right: Metal lobster traps are loaded onto a boat for a run to the fishing grounds.

that illusive sunset shot of the Yarmouth Light. Pretty pictures are important, but for a photojournalist it is also the story and the people behind the images which attract, and for that reason Yarmouth County continues to provide a rich treasure trove of photographic material.

It is amazing what delights you can discover, like the charming woman we met at The Tittle, or the humour of quilter Louise Vincelli's lifelike mannequins. There is the unusual multi-million dollar export industry stemming from the back-breaking work of blood worm diggers so often seen on the salt-water flats at low tide; the tranquil existence of the monks at Nova Nada; the ties that bind the Cooks Dairy family together—all are examples of the many interesting stories we encountered.

Of course, my daughter says she could write a few stories about what took place behind the photography for this book and the amount of time and effort we spent capturing certain pictures. Wiggling worms, strafing seagulls, dodging traffic, climbing ladders, rising on forklifts and laying in mud were all part of the experience.

For me, one of the most unique experiences was the shoot of the d'Entremont family portrait in West Pubnico, a photograph I had always wanted to attempt. What I nicknamed "the d'Entremont Ben-Hur production," was shot following Mass during the colourful Acadian Festival from the bucket of a power truck high above the group of more than five hundred descendants of Pubnico founder Philippe d'Entremont. The incredible cooperation I received in order to make that dream photograph a reality was a good example of the friendliness and sincere generosity I have always found in Yarmouth County.

This book only scratched the surface of the photographic joys offered in Yarmouth County, but my recent shooting confirmed what I have always known. Whether making their living from the ocean or land, the inhabitants of Yarmouth County demonstrate a resourcefulness, spirit and pride that I greatly admire. It is the people of Yarmouth County who make it what it is. I hope that I have portrayed the county and its people well and done them justice, for I have felt awfully proud to do so.

Bob Brooks, MPA

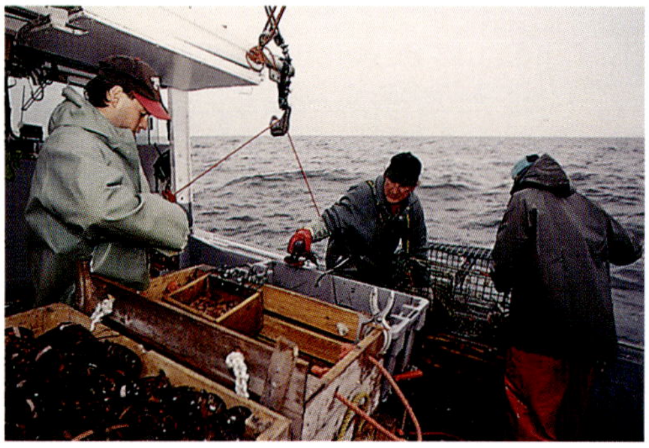

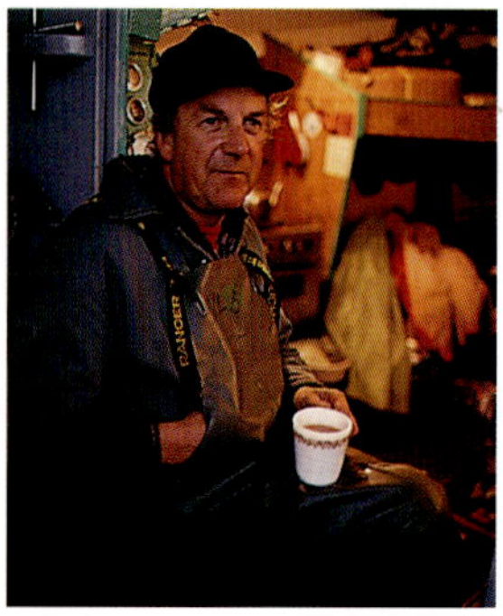

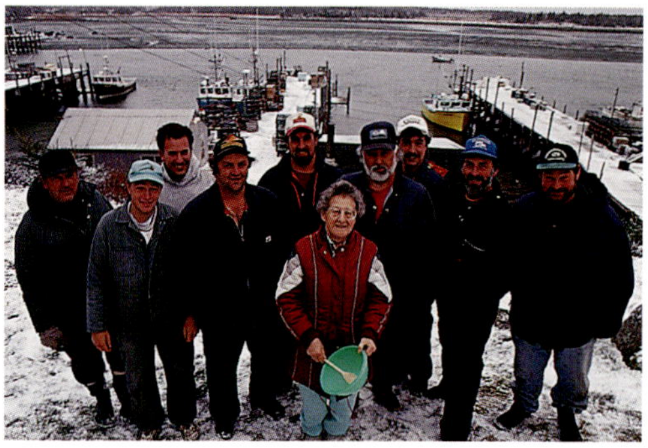

Above, left: Split-second timing is essential in setting the 300 traps Captain LeBlanc and his crew haul each day.

Above, centre: Captain Victor LeBlanc pauses in the wheelhouse of his boat, The Provider, *for a "mug up."*

Above, right: Seasonal residents of Harris Island pose with their cook for a picture. Left to right: Captain Victor LeBlanc, Jonathan Manser, Floyd LeBlanc, Ted Saulnier, Derrick Jacquard, Alice Jacquard, Captain Patrick Jacquard, Devin Boudreau, Roland Boudreau, Captain Raymond Boudreau.

Introduction

When those who leave Yarmouth reminisce about the things they miss most, they inevitably get around to mentioning the sounds of the sea.

The sounds of Yarmouth tell a great deal about the triangular-shaped county nestled at the southwestern tip of Nova Scotia between Digby and Shelburne which is home to twenty-seven thousand people. There is the crash of waves against the rocky coast, the lapping of waves against the shoreline from the wake of fishing vessels heading out to sea. Ships from Yarmouth ports have been going to sea for centuries. There is the sound of children running along the sandy beach at Port Maitland and the haunting sound of the Yarmouth Lighthouse's foghorn blaring every ten seconds—as it did one year for five hundred straight hours—warning approaching vessels to be cautious as they approach Yarmouth Harbour.

Although you can't photograph a sound, you can photograph the places where familiar sounds have long been part of everyday life. And that's what photographer Bob Brooks has done in this book about Yarmouth County, a place he has long called home. There is lots to see in Yarmouth County, and Bob Brooks and his camera have seen it all.

Brooks has depicted tiny treasures like the world's smallest drawbridge in Sandford where the cries of seagulls fill the air. His camera has focused on larger things as well, like the brightly decorated ox teams at the Western Nova Scotia Exhibition in the town of Yarmouth whose owners have invariably named them Bright and Lion.

There are the tree-lined town streets forming umbrellas of overhead leaves. The rainbow of ground level colours created by lupins heralding summer in places like South Ohio.

Magnificent architecture so amazes visitors that the locals often watch from the windows of old captains' houses as tourists walk by craning their necks to admire things like porthole windows, braided wooden trim, elaborate gingerbread accents that run up the corners of old houses, and of course, the fancy rooftop cupolas that face the harbour.

One of the county's largest villages, Wedgeport, is jammed with fishing vessels and abounds in tales of the days when anglers from around the world converged on this area in search of the giant bluefin tuna. Wedgeport's links to the past are preserved with the recent opening of a tuna sport fishing museum just yards away from the bustling village's famous tuna wharf.

Brightly painted fishing boats with names like *Seawife* and *Wishful Thinking* fill every county harbour with colourful reminders of life on the water along with well-worn fishing nets gracefully clinging to wharfs.

Brooks also captures on film Yarmouth's people and its cultures. Some county villages like the Pubnicos are primarily famous for their Acadian heritage. Skim through the telephone directory for West Pubnico and you'll see column after column of D'Entremonts and D'Eons, two families that have played vital roles in the development of the Acadian presence in this end of Nova Scotia. Acadian heritage is celebrated each summer season in Yarmouth County during festivals in Ste.-Anne-du-Ruisseau, West Pubnico, and Wedgeport where the age old traditions are kept alive.

Yarmouth is proud of its history. Museums abound in several county centres highlighting the area's famous shipping era. In West Pubnico there are plans to develop an historic Acadian Village.

Yarmouth folk are friendly people. This is a place where, every year, tourists write letters to the local newspaper thanking strangers who came to their aid when their car broke down, or when they were lost on one of the county roads. People here care about each other as well as those who pass through.

All along the coast, fishermen have worked for generations to make the region one of the most lucrative fishing areas in North America.

In recent years, the lobster catch in District 34, which includes Yarmouth County, has brought in over $100 million annually to the local economy. The sign at the foot of Forest Street in Yarmouth welcoming the thousands of tourists who each year come through the International Ferry Terminal tells them they've arrived at the lobster capital of Nova Scotia. In an age of hyperbole this is no idle boast. It's a classical understatement that only one sign mentions the county's outstanding accomplishment.

As you travel from village to village along the coast, you come to realize that while fishing is the backbone of the community, Yarmouth County has also hosted other significant industries.

At the head of Yarmouth harbour stands the longest building in the county, the former site of one of Canada's major cotton mills. The relatively remote East Kemptville region was home to North America's only tin mine. Minard's Liniment, the famous ointment for aches and pains, became a Canada-wide household staple from a manufacturing plant in downtown Yarmouth.

Indeed, Yarmouth is used to making its mark on the world stage. There was Izaak Walton Killam who, as an enterprising youngster, was a familiar face along Yarmouth's main business streets hawking newspapers.

He grew up to become a world figure in numerous business endeavours including the pulp and paper and securities fields. When he died in the 1950s he was Canada's wealthiest man. So many schools, libraries, and hospitals have been named after Killam that a new generation of Nova Scotians know his name. In fact, taxes on the Killam fortune were part of the funding used to establish the Canada Council, which today fuels the nation's arts community.

General George Kenney, who became General Douglas MacArthur's right-hand man in World War II, was also born in Yarmouth County. As was John Patch, credited with inventing the screw propeller and thereby revolutionizing shipping. Patch died a pauper, never having gained the financial benefits such an important invention should have brought because of a patent snafu.

Not only has Yarmouth produced more than its share of leaders in the world of commerce, the military and industry, those in the arts community have also gone on to make their mark. People like Connie Tomlinson, daughter of a Yarmouth clergyman, who went to Paris and became a dancer with the Foilles Berger. She wrote the 1955 book *Les Girls* which, after considerable critical acclaim in *Atlantic Monthly* and *New Yorker* magazines, became the basis for a movie staring Mitzi Gaynor and Gene Kelley.

Hilda Kay Grant, a Yarmouth County native, became a prolific author under the pseudonym Jan Hilliard and received Canada's Stephen Leacock Memorial Medal for her book *The Saltbox*.

One of Yarmouth's most famous artists, Maud Lewis, was born in South Ohio, Yarmouth County, and lived with her family on Hawthorn Street one block away from Yarmouth's famous waterfront.

Today's Yarmouth is home to many artists who have "come from away," but live here by choice, inspired by the beauty and serenity of this seaside environment.

The entrepreneurial spirit has always thrived here. Hundred-year-old family firms are not unusual and, although some of the important industries like the cotton mill and the tin mine have disappeared, others have taken their place.

This is a place where you are never far from the past. Many families trace their Yarmouth roots back to the 1700s, often with many having connections to the New England Pilgrims and the *Mayflower.*

Ships from foreign lands that pull into the docks are greeted by people with strong ties to the sea. Yarmouth's history owes much to the sea and to the mariners who plied the water between Nova Scotia and ports all over the world carrying a rich variety of cargo.

As the seaport that links New England with Canada, thousands of tourists every year disembark at the International Ferry Terminal. Long known as the Gateway Town, tourism played an important role in the area's history. A monument in front of the Yarmouth tourist information centre celebrates the fact that a native son, Loran Baker, was the father of this province's tourism industry.

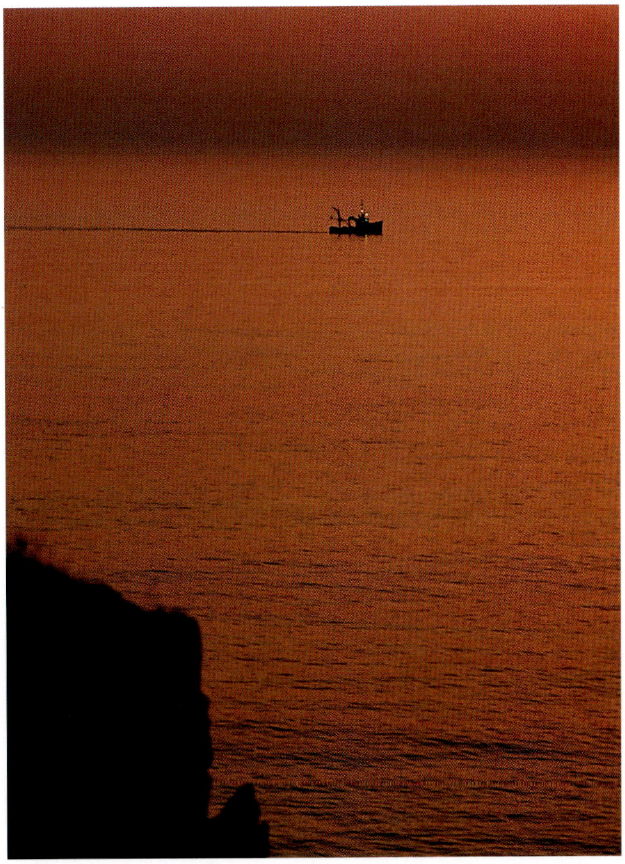

A fishing dragger heads out to sea at sunset.

Although today there are fewer wharfs along Yarmouth's shoreline, the town's waterfront area has enjoyed a resurgence thanks to a redevelopment programme. It has regained some of its former glory as an integral, vibrant part of the community, which has been greatly enhanced by Yarmouth's new high-speed catamaran ferry, *The Cat,* which began its service between Yarmouth and Bar Harbour in spring 1998.

Although it's true that Yarmouth has its share of Maritime precipitation, those of us who live here don't mind our grey days as much as some visitors may. Even on the foggiest of days, the familiar sounds are all around us—seagulls, foghorns, crashing waves —and we know that they help make Yarmouth what it is.

Once you become familiar with Yarmouth County you will remember it forever. Leave, and your memories, especially those of the sounds, will call you back.

As Bob Brooks' wonderful photography clearly illustrates, you will find no better place.

FRED HATFIELD
Yarmouth, N.S.
January, 1998

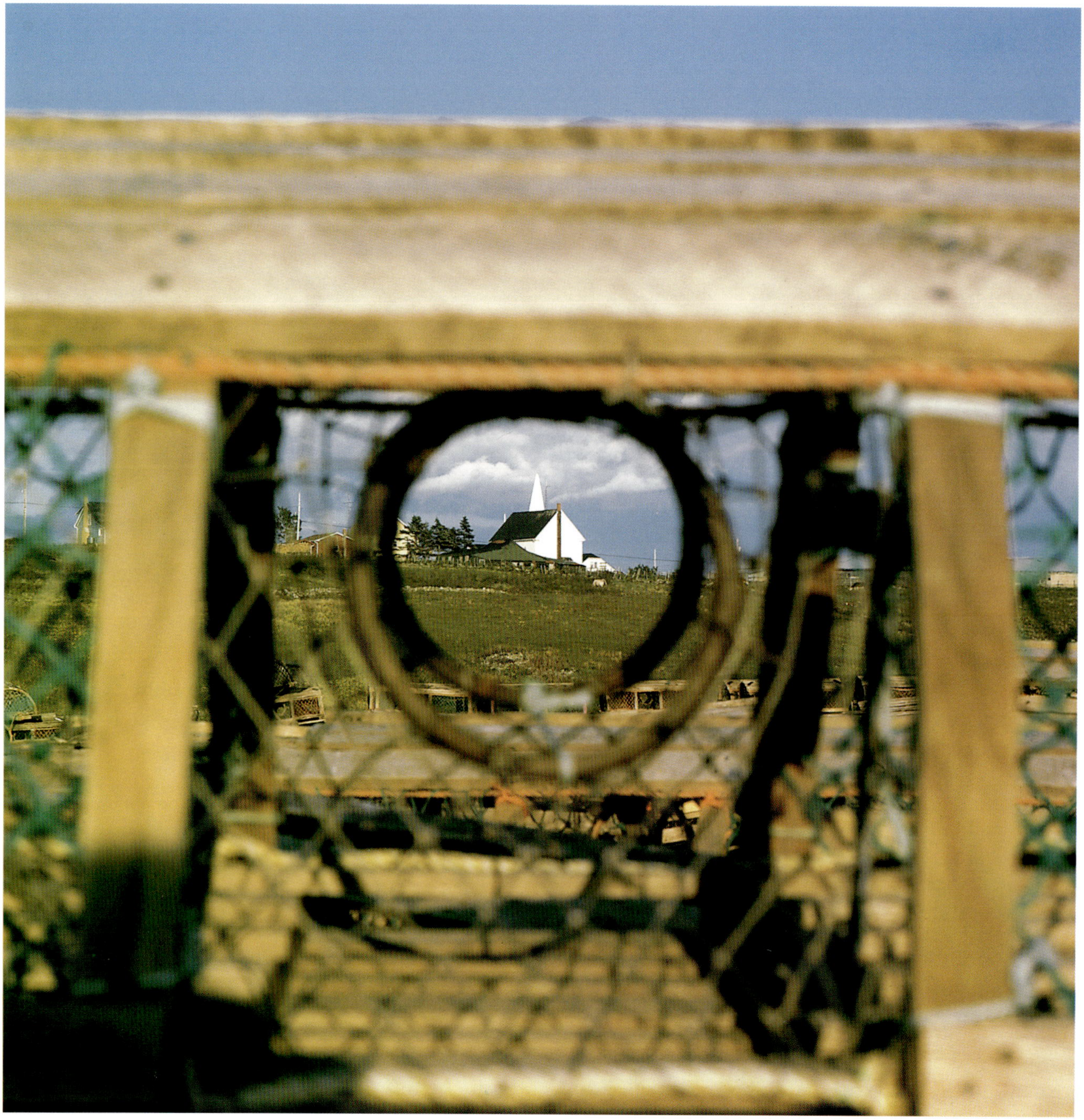

A lobster trap creates a Maritime frame for a gleaming church at Sandford.

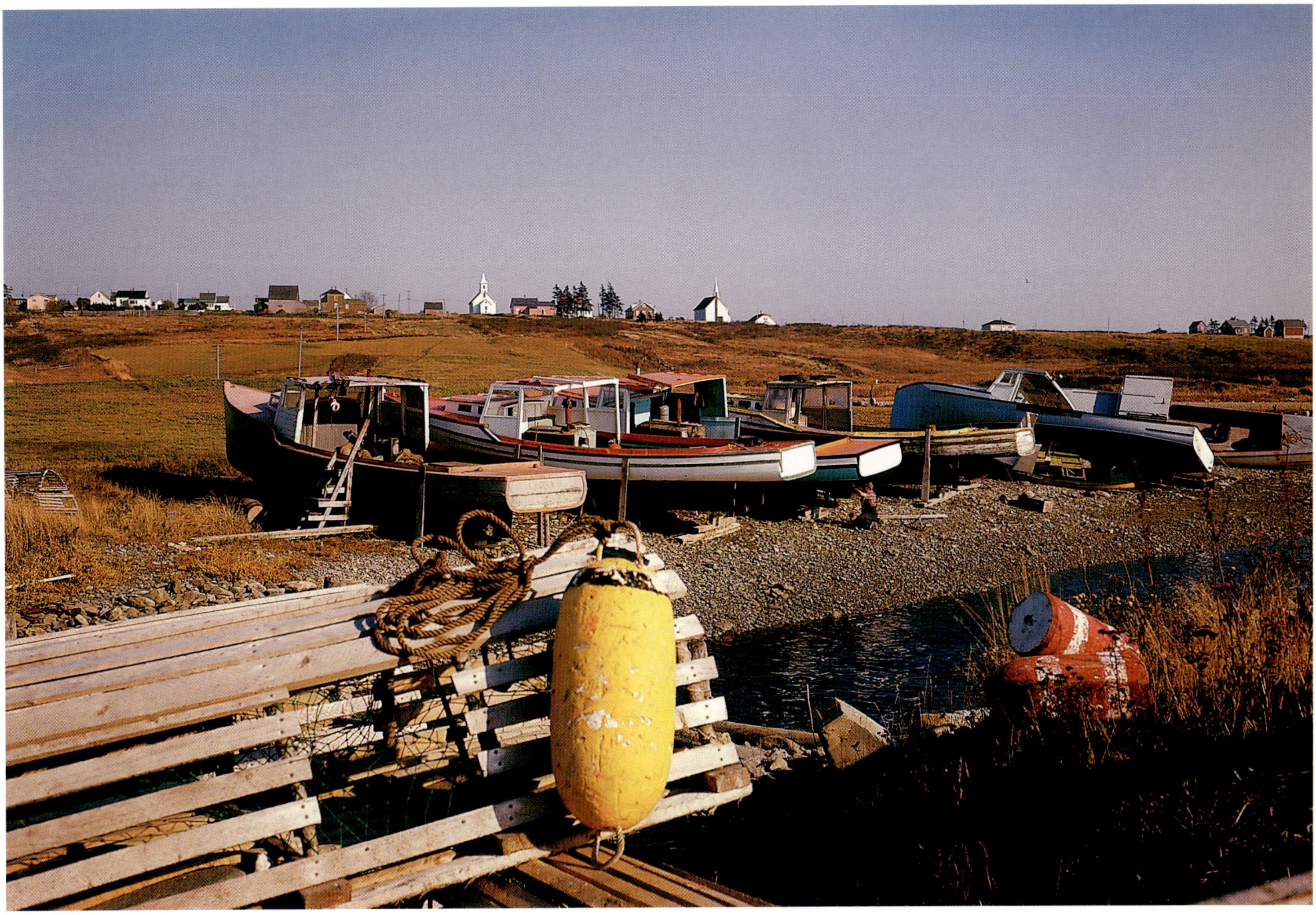

Lobster boats are pulled up during the off-season for repairs and a fresh coat of paint.

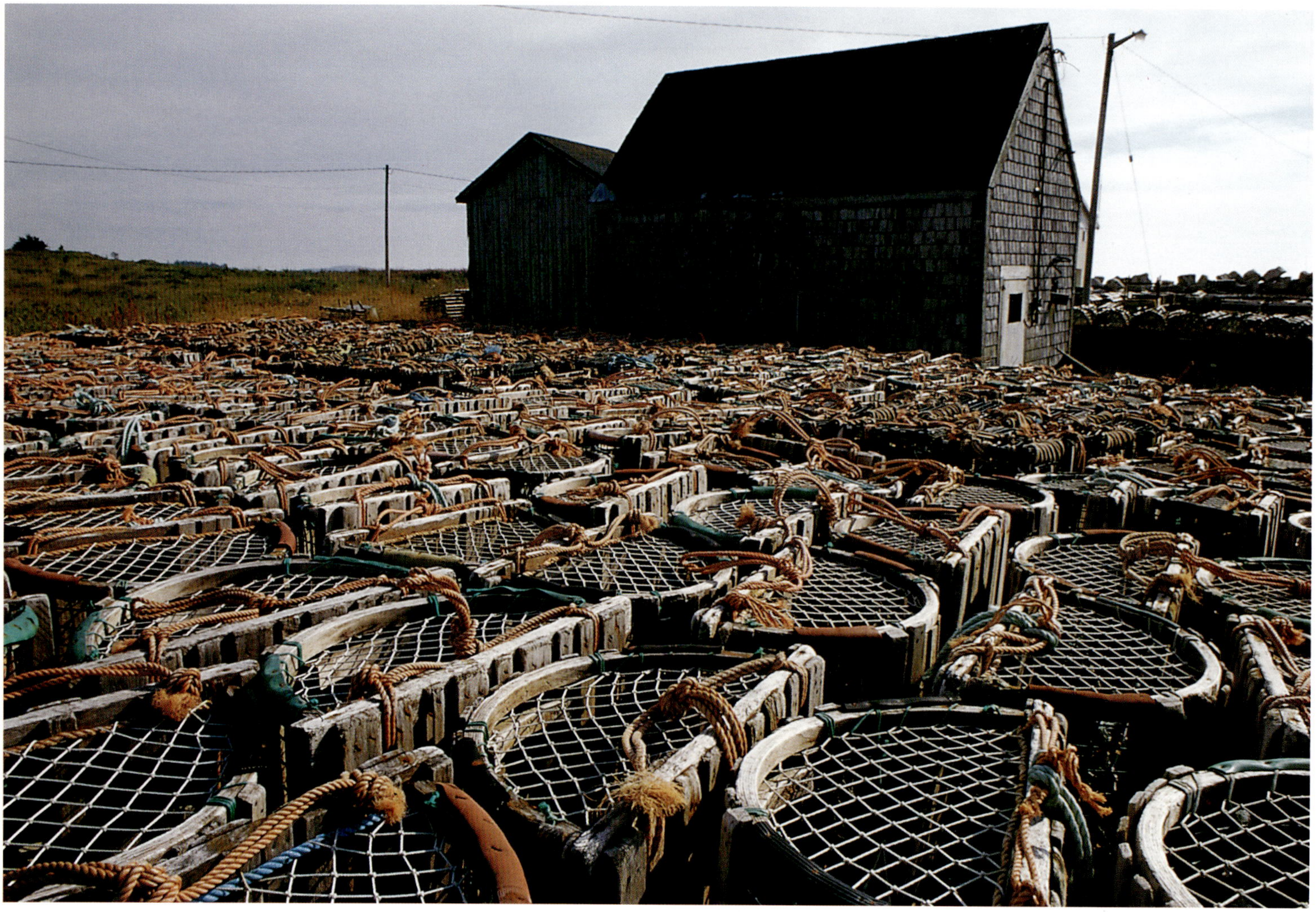

Scores of lobster traps at Pembroke are ready for the first day of the season. In southwest Nova Scotia, the lobster season runs during the harshest months of November through May.

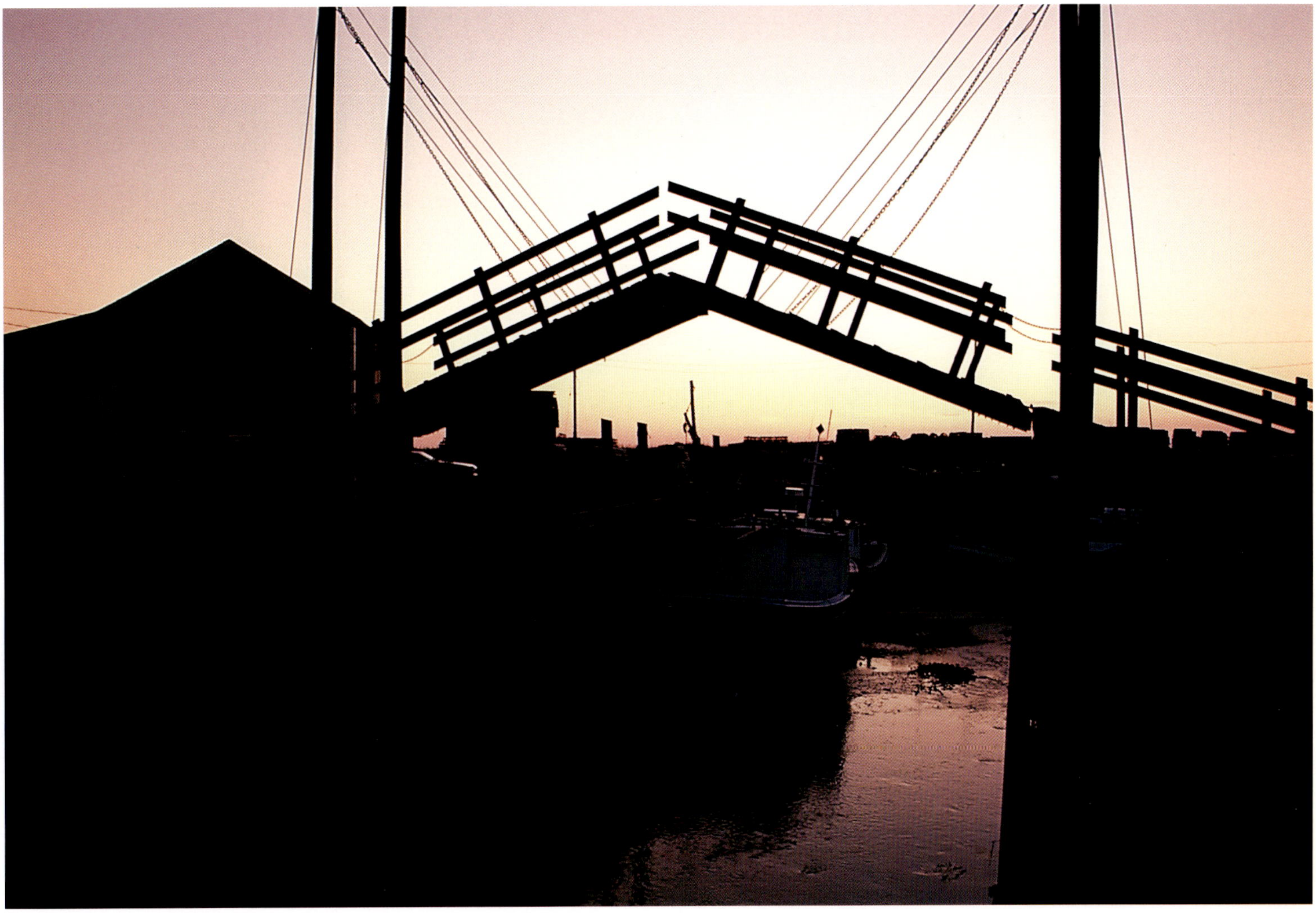

The smallest wooden lift-bridge in the world cuts a stark silhouette against the evening sky. Having been moved from its original site due to the taller electronic masts of modern vessels, Sandford's bridge is still a popular tourist attraction.

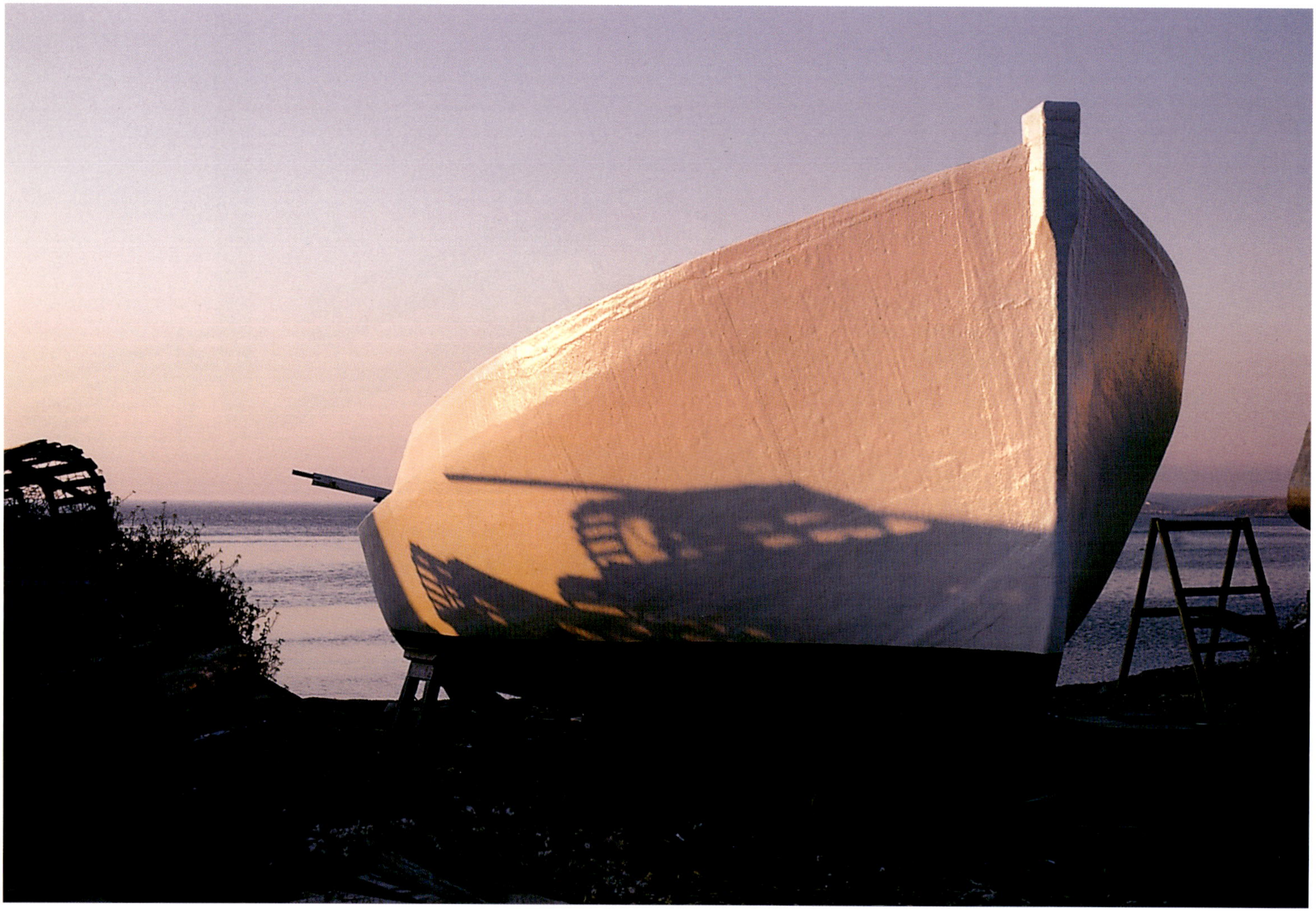

Lobster traps cast evening shadows across the bow of a 'hauled-up' boat.

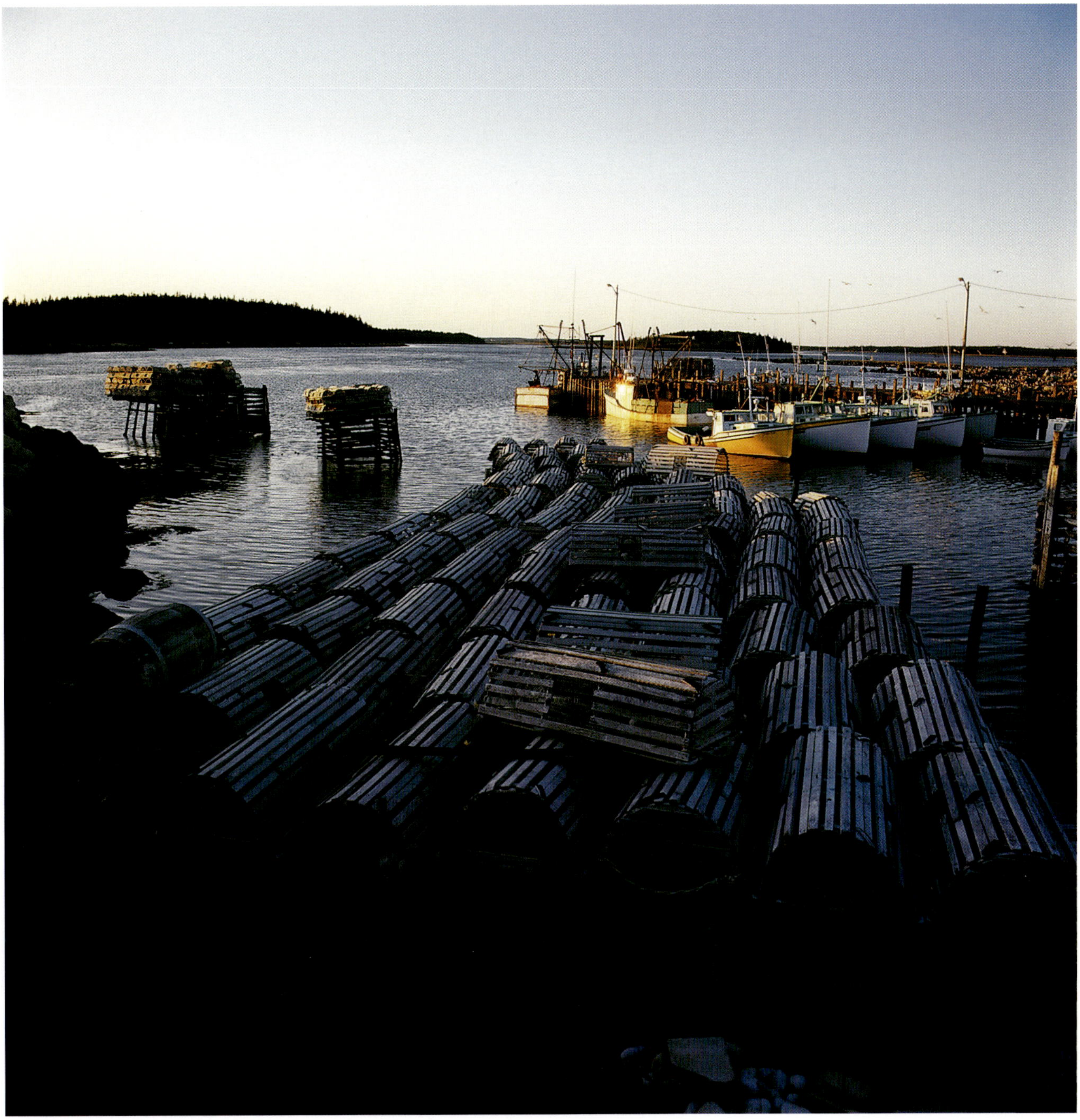

Ready for loading, traps cover a wharf during low light at Little River Harbour.

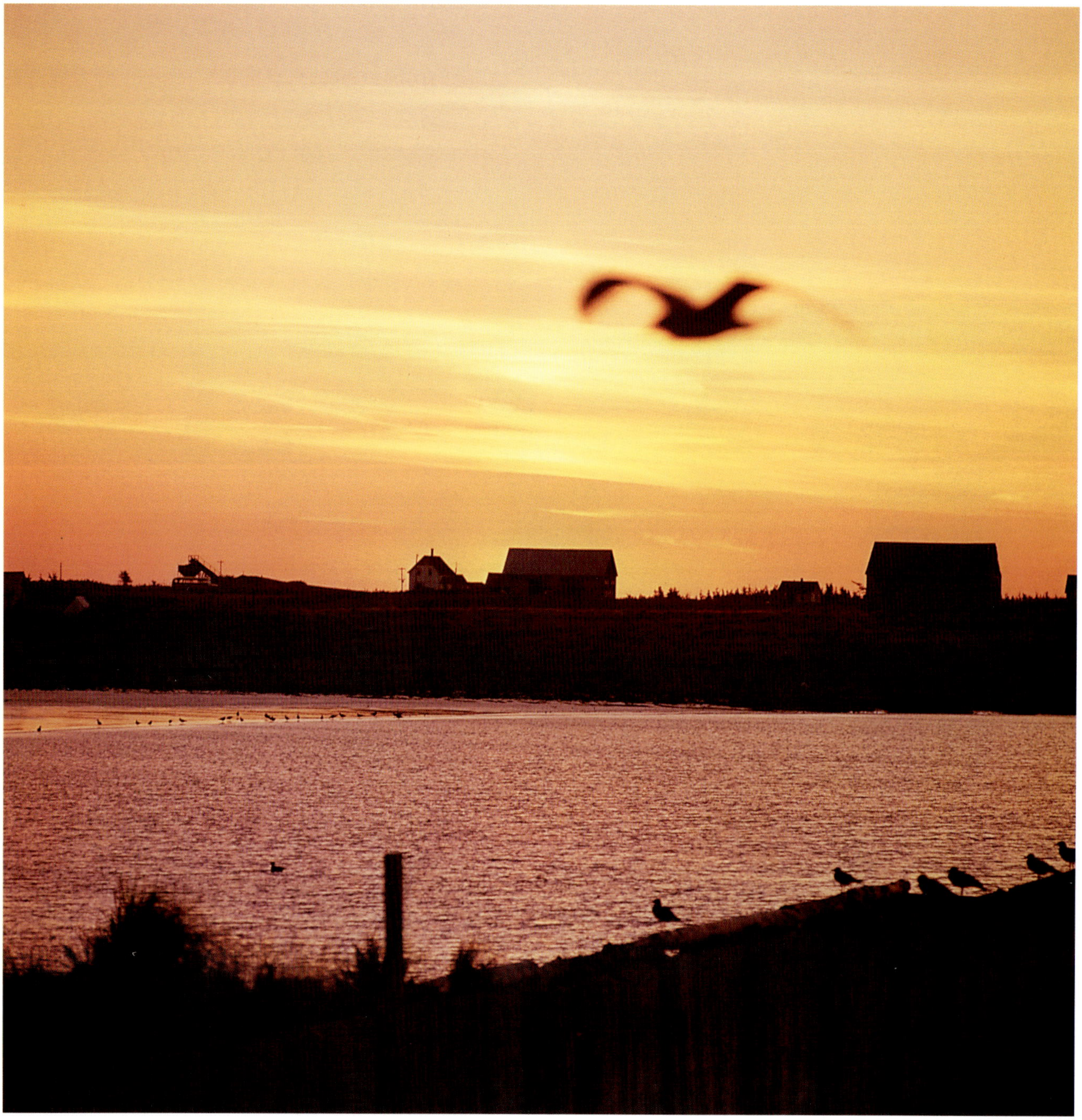

A gull is caught in mid-flight as it glides towards Pembroke.

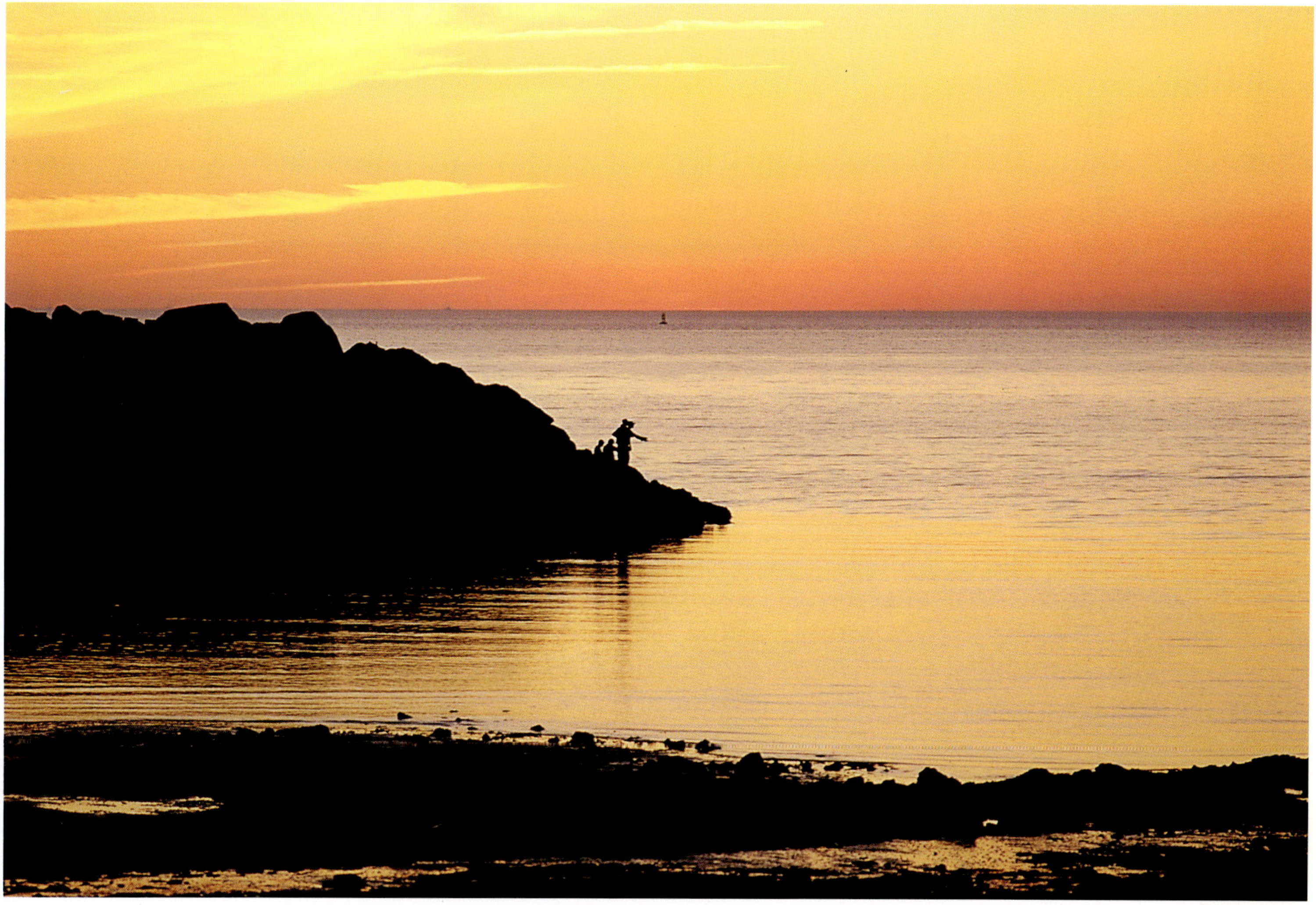

Young fishermen try their luck from the shore at Sandford during dusk.

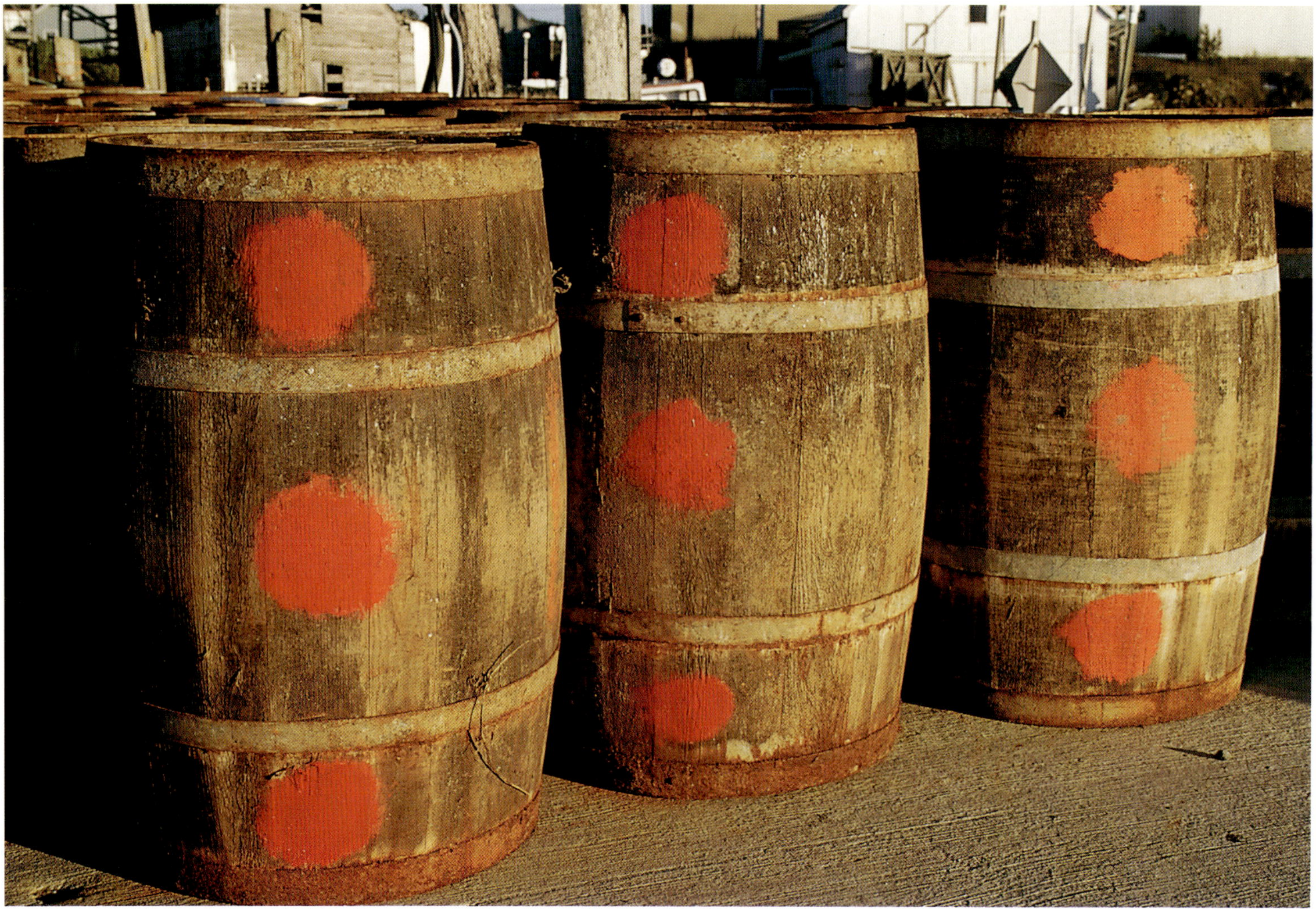

Colourful and distinctive designs are often used to identify barrels and buoys, such as these at Port Maitland.

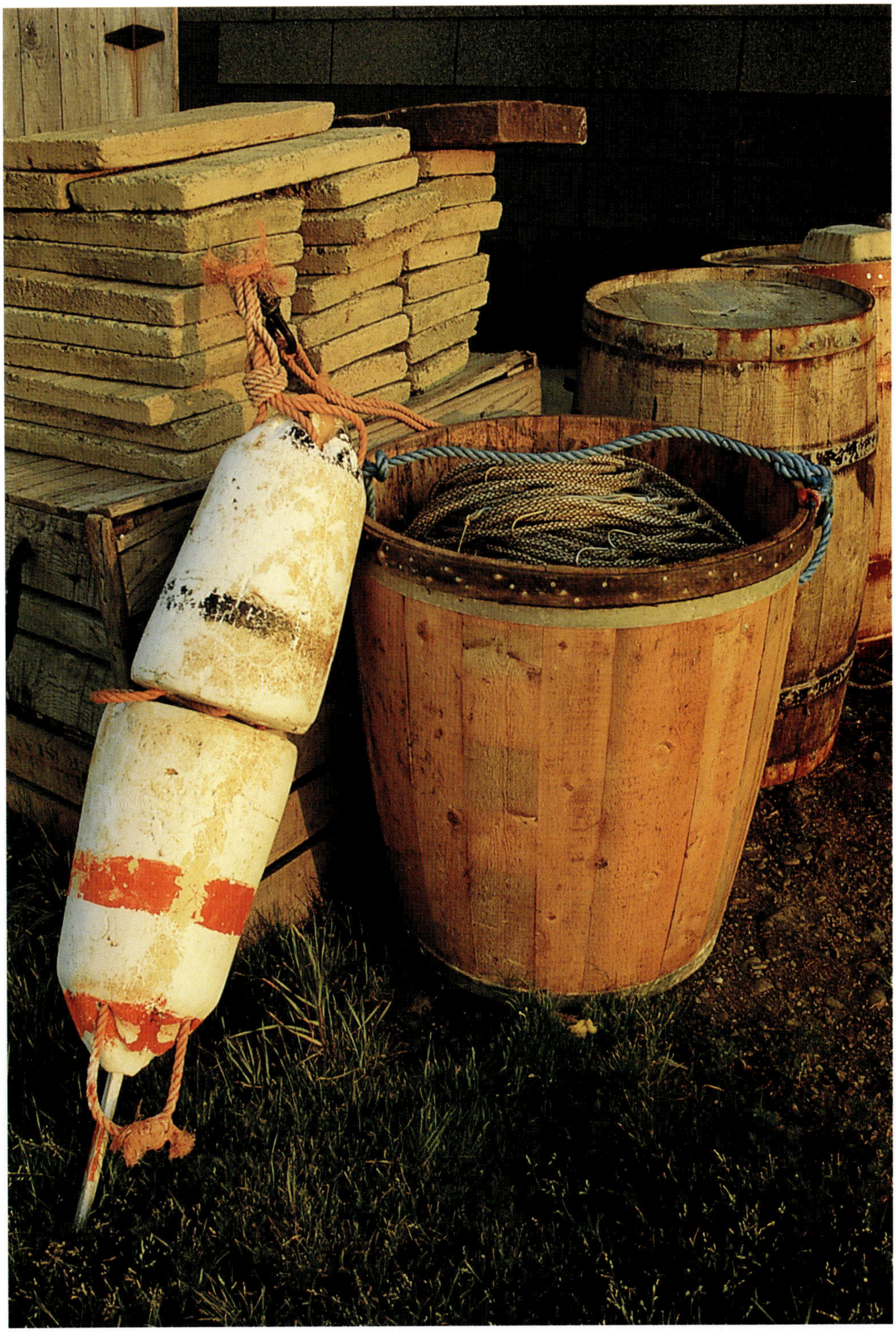

Some tools of the lobster trade: buoys, coiled rope, and a neat stack of ballast to weigh down the lobster traps. Ballast ranges from the "modern" cement variety, to nothing more than flat beach stones.

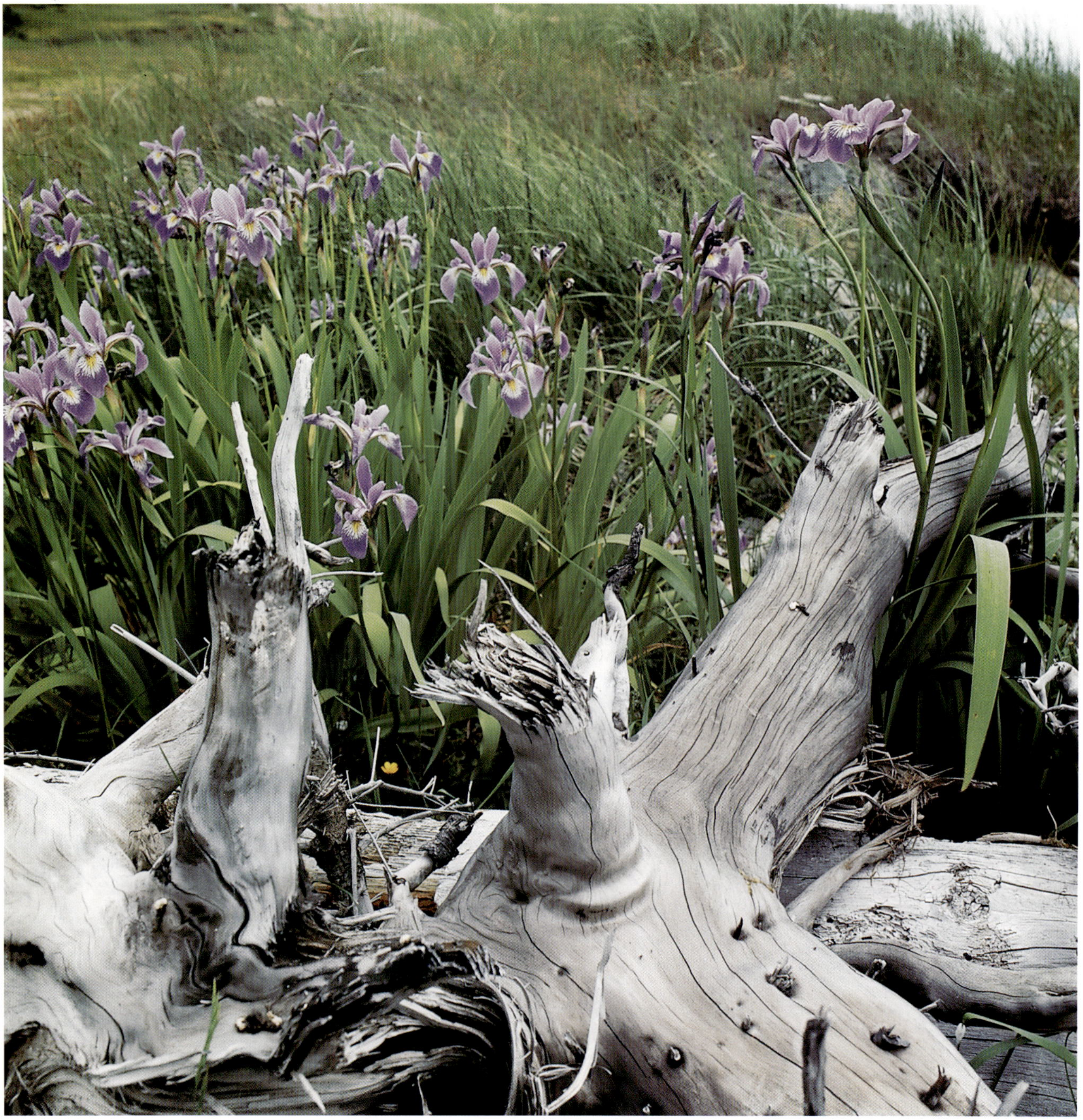

Wild iris and driftwood create a natural still life.

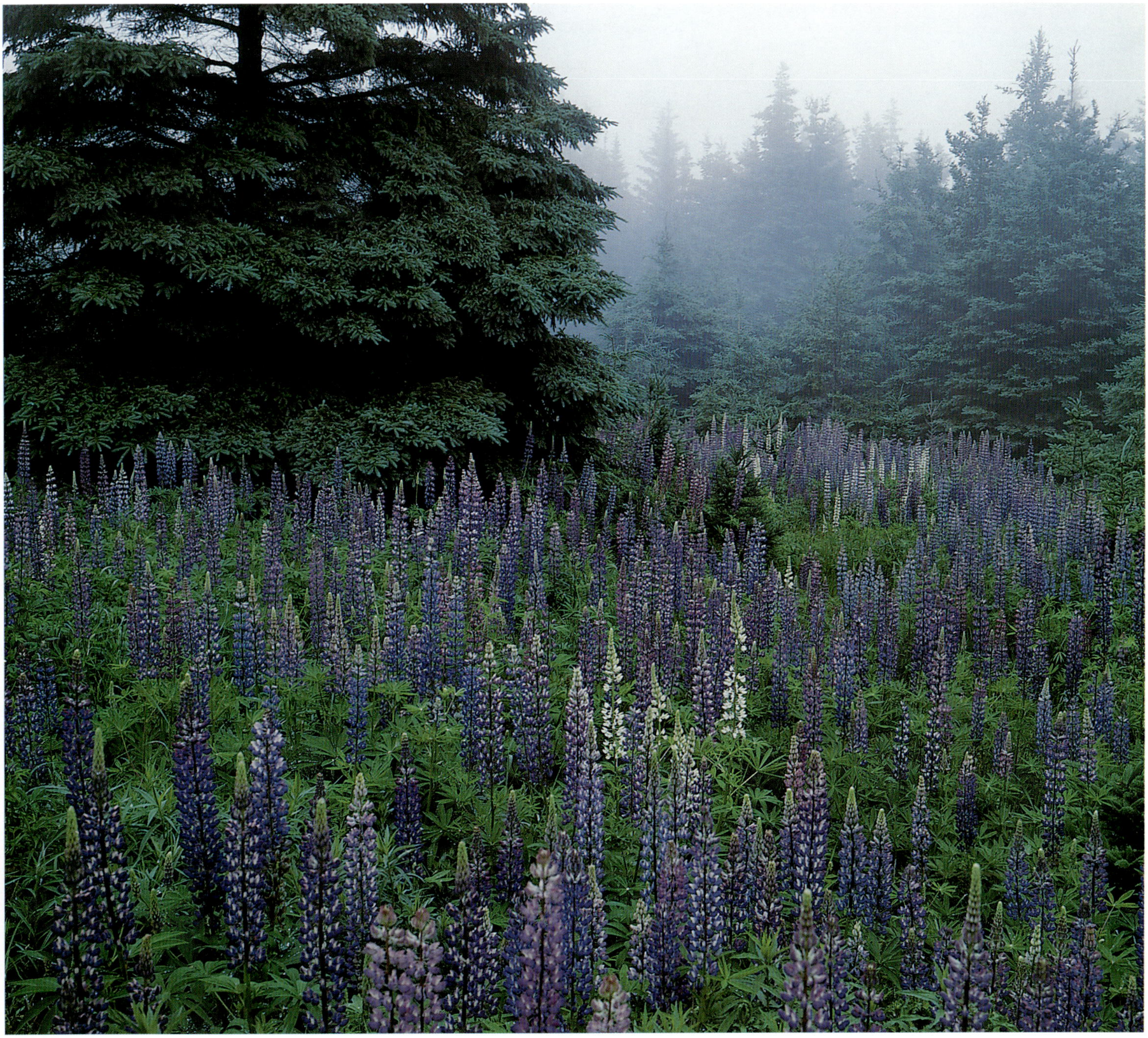

Deep purple, mauve, and pink lupins thrive in fields, woods, and along roadsides throughout Yarmouth County during the month of June.

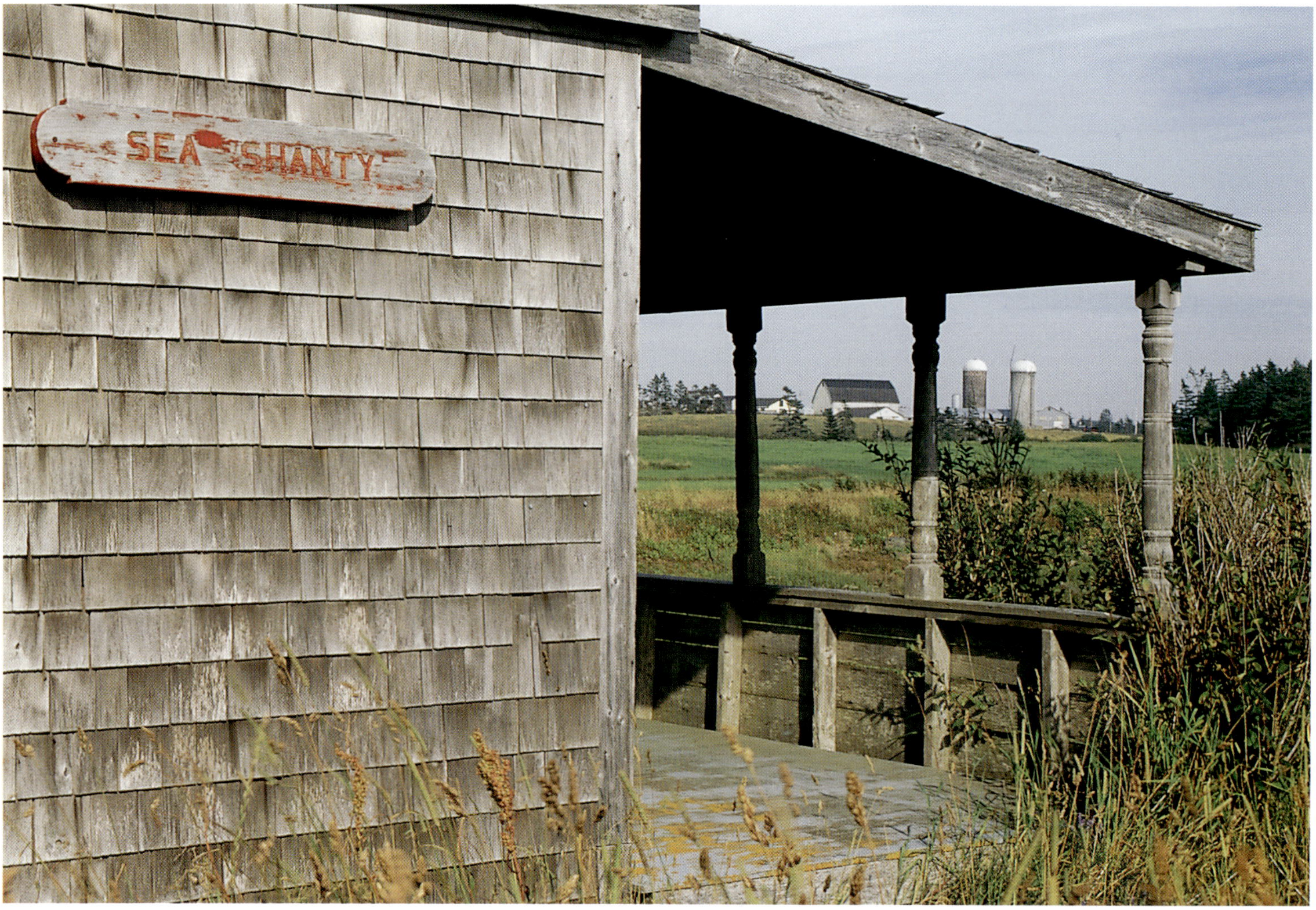

A farm is framed by this weather-seasoned building at Pembroke.

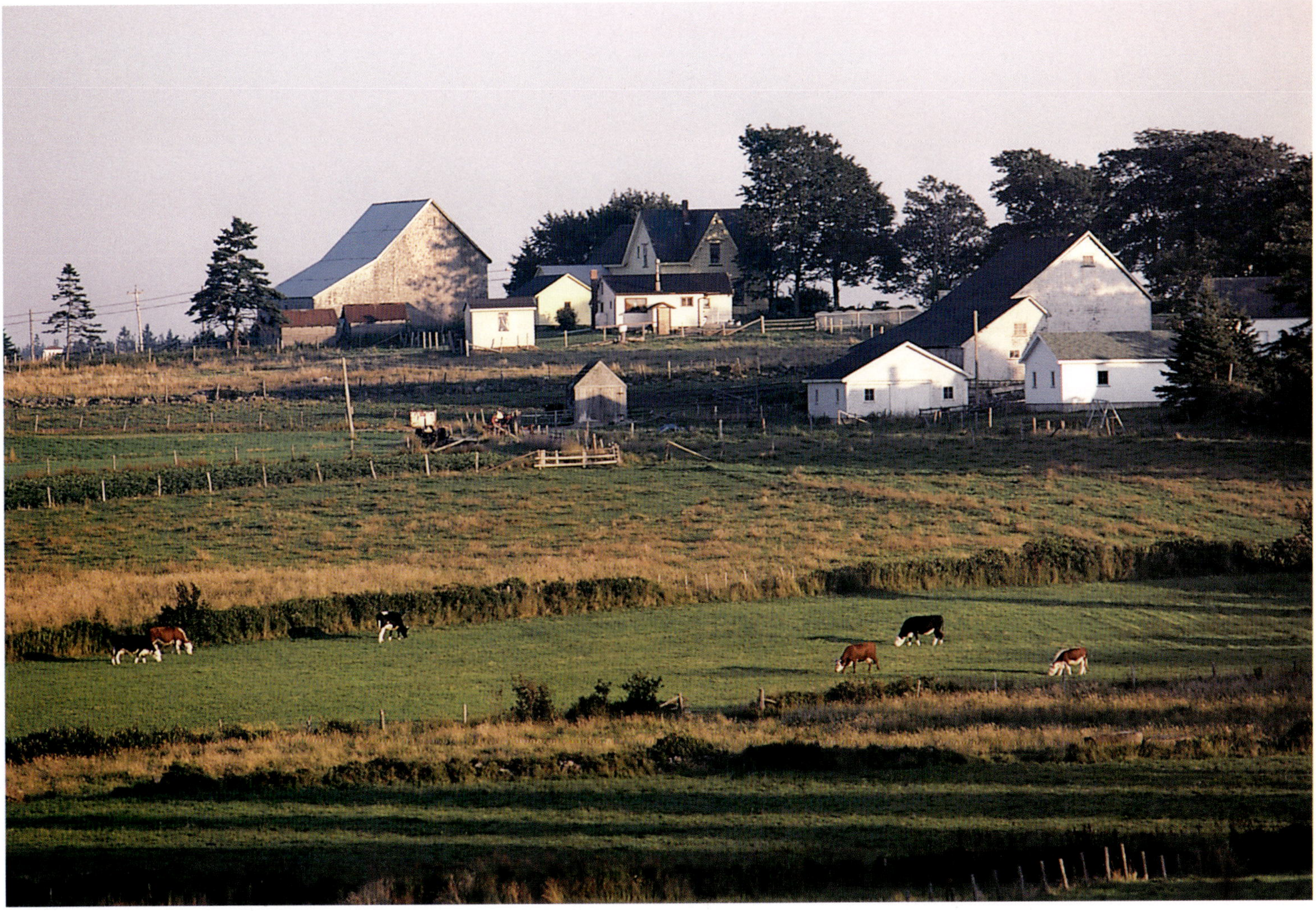

Rural peacefulness near Port Maitland.

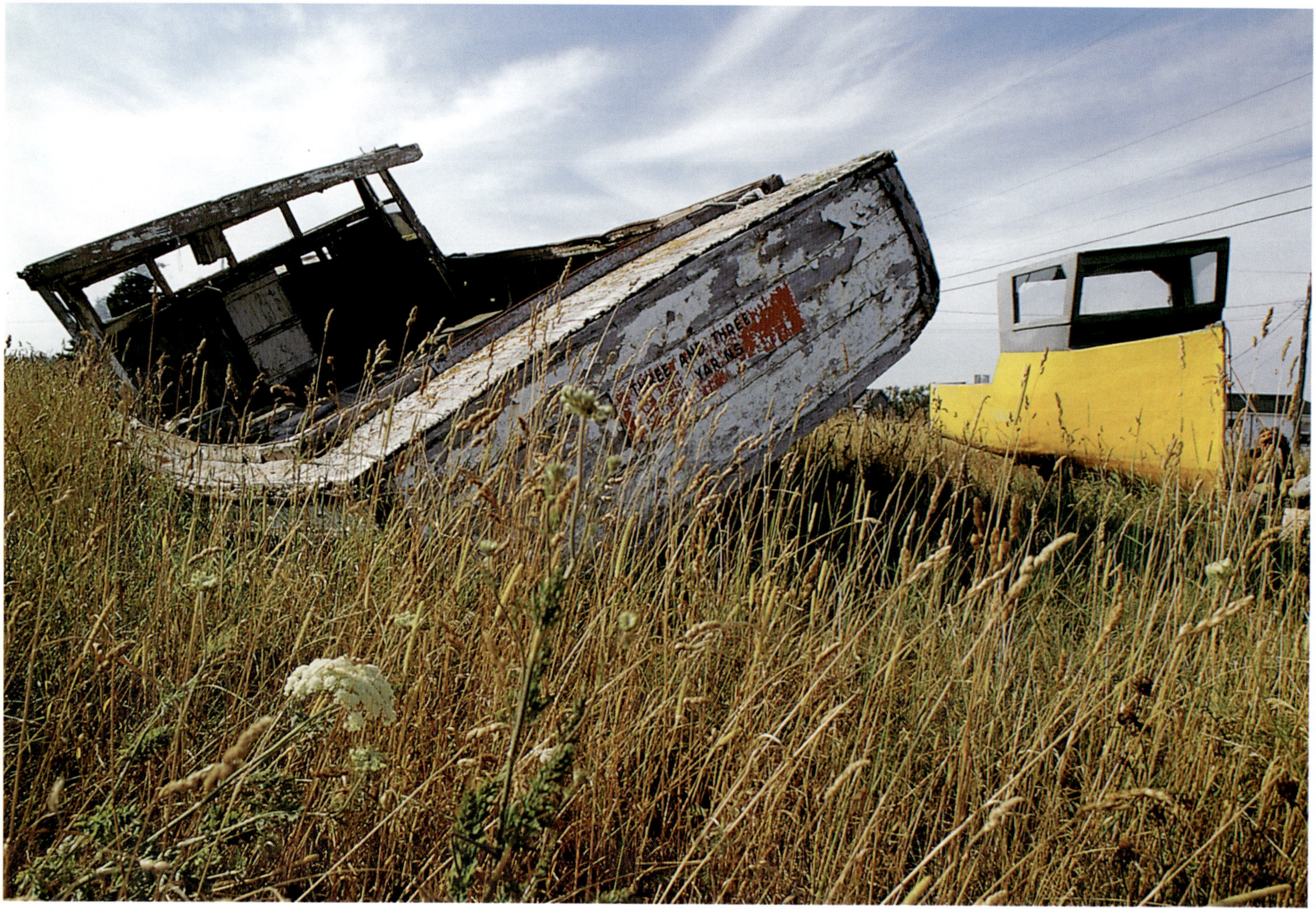

A freshly painted boat stands proudly next to one which has seen better days.

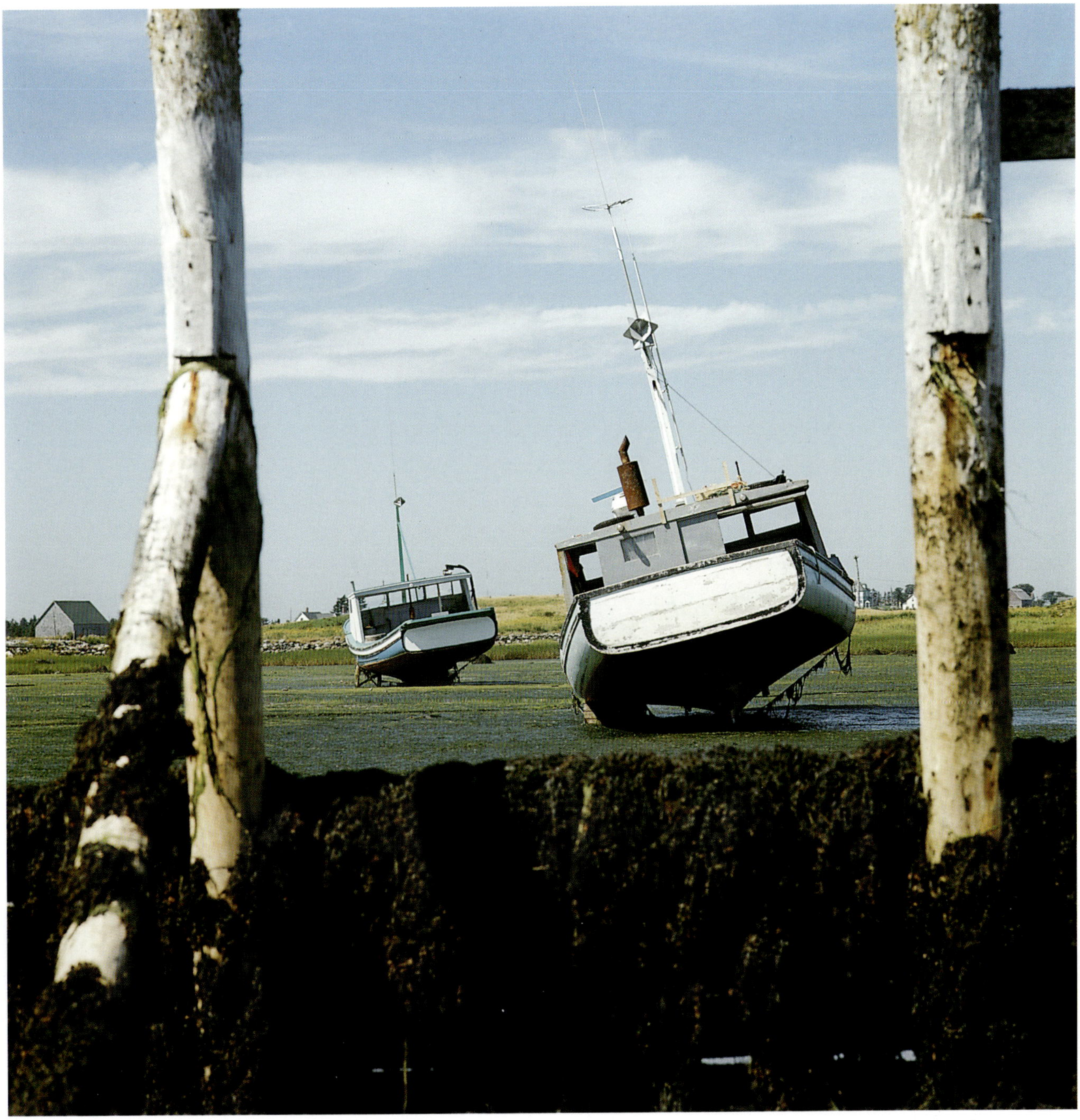

Cape Island fishing boats rest on the flats at low tide in Yarmouth Harbour.

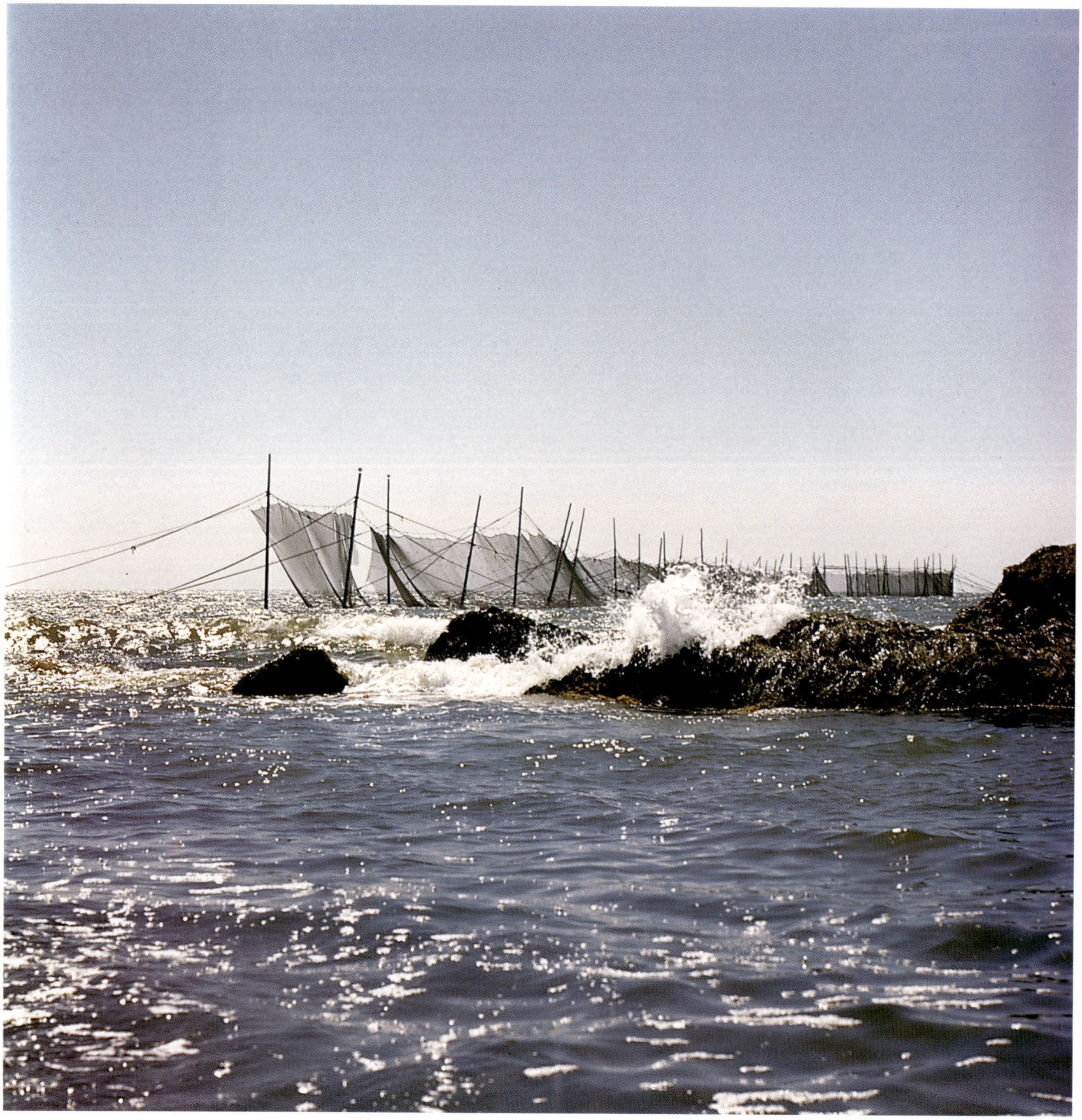

Seemingly delicate fish weirs are able to withstand tides and pounding surf.

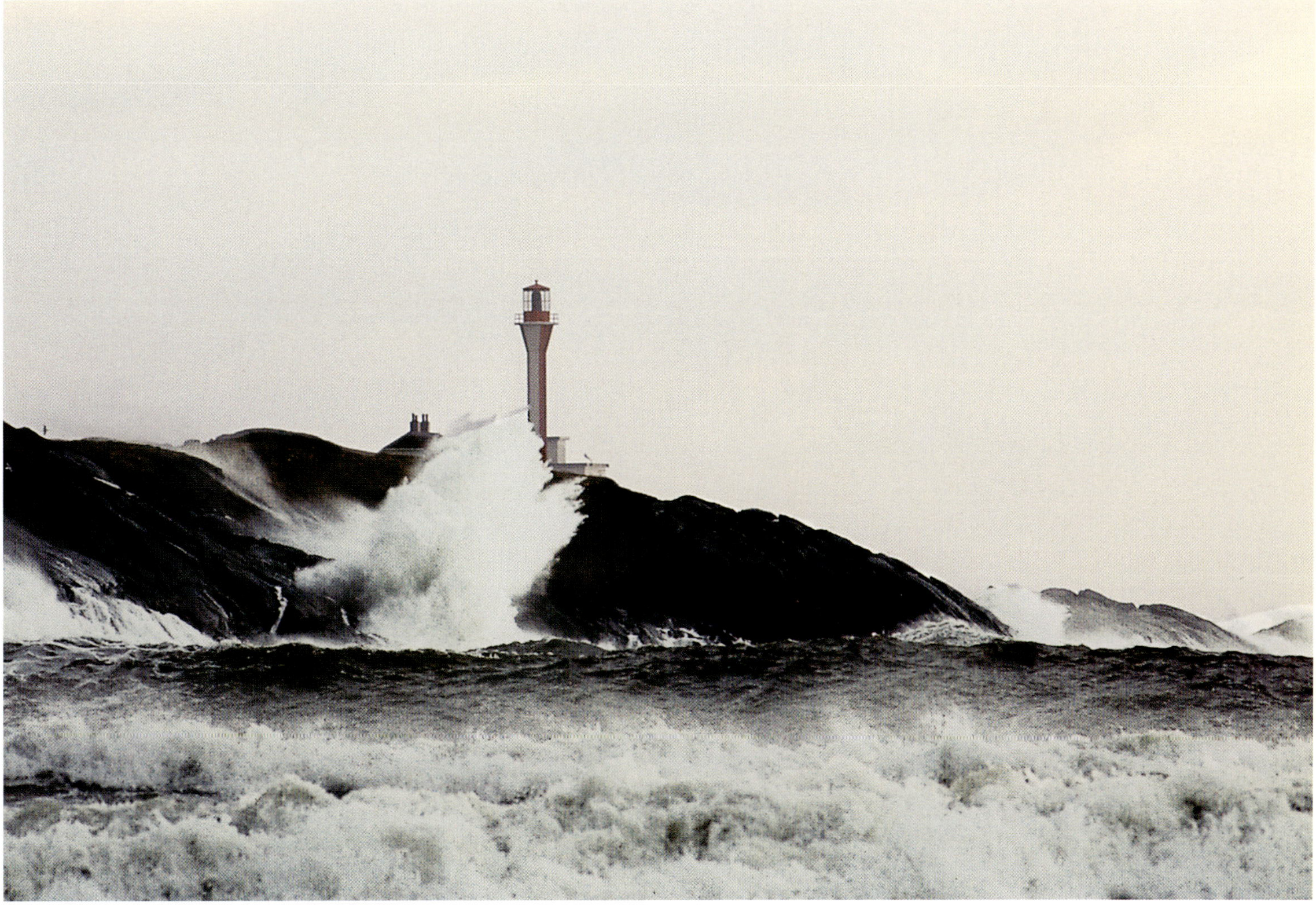

The sea smashes into the rocks of False Harbour. Watching the surf is a common pastime for Yarmouth County residents, but one not without its dangers. Waves have been known to whip right over the high perch of the Yarmouth Light and cut off travel across the causeway leading to Cape Forchu.

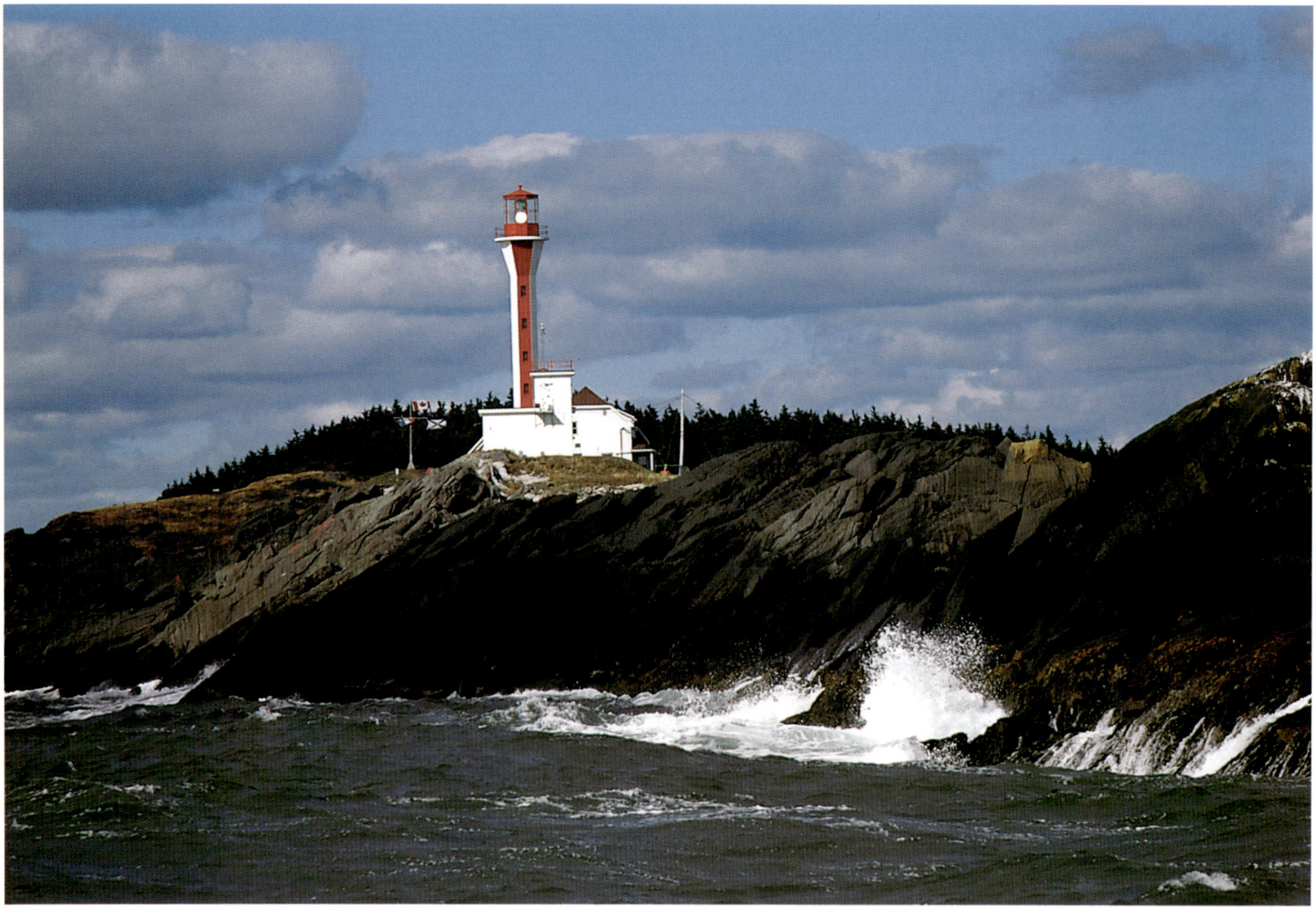

Yarmouth Lighthouse on Cape Forchu, at the mouth of Yarmouth Harbour, is the county's most familiar landmark. The original lighthouse, built in 1839, was replaced in 1961 with the unique structure standing today.

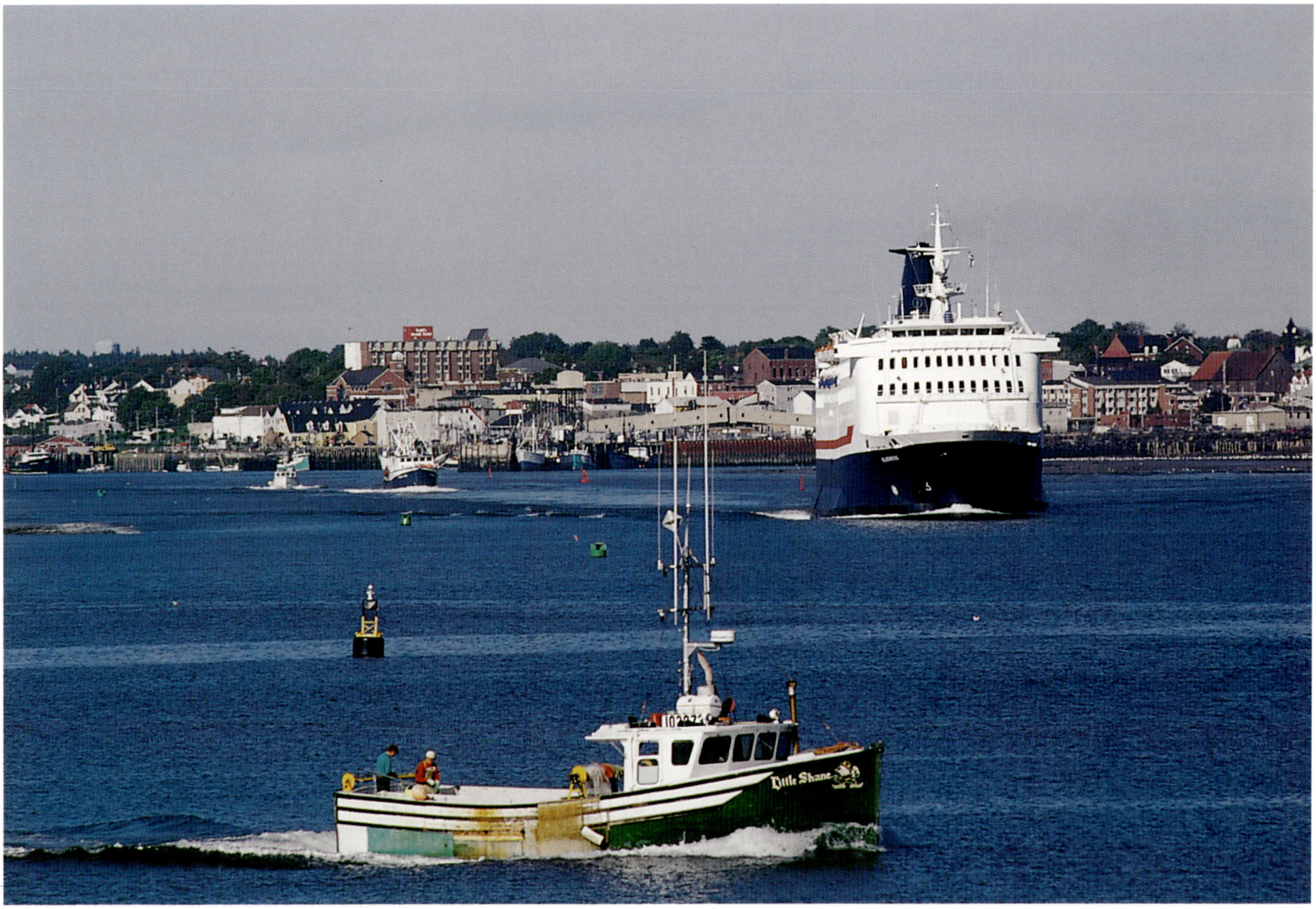

With the town of Yarmouth in the background, fishing boats share the harbour with the passenger ferries that link Nova Scotia with New England.

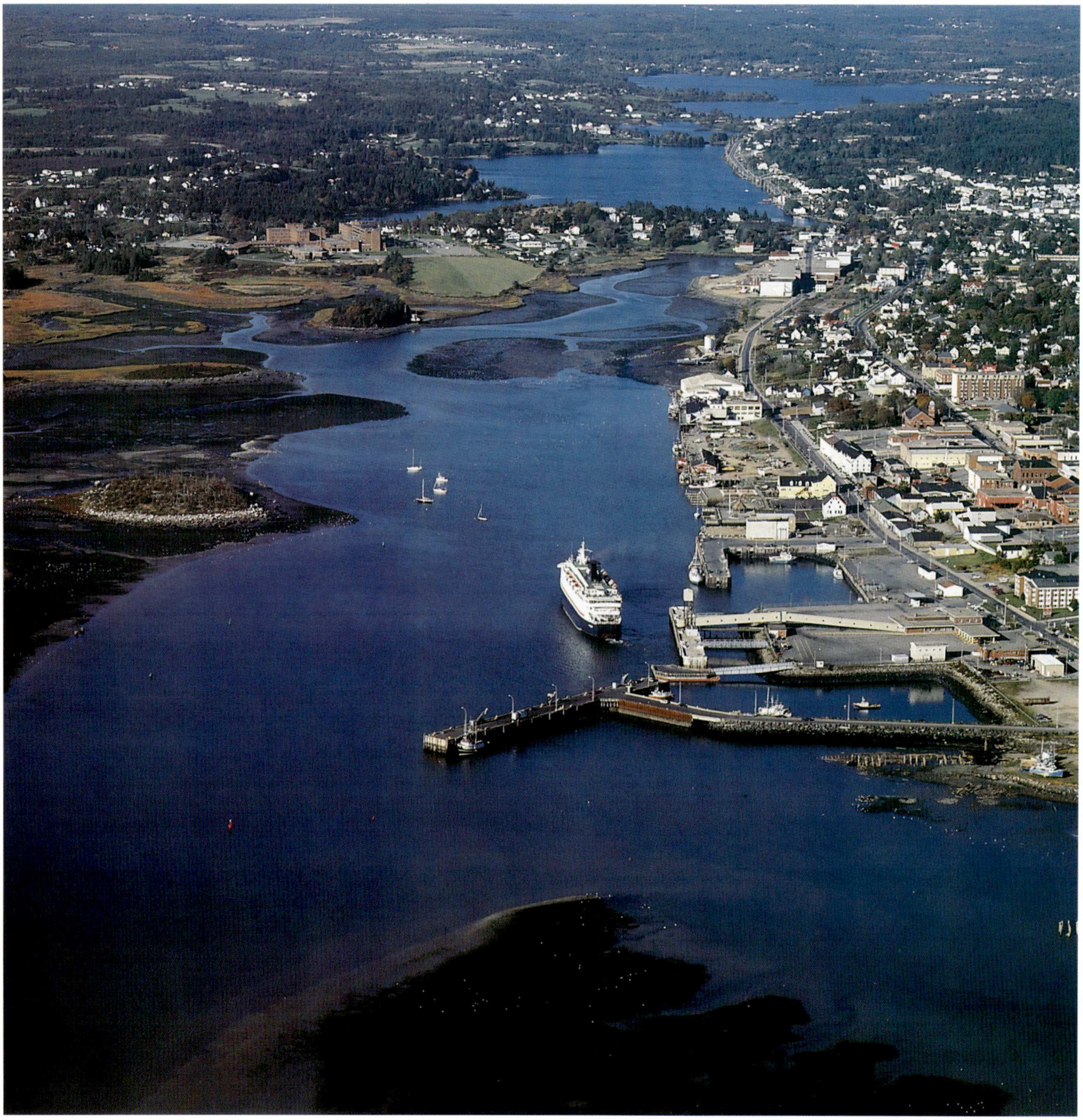

A bird's-eye view showing part of the harbour and town of Yarmouth. A passenger ferry pulls out from its berth to begin the journey to Maine.

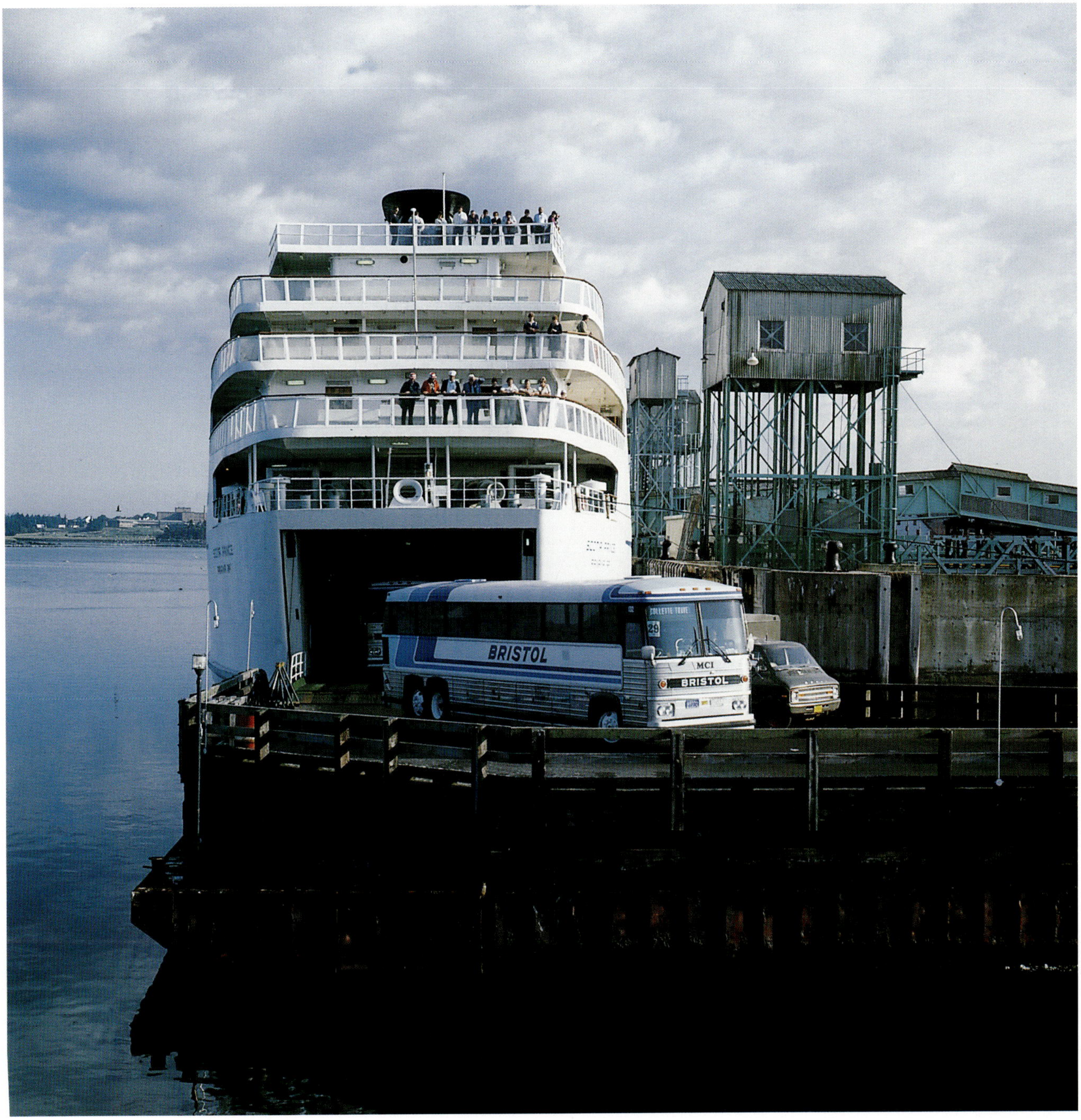

After an overnight voyage from New England, a tour bus unloads. Passengers stake their positions along the rail up top for the scenic cruise out the Yarmouth Harbour.

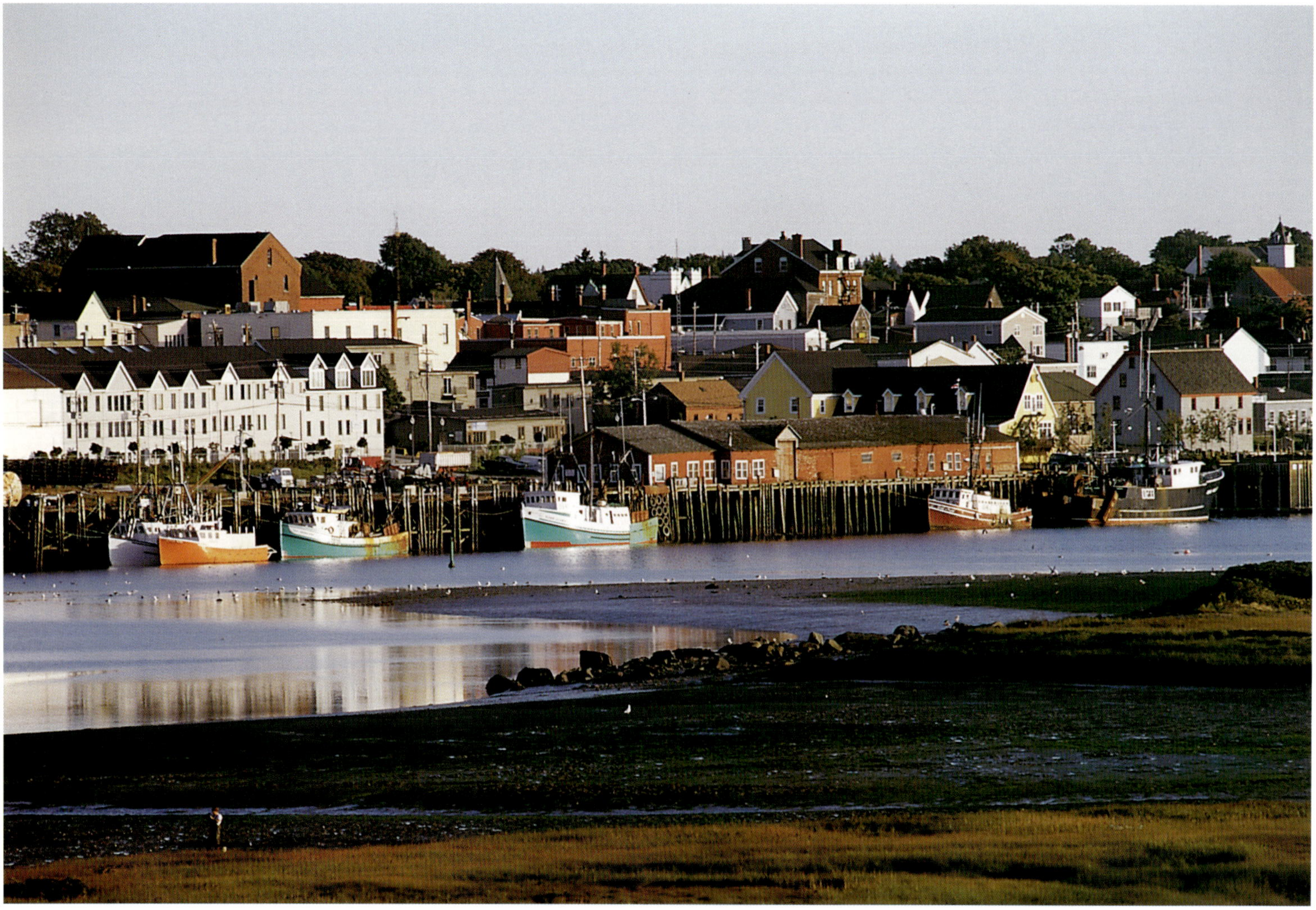

The late-afternoon sun across the harbour at low tide illuminates Yarmouth's rejuvenated historic waterfront. On the mud-flats, a sole blood-worm digger can be seen working.

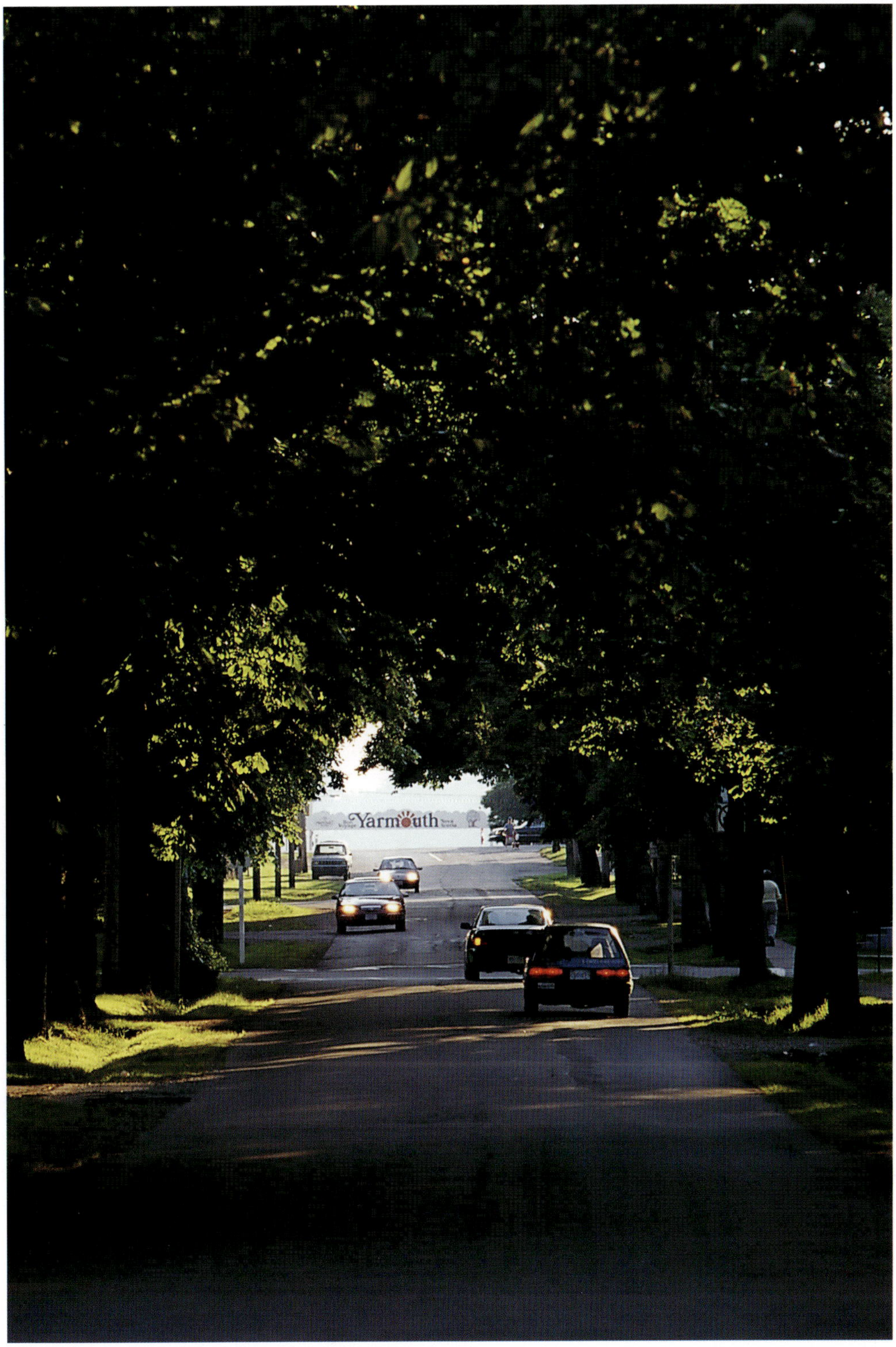

The dense canopy of leaves along the aptly named Forest Street creates a dramatic tunnel leading to the sign welcoming visitors to Yarmouth. The town's many tree-lined streets and picturesque homes make the popular walking tour one of Yarmouth's main attractions.

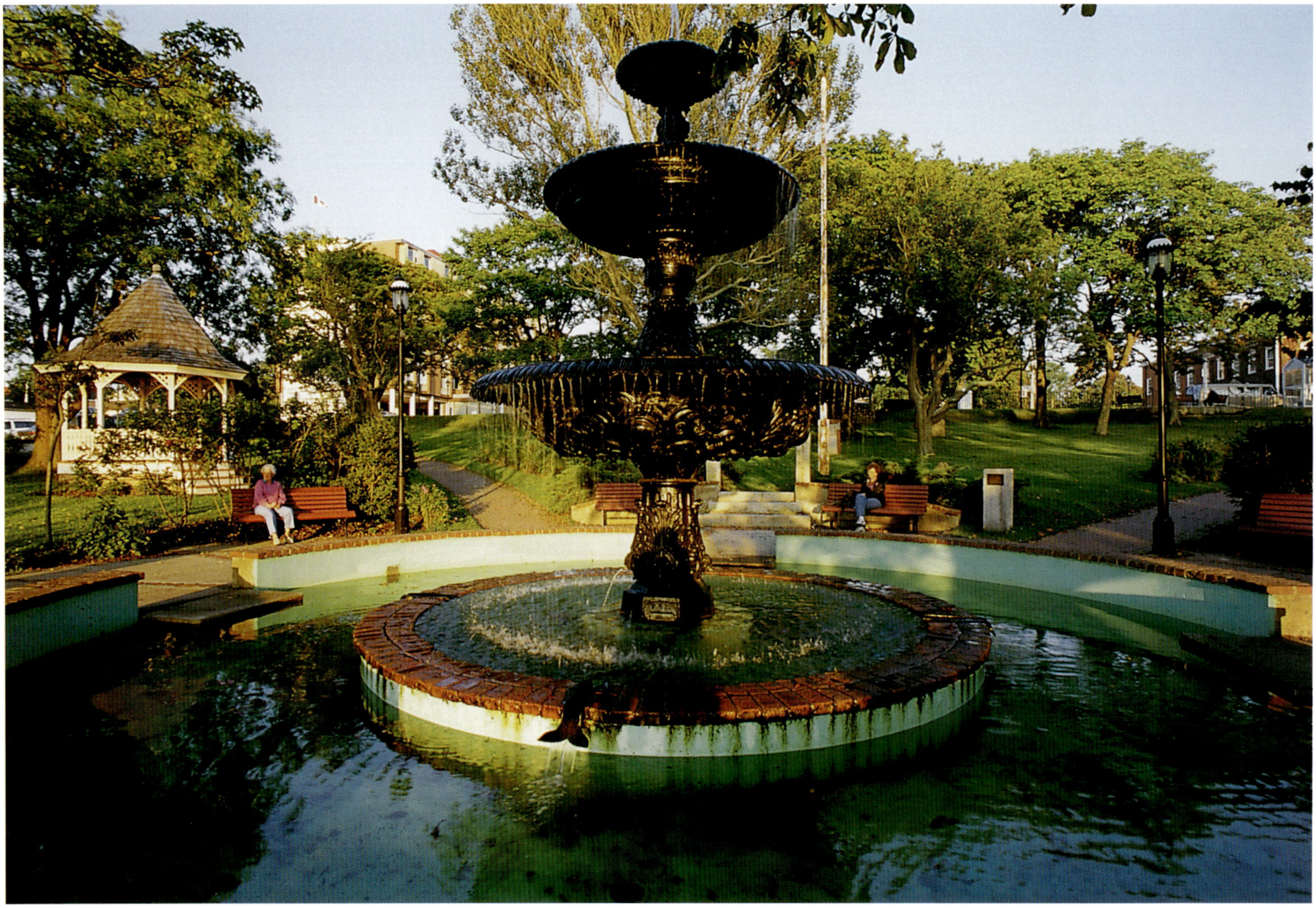

Frost Park provides a tranquil setting in the evening sun.

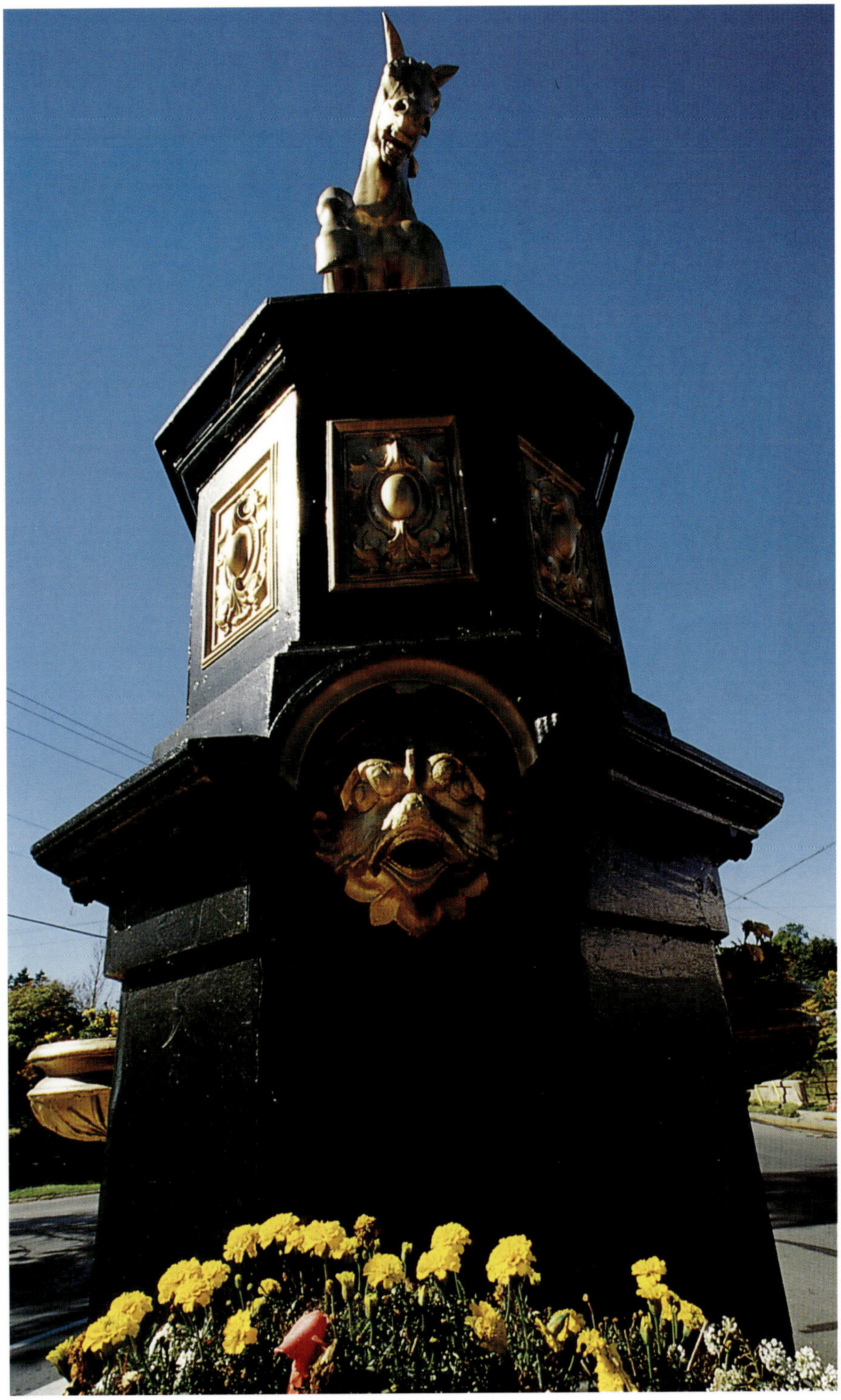

Once a stop for thirsty horses, flowers now spill out of this Milton landmark.

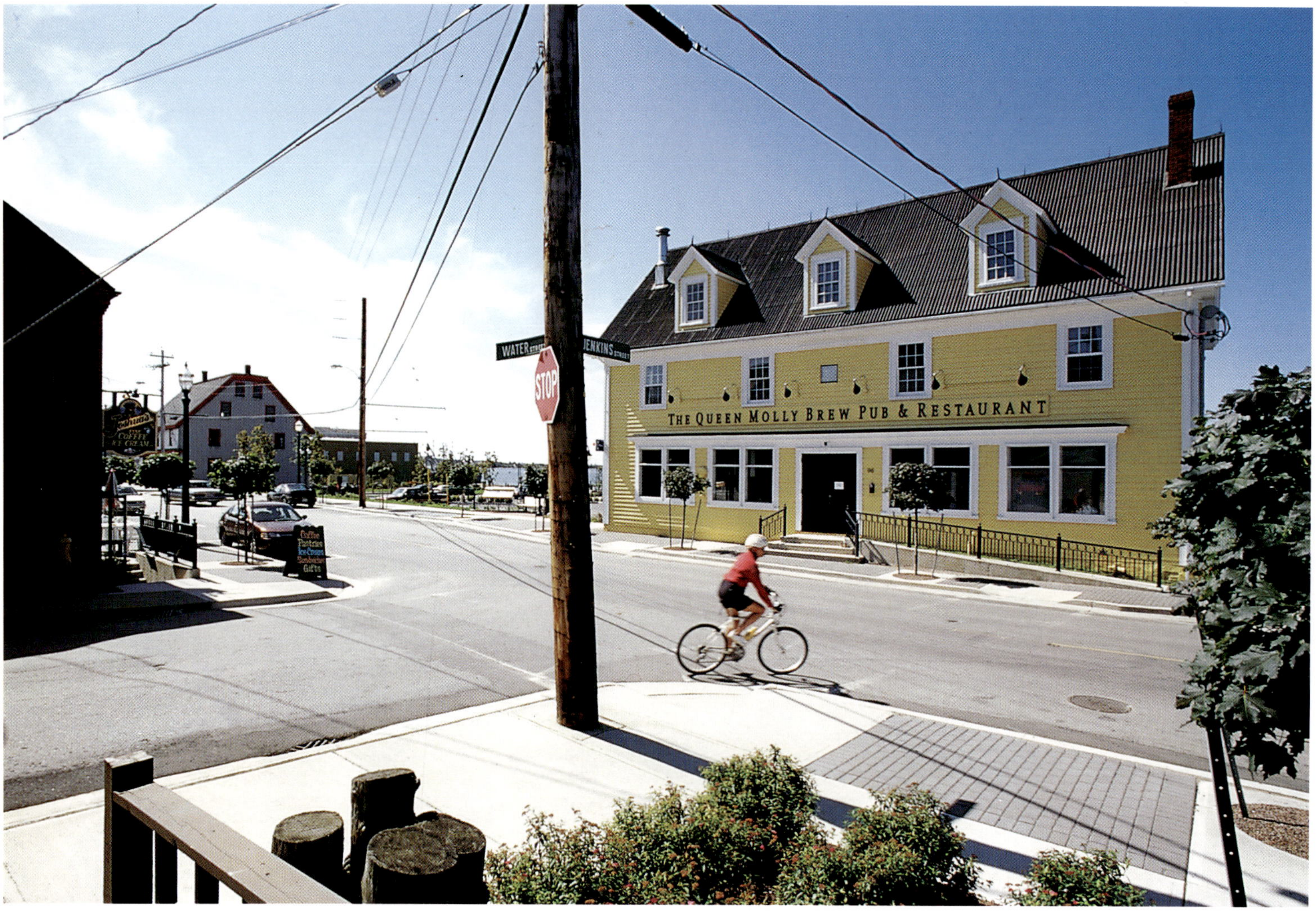

A cyclist cruises past Joshua's and The Queen Molly Brew Pub on Yarmouth's rejuvenated waterfront.

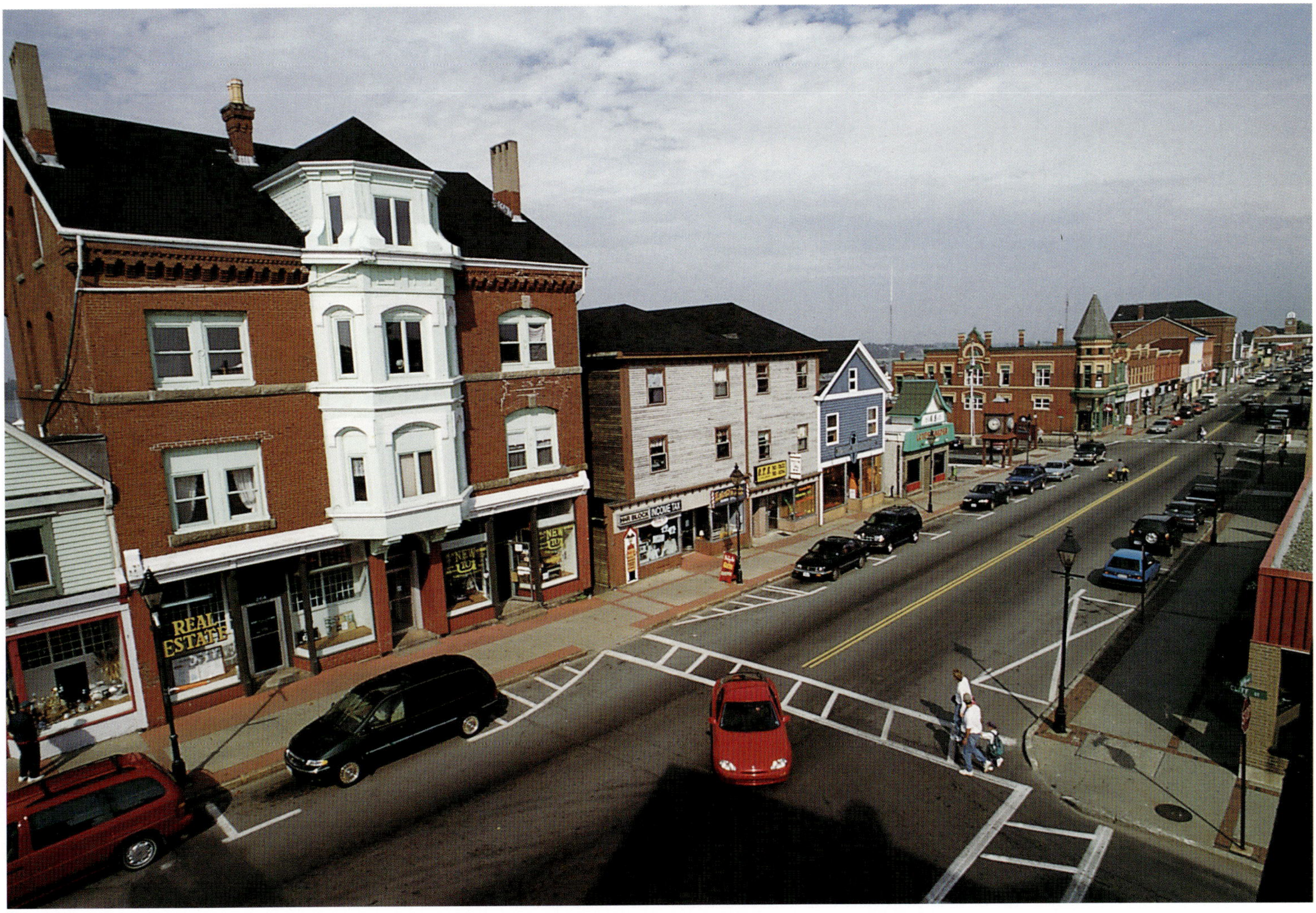

Architecture provides many reminders of Yarmouth's past. Looking north down Main Street, one sees a building from the 1860s and, farther along, a towered structure from the 1880s.

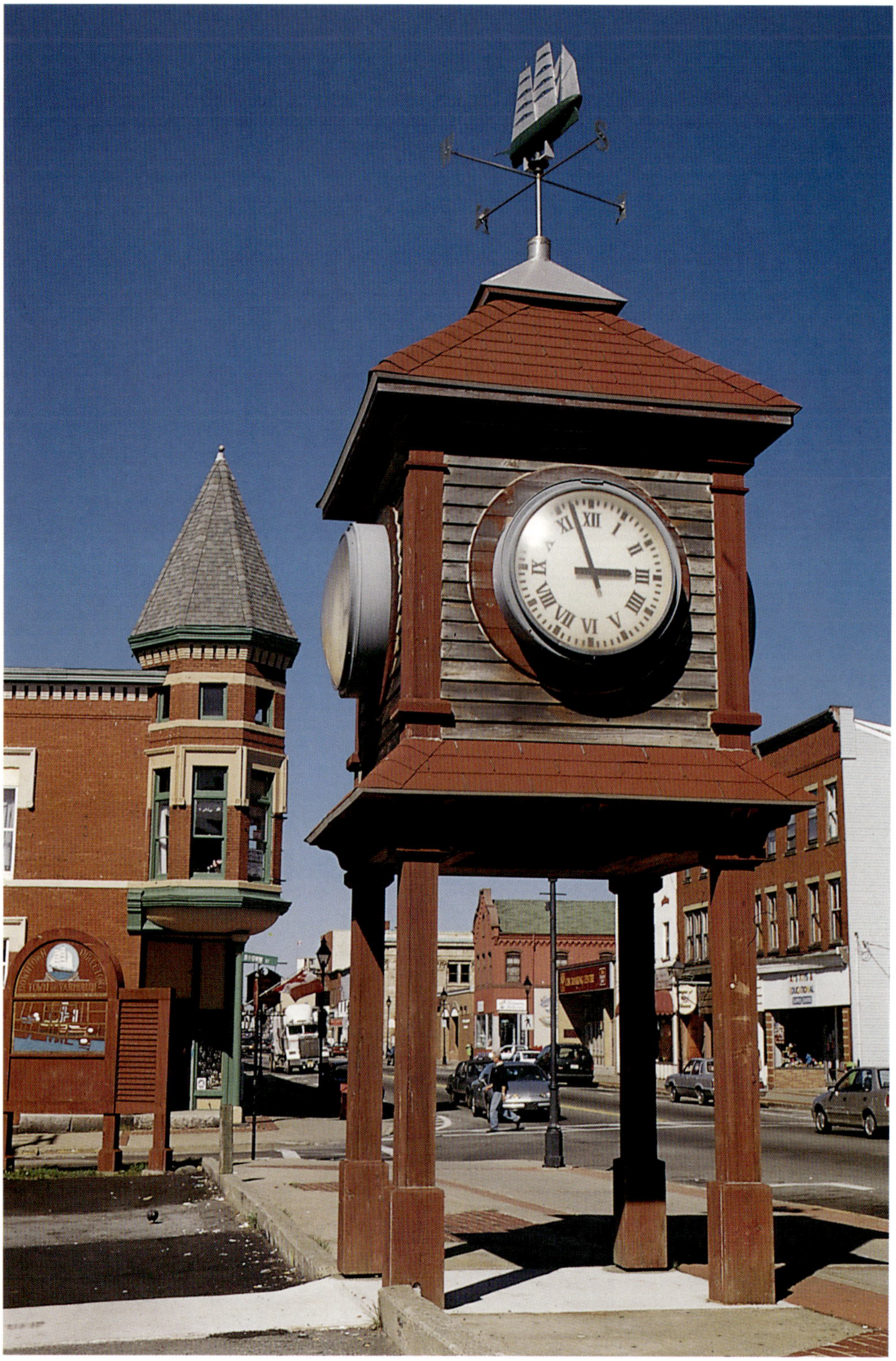

Time stands still on Main Street where a modern-day treatment to a clock is situated near an architectural marvel from another era.

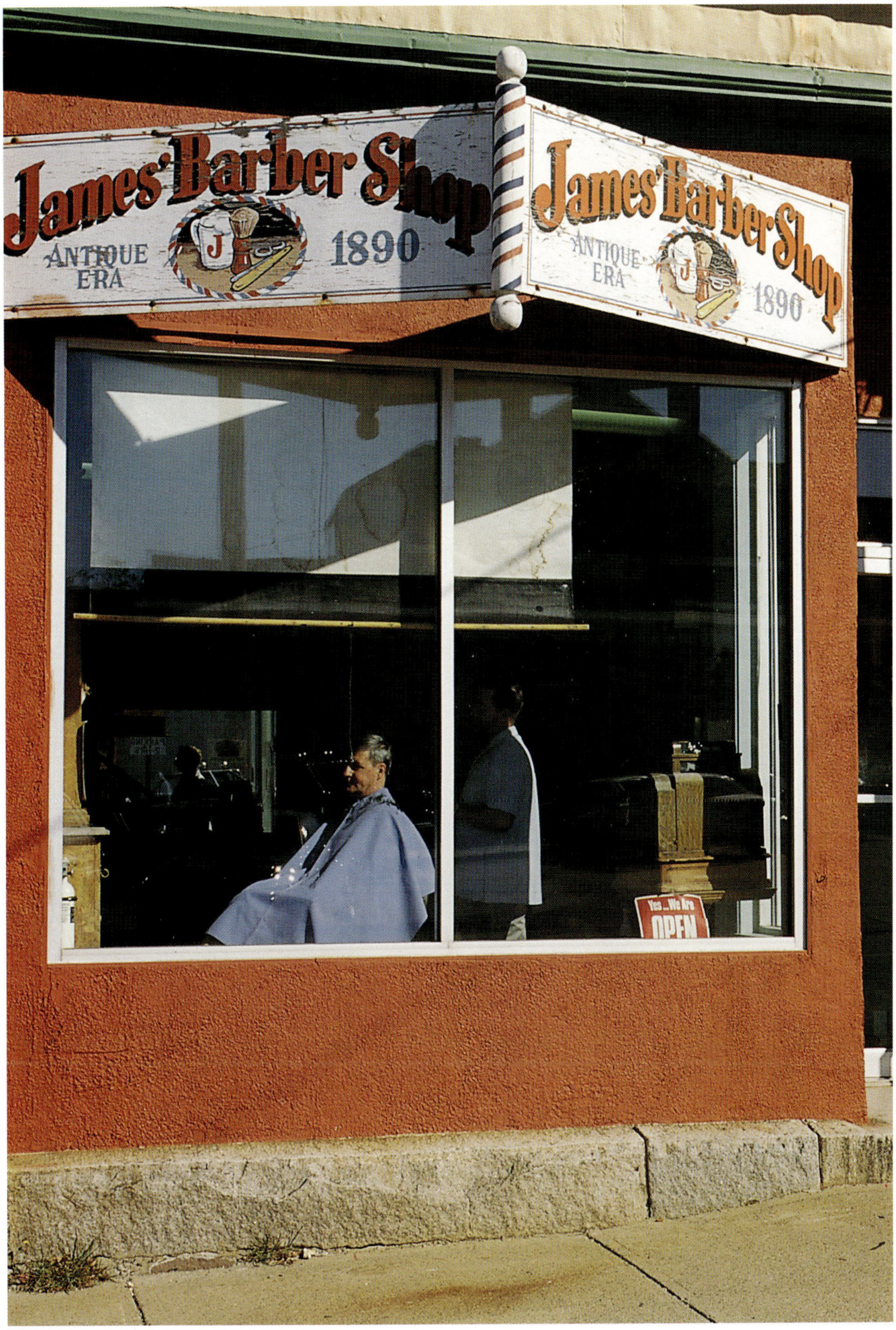

This barber shop has heard its share of gossip since 1890.

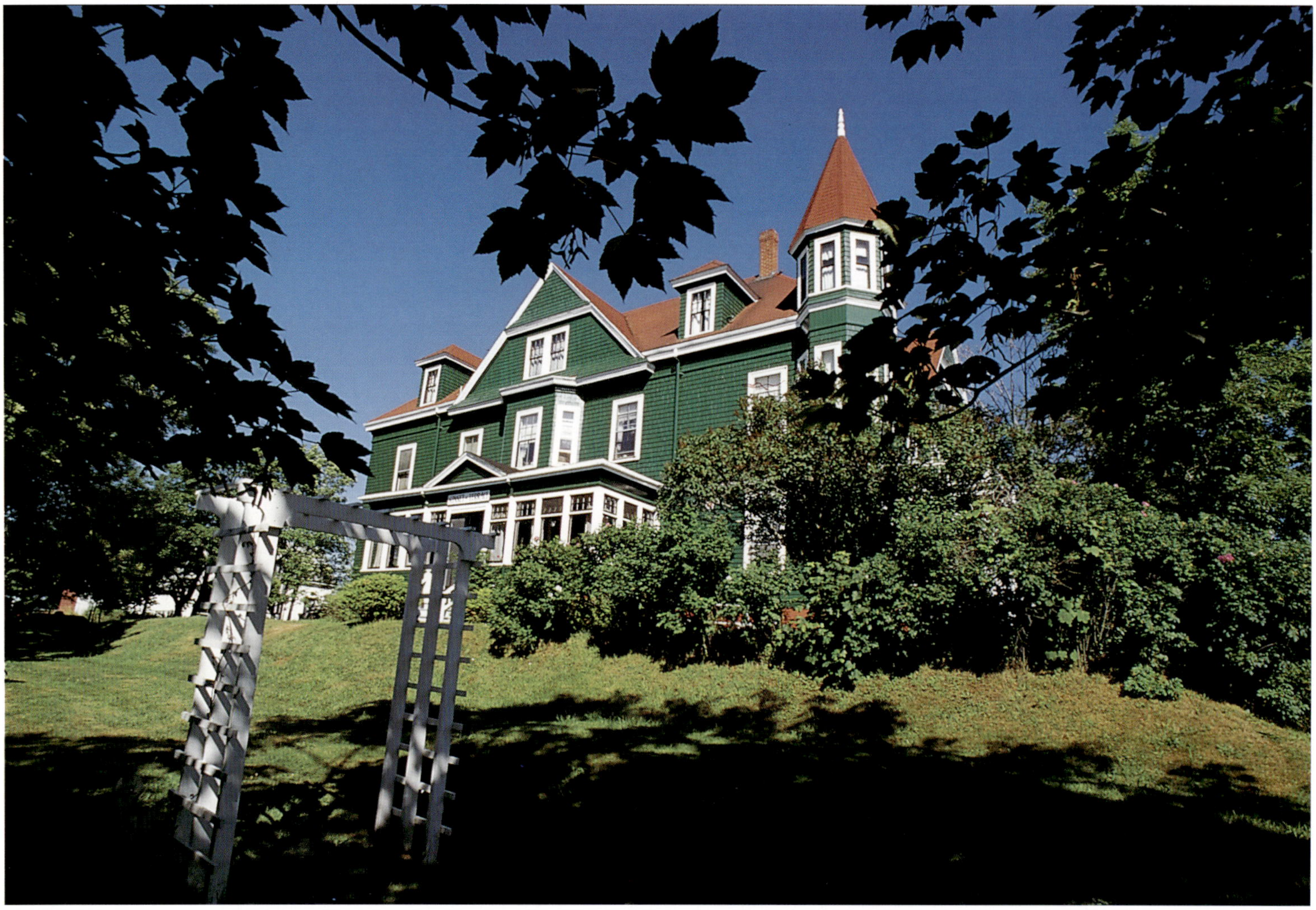

Sunset Terrace, a seniors' home, enjoys a beautiful setting.

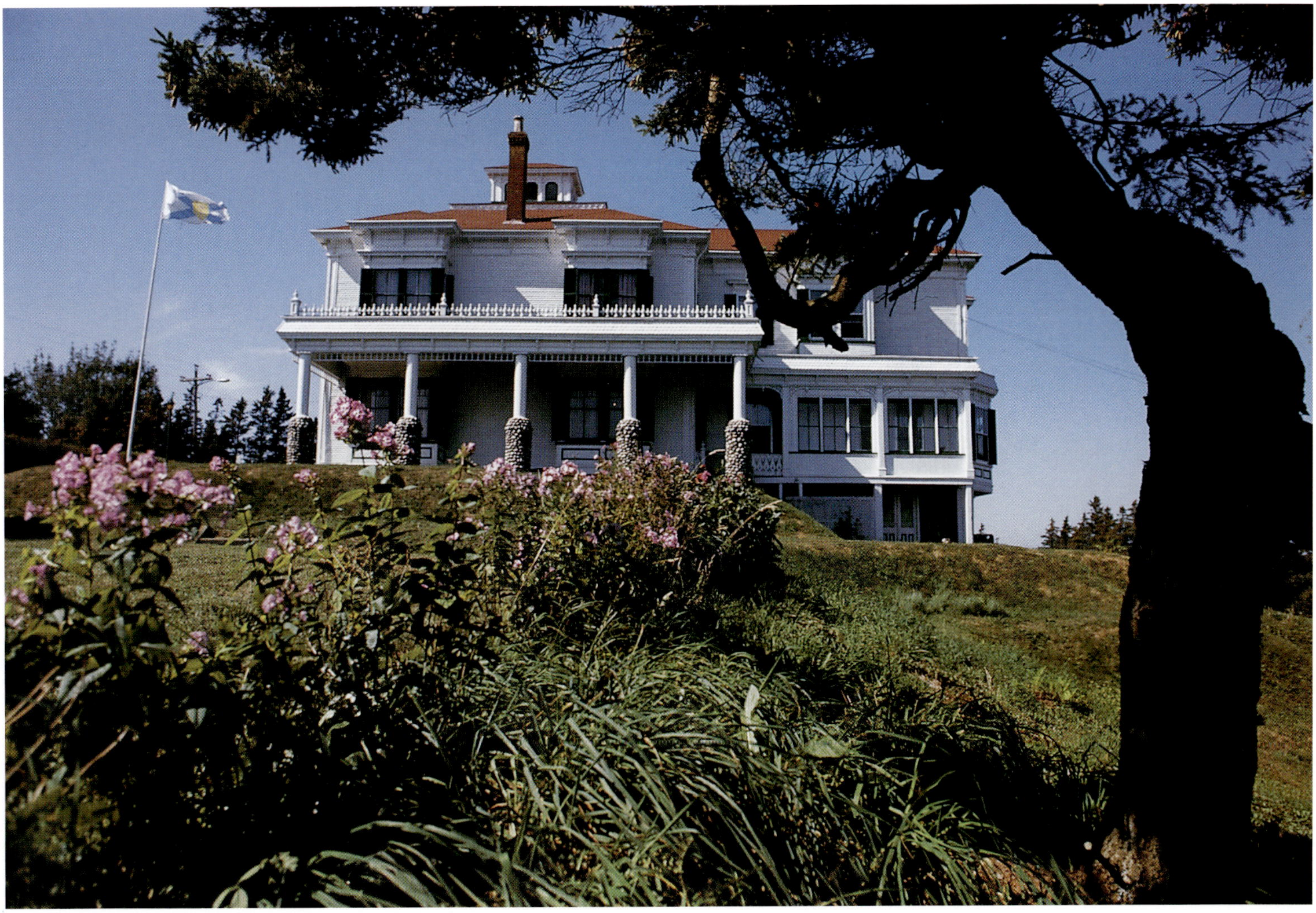

The magnificent and historic Churchill Mansion, now a country inn, is topped with a widow's walk overlooking Darlings Lake and the Bay of Fundy.

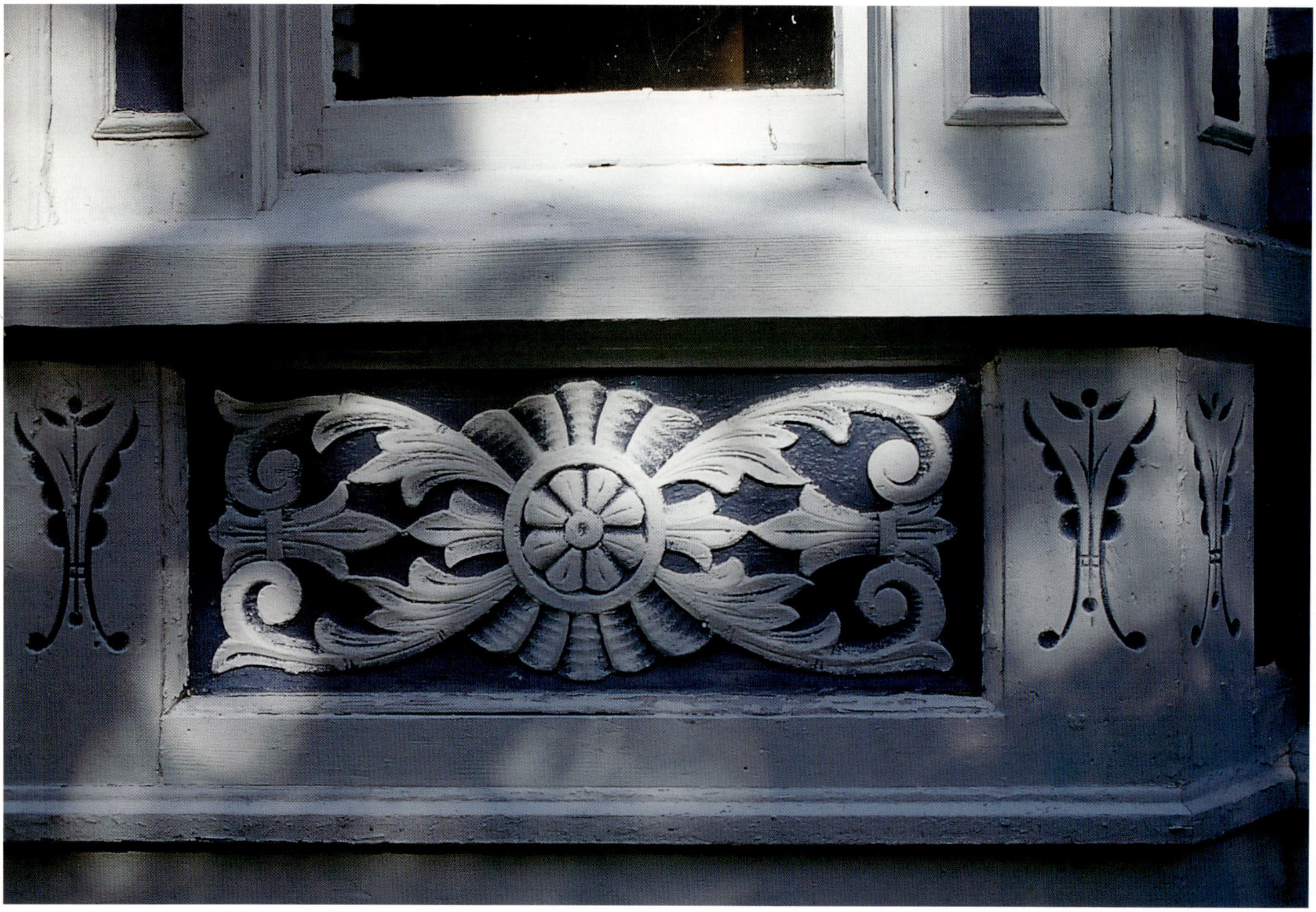

Architectural flourishes on one of the many historical homes to be seen on Collins Street delight the eye.

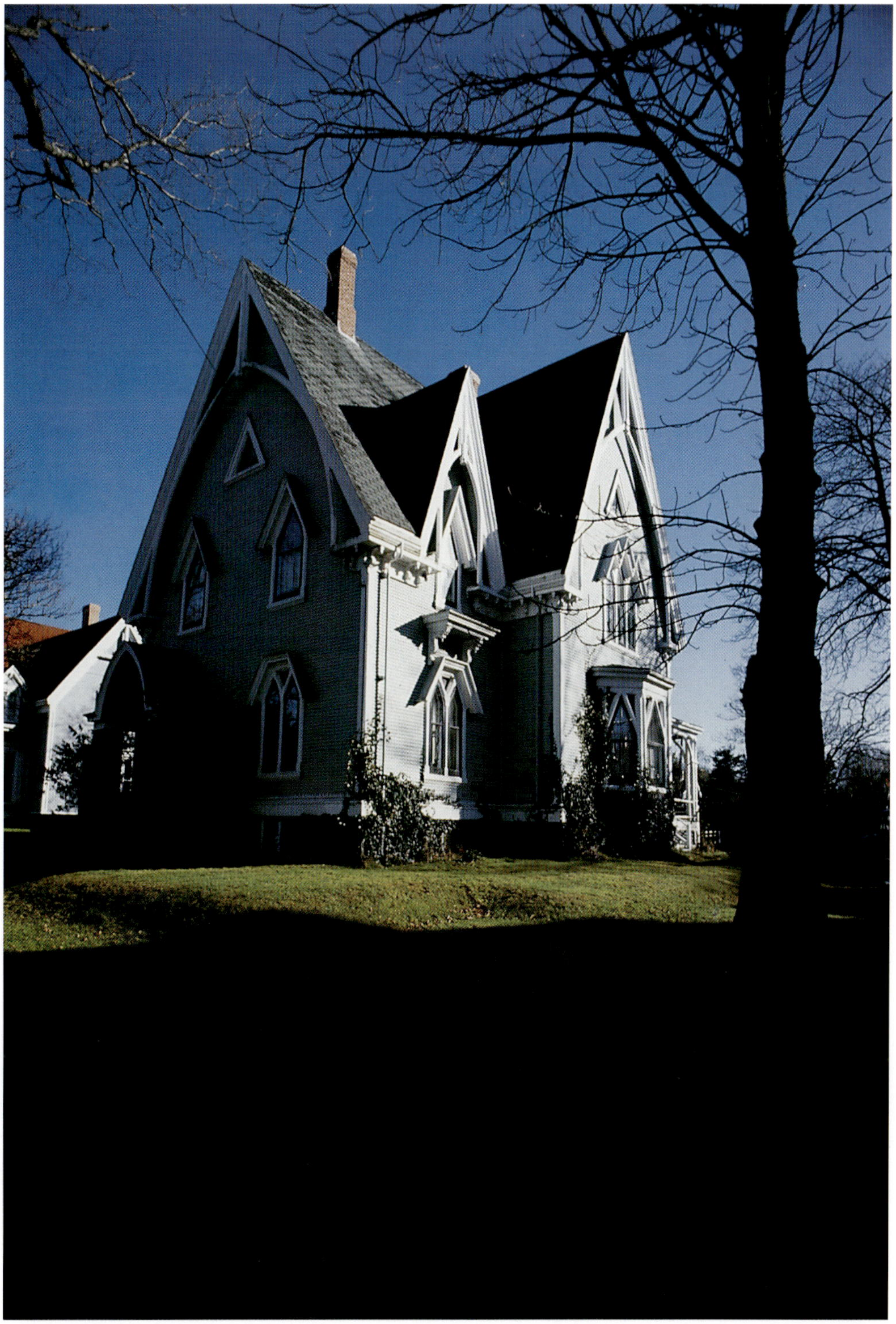

The steep pitches of this Gothic Revival house on Williams Street draw much attention on Yarmouth's popular walking tour.

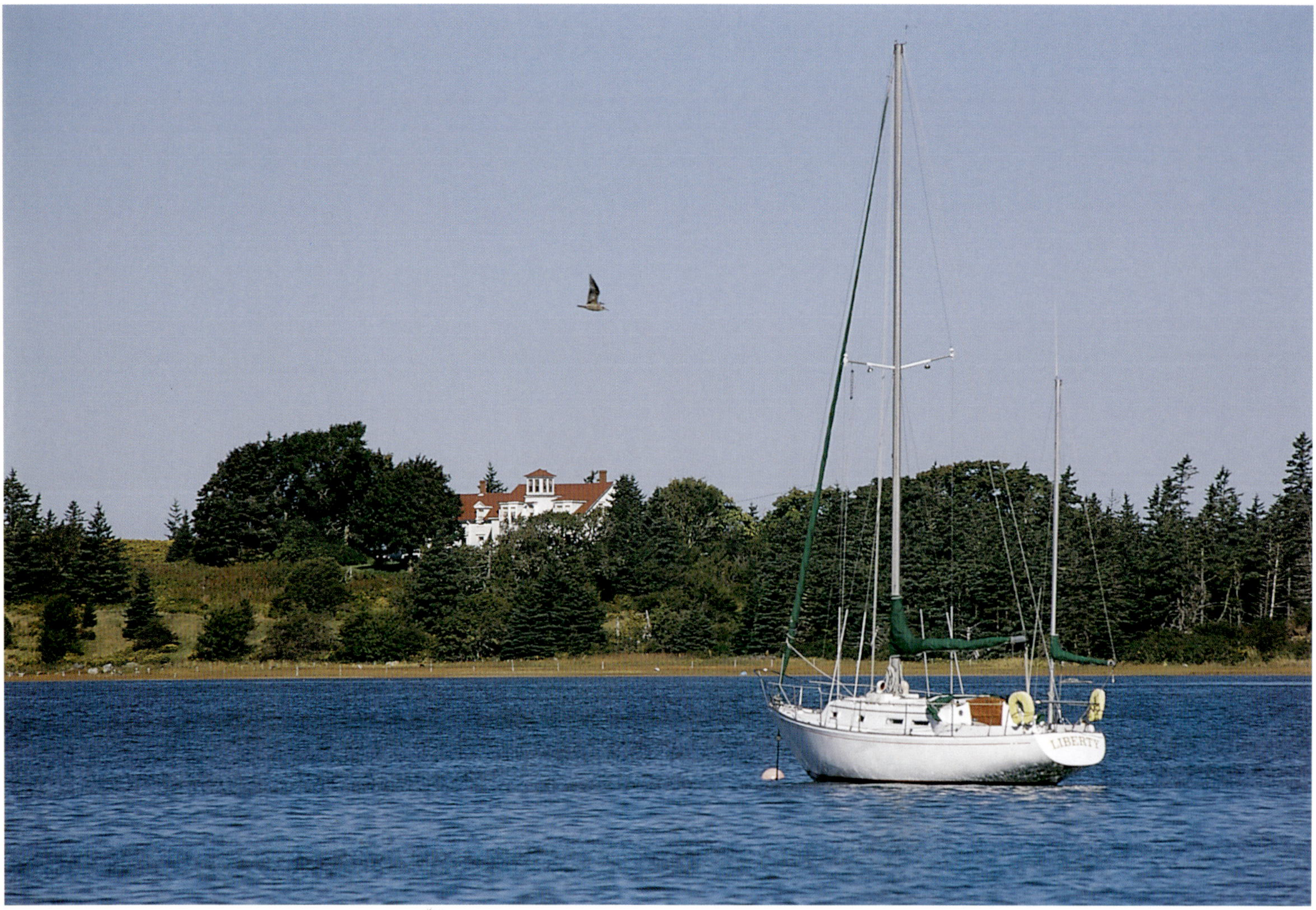

A stately nineteenth-century home complete with widow's walk keeps watch on all who sail in Yarmouth Harbour.

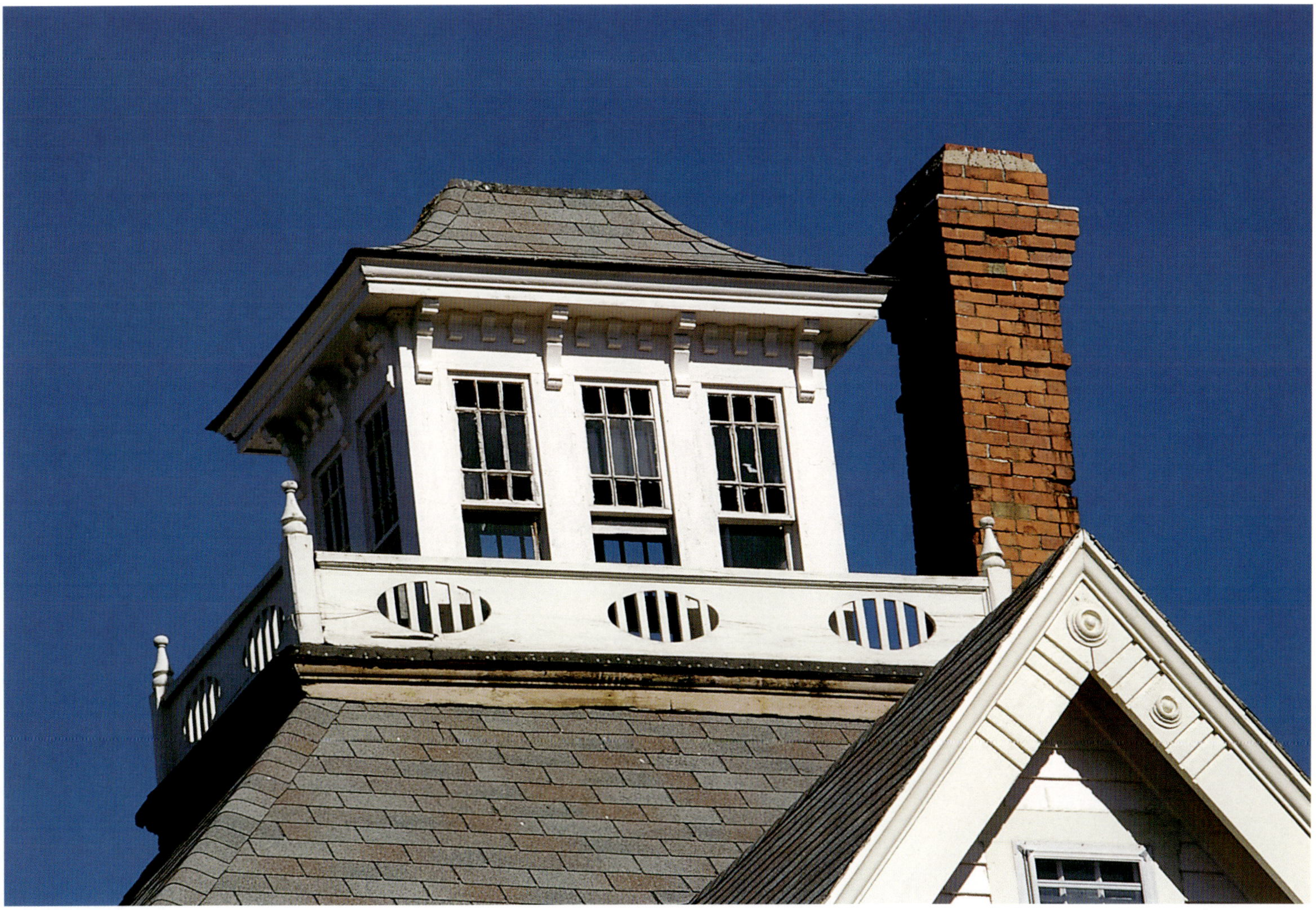

The widow's walks of Yarmouth are a romantic architectural link to its rich, seafaring past.

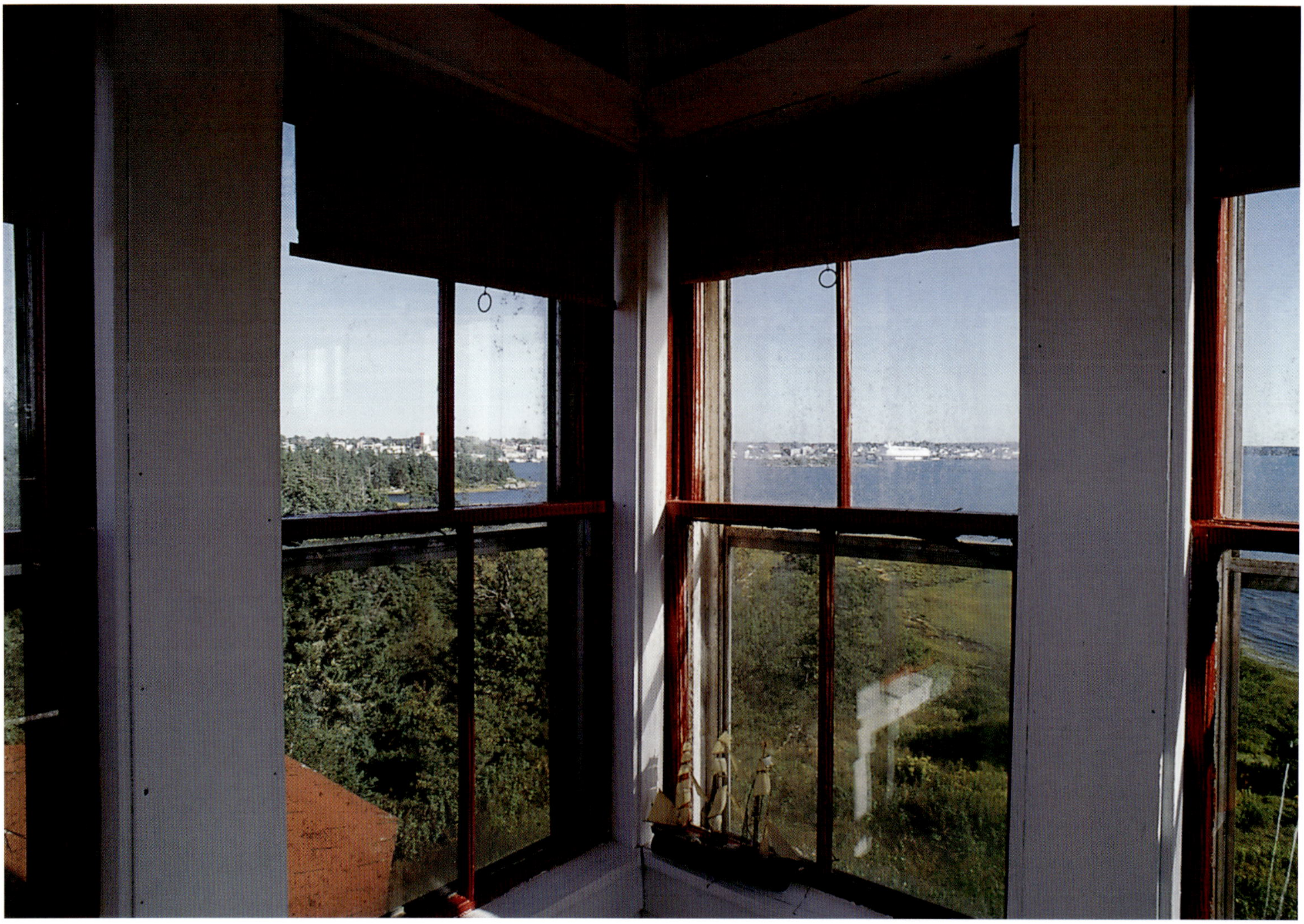

The commanding view from this widow's walk gives a breathtaking 360°-sweep of the town, harbour, and surrounding countryside.

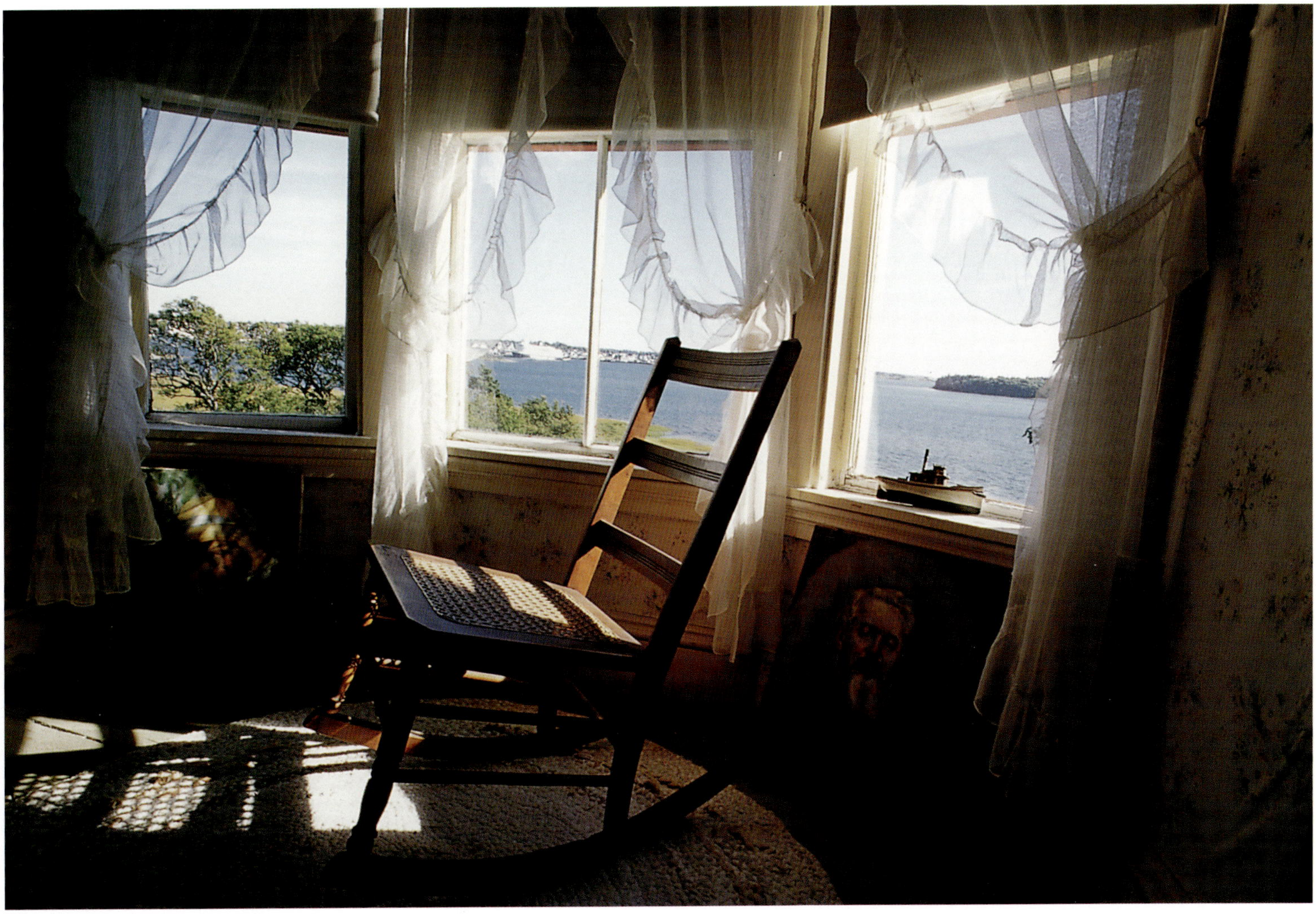

A tranquil setting for an old sea captain's home, overlooking Yarmouth Harbour.

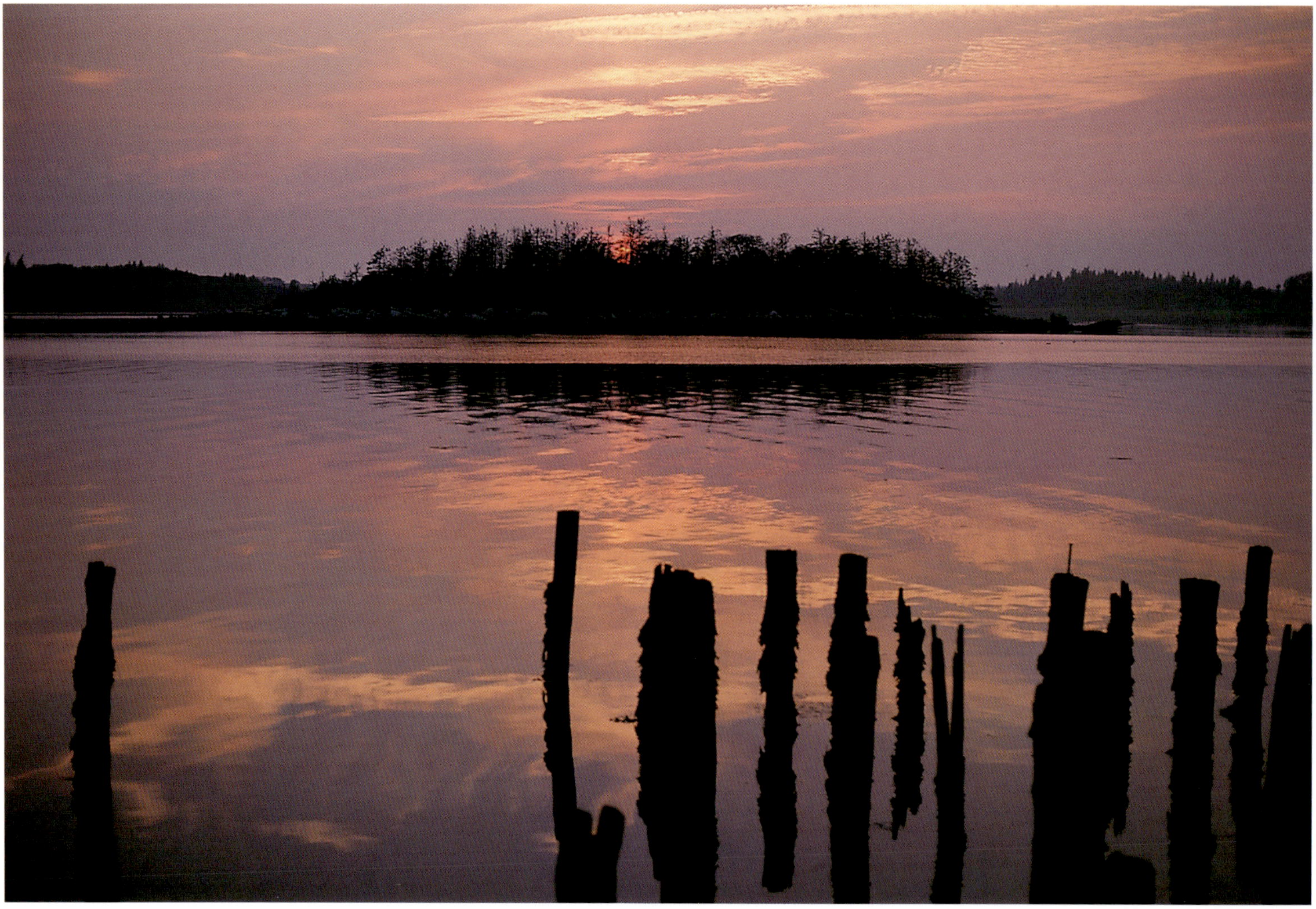

The sun sets behind Doctor Island in Yarmouth Harbour.

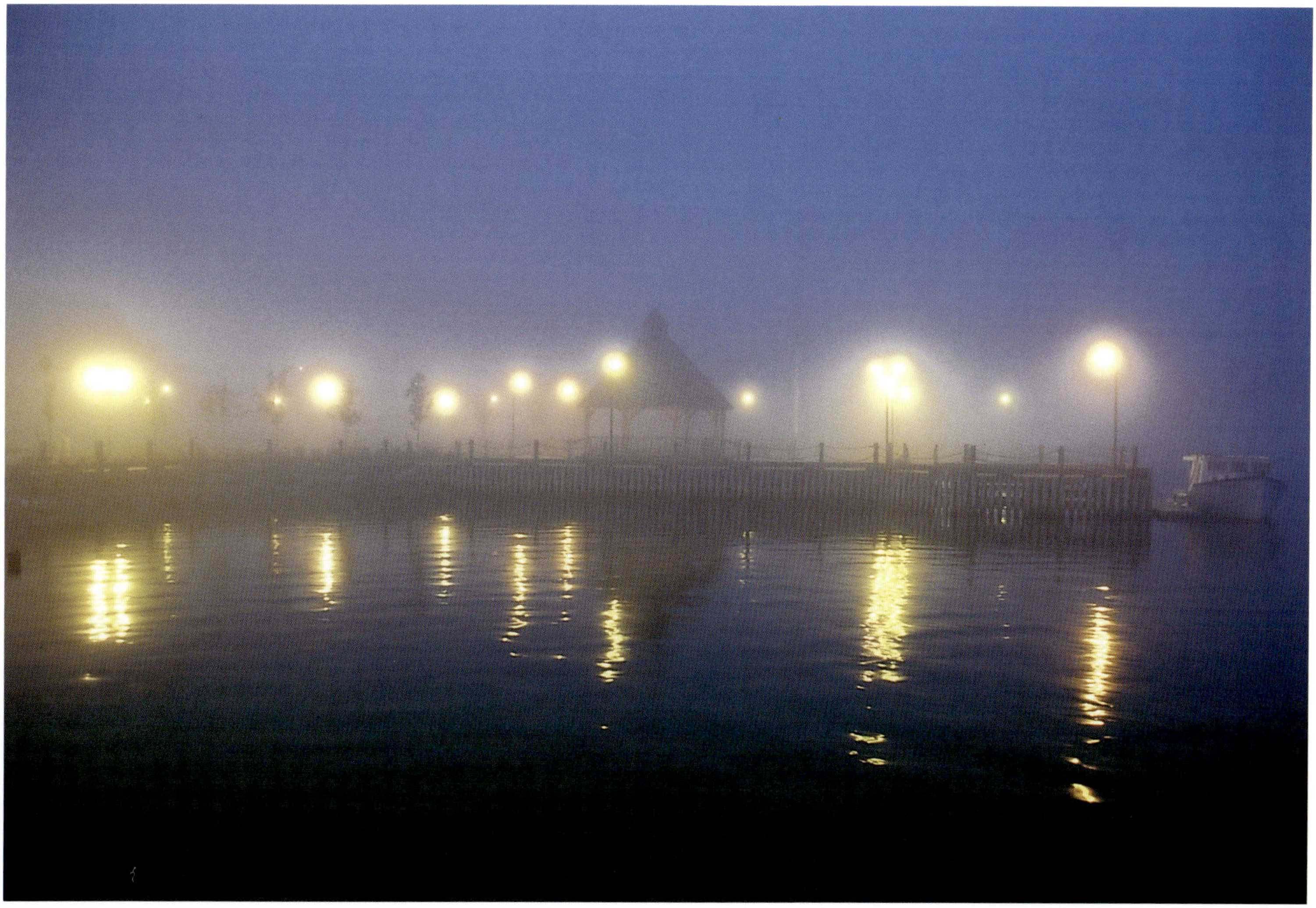

A curtain of fog shrouds this gazebo on the waterfront, creating an eerie atmosphere.

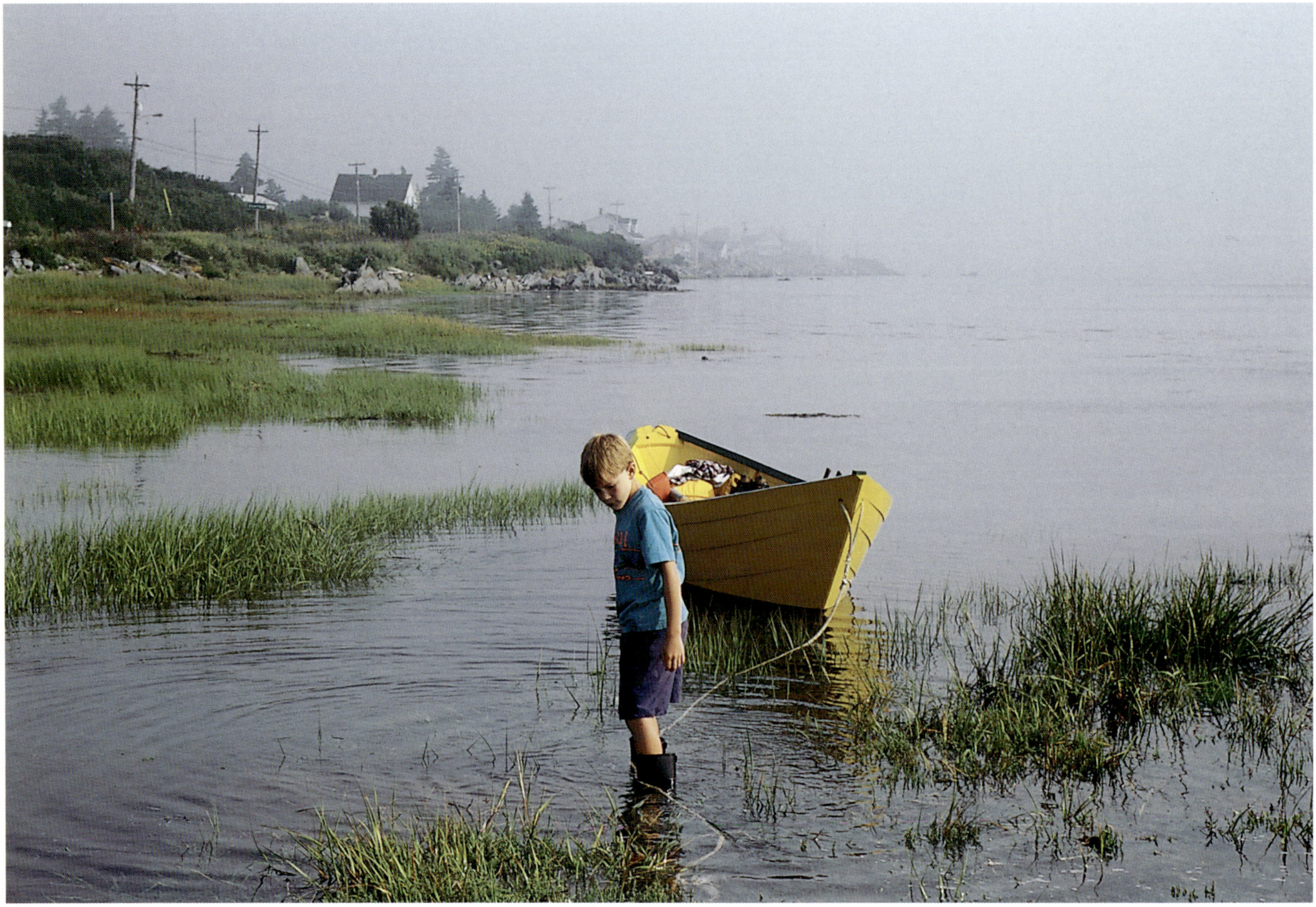

A young boy wades alongside his adult-sized dory at the Yarmouth Bar.

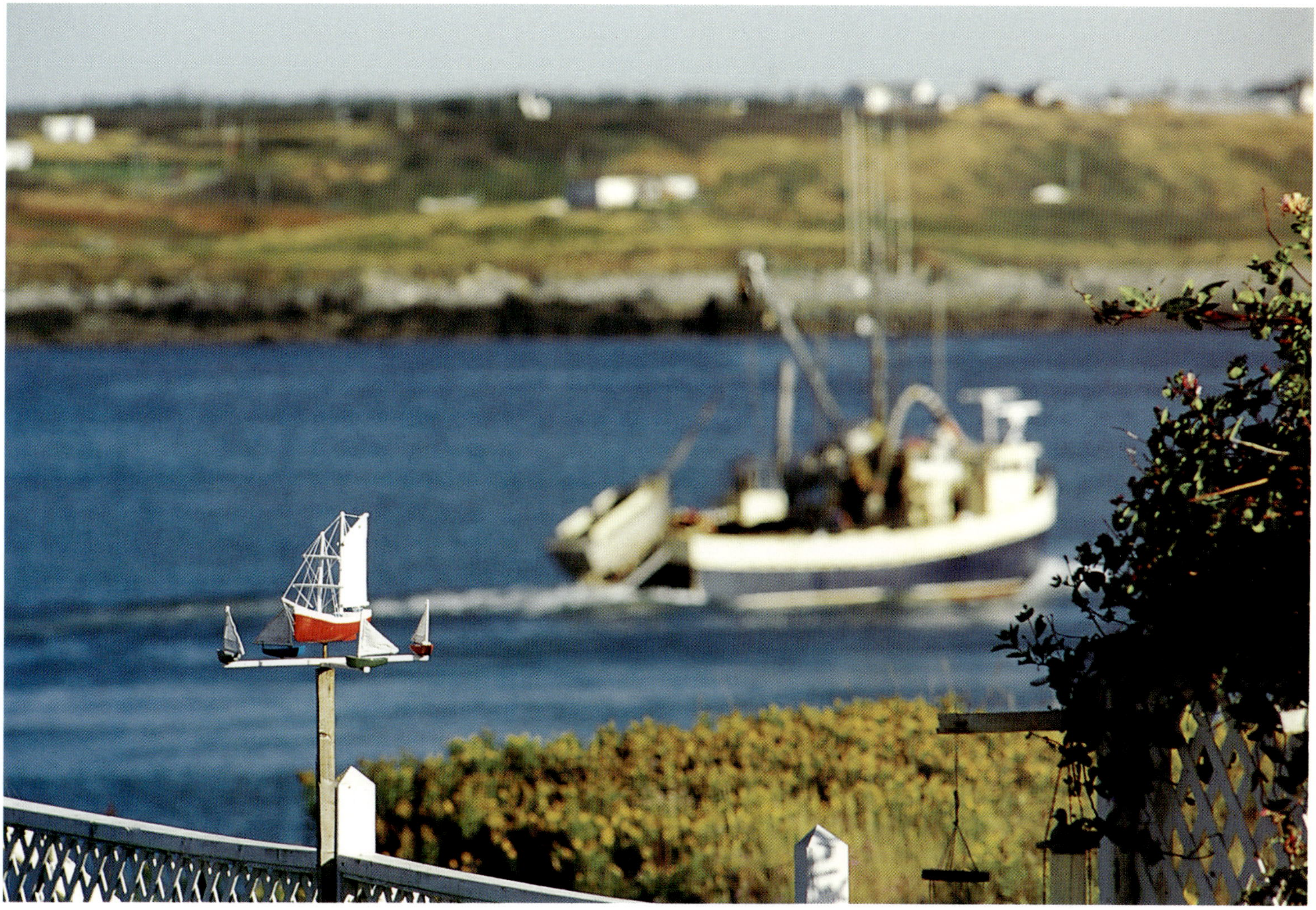

The whirligig's toylike boat plays in the breeze as a herring seiner heads out to sea.

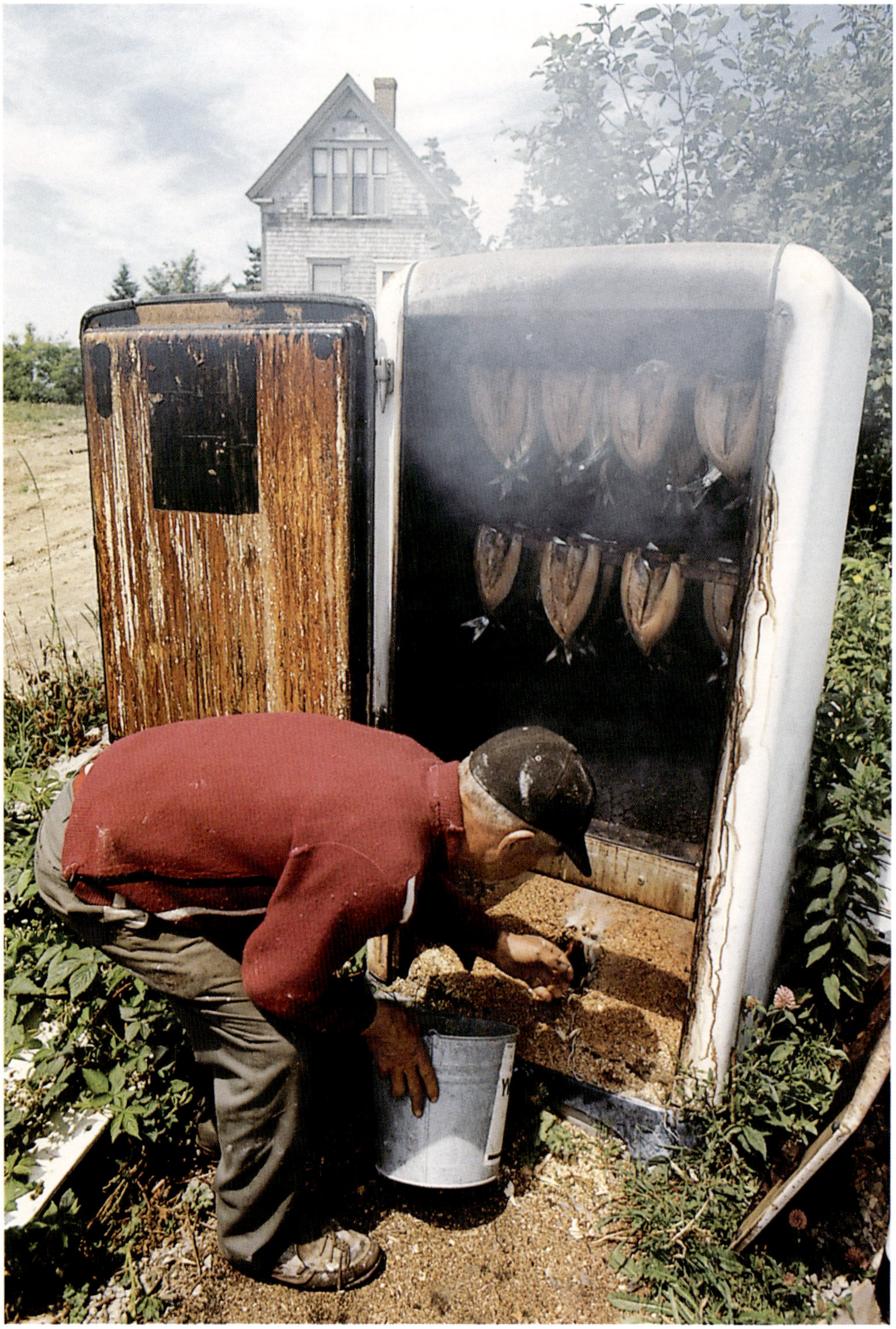

The late Owen Sweeney demonstrates his ingenious method for smoking fresh local fish, a technique still practised by his wife, Katherine. A regular clientele stops by her buoy-decorated home in Markland to buy kippers.

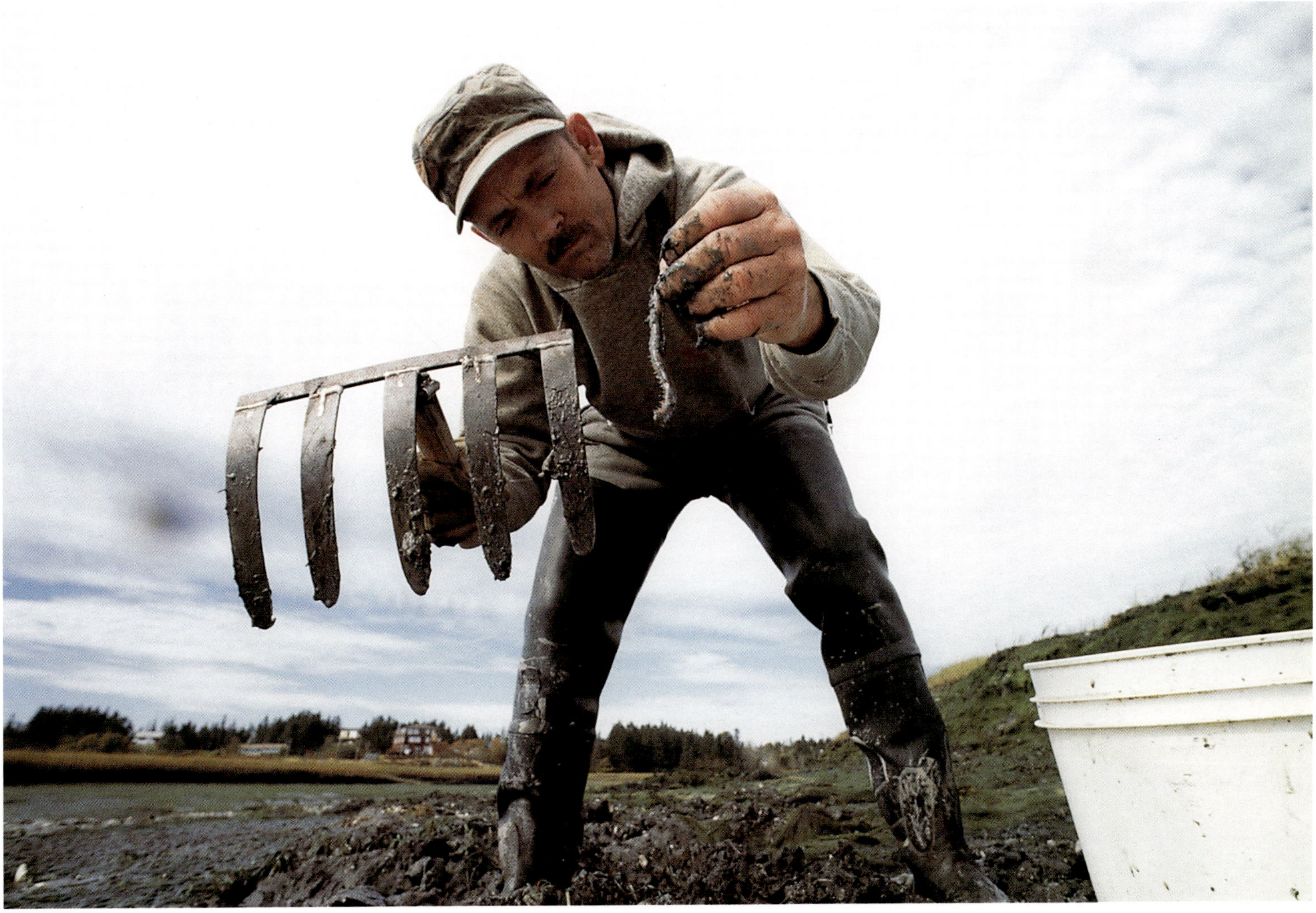

Veteran digger Brian Thompson checks the quality of one of over seven-hundred blood-worms he digs for on the mud-flats around Yarmouth County during each low tide. Blood-worms are sorted at processors, packed in seaweed and shipped live to markets as far away as Virginia, where they are in great demand as sport-fishing bait. Some 110 diggers engage in this back-breaking and competitive work, contributing to a blood-worm industry that, overall, brings in an impressive $4 million a year to Yarmouth County's economy.

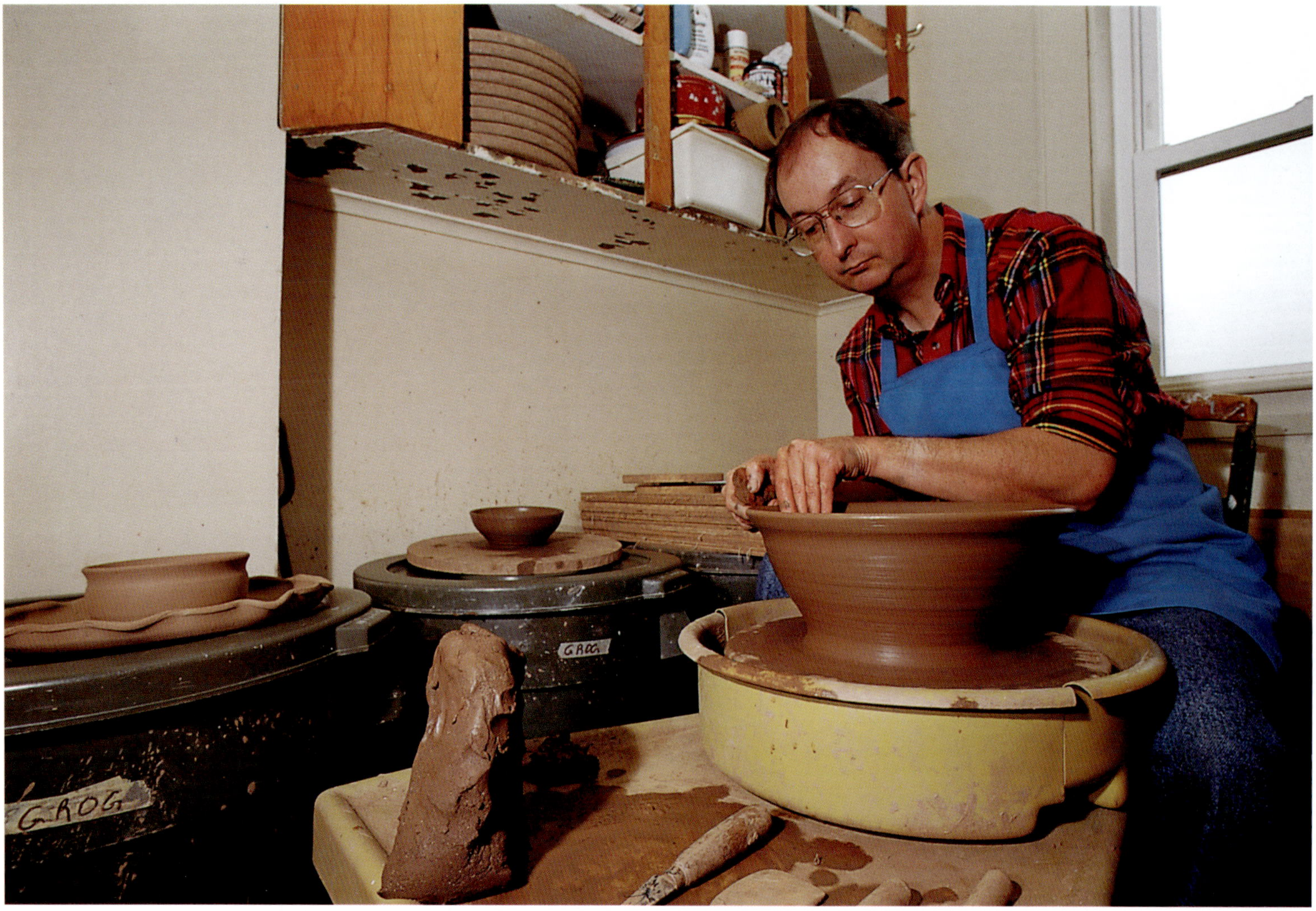

Creativity abounds throughout Yarmouth County as clay takes shape under the skilled hands of Michael Morris at Morris Pottery in Dayton.

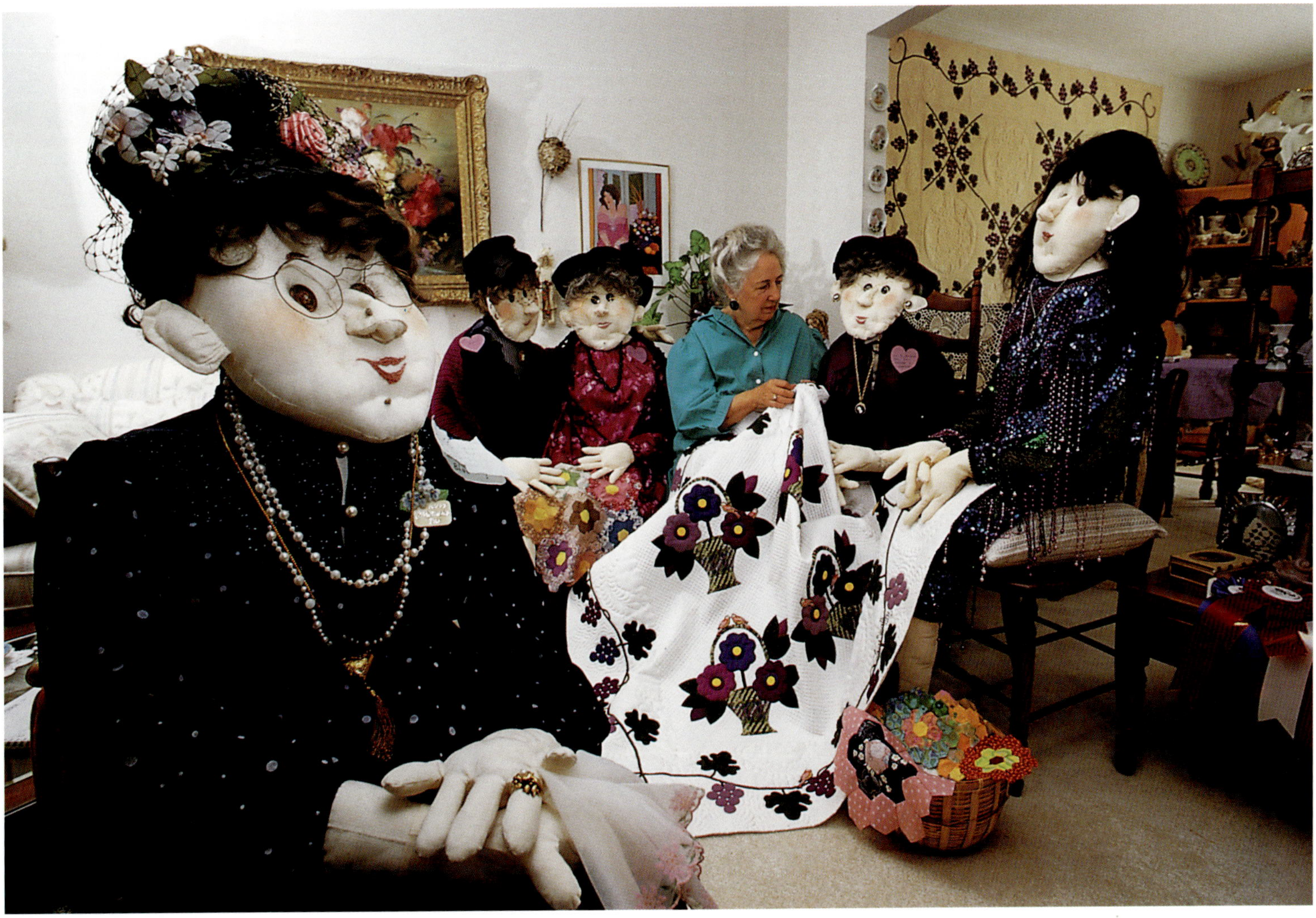

Sporting elaborate outfits, talented Louise Vincelli's "people" get a lesson in stitching from this award-winning quilter.

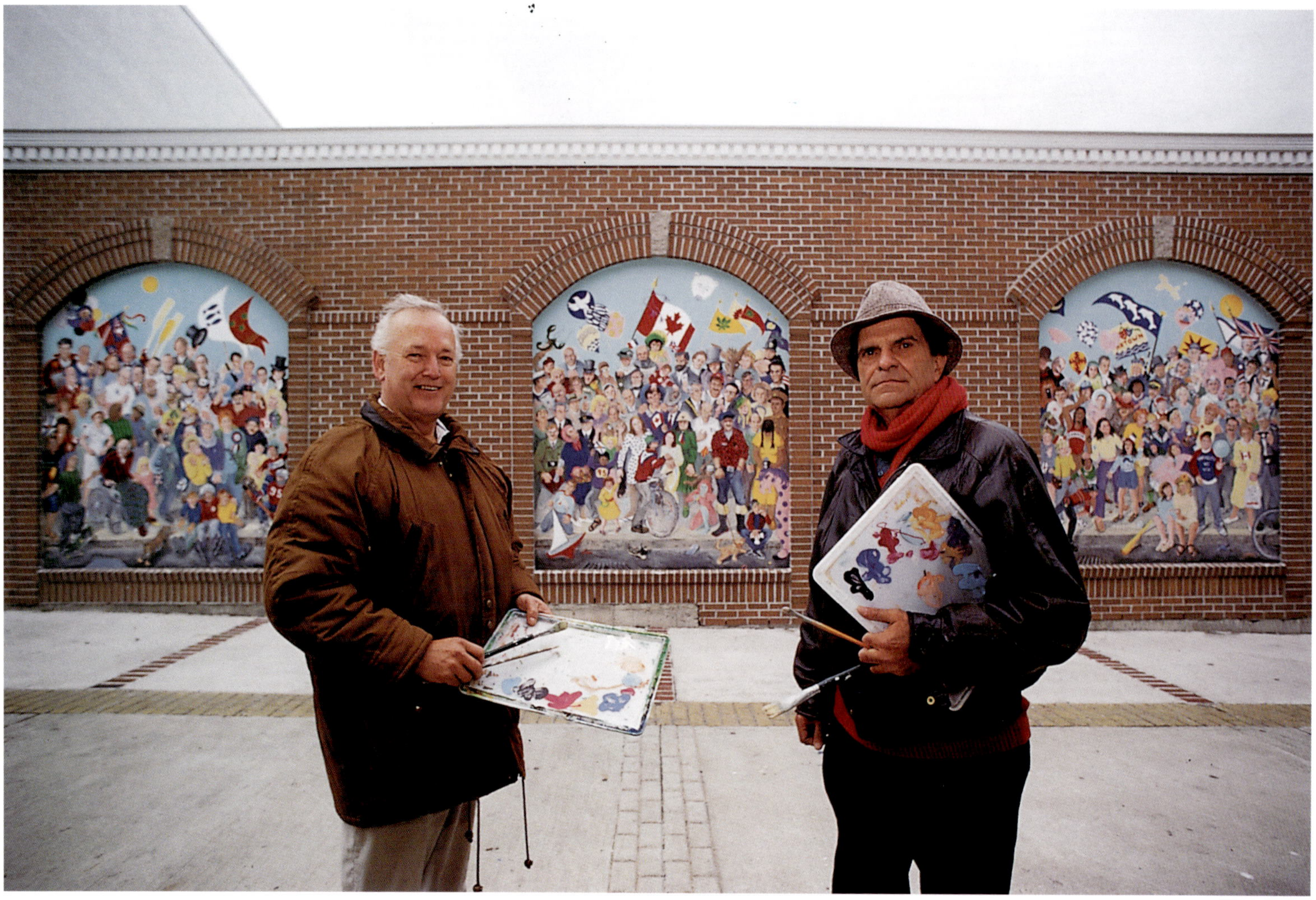

Well-known Yarmouth artists Hugh Eamon and Alex Gigeroff pose in front of their colourful mural in Alma Court, Yarmouth.

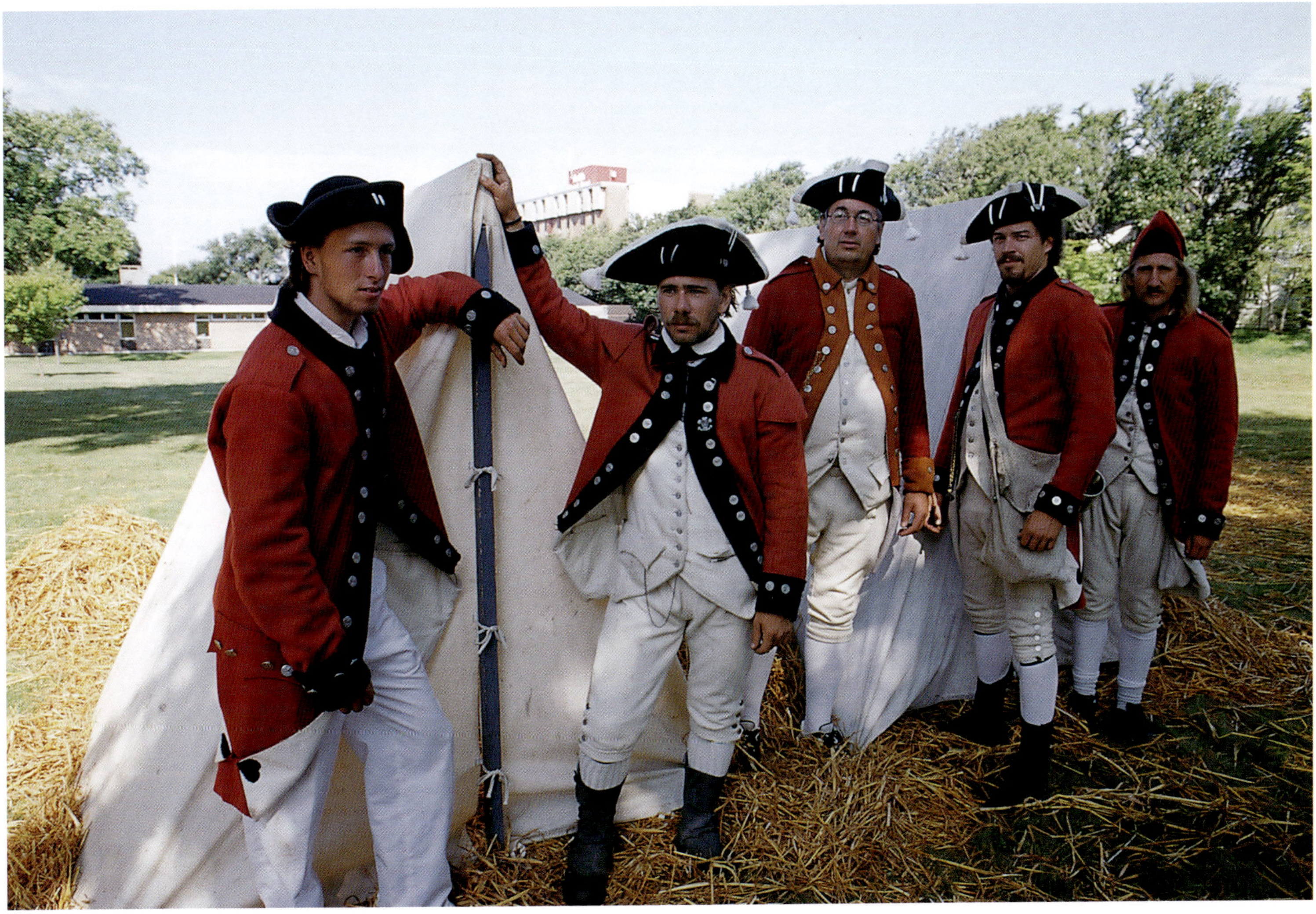

Past meets present at an encampment by reenactment troops of the Prince of Wales American Regiment.

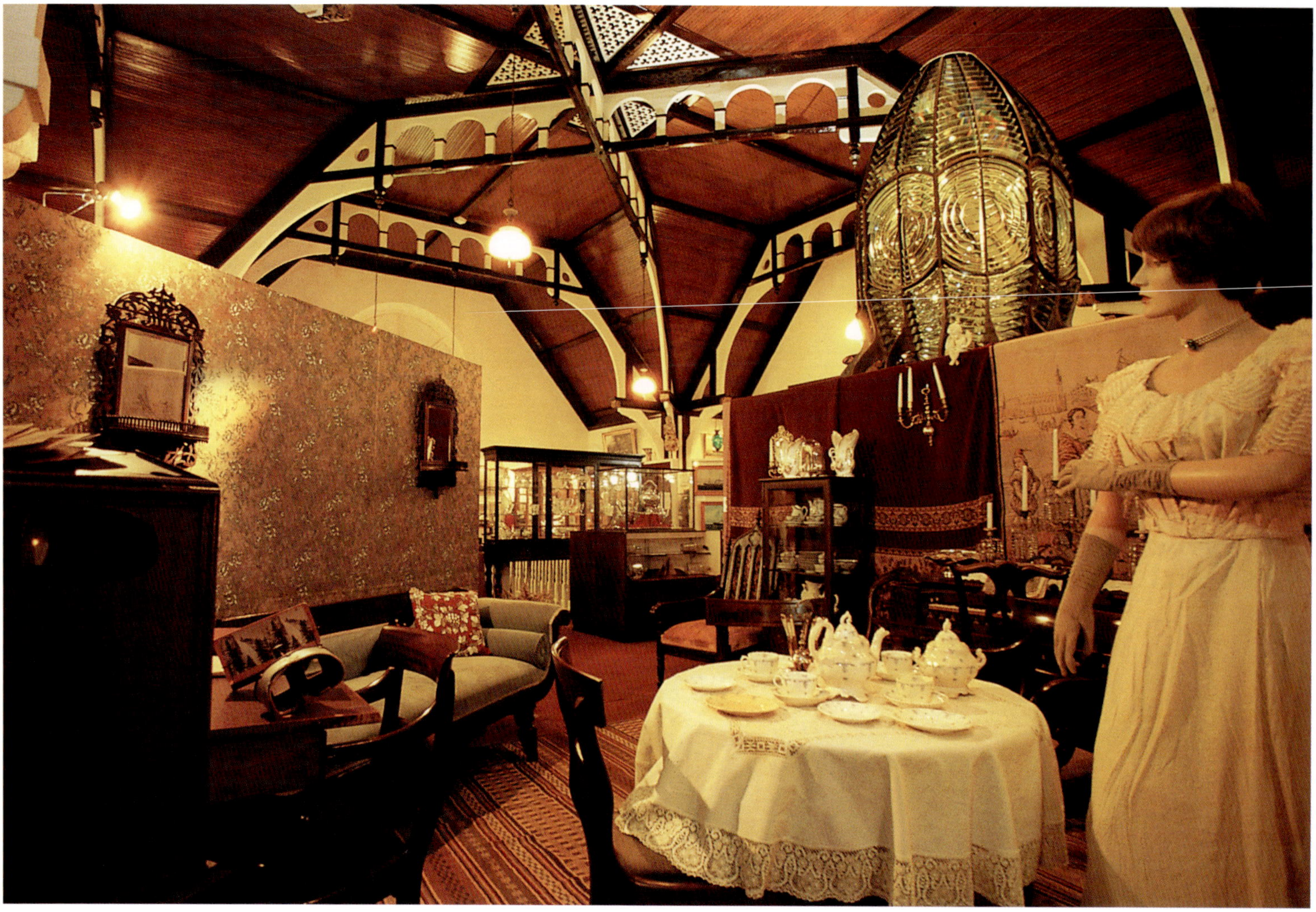

The old Yarmouth Light stands guard over the impressive collections of the Yarmouth County Museum.

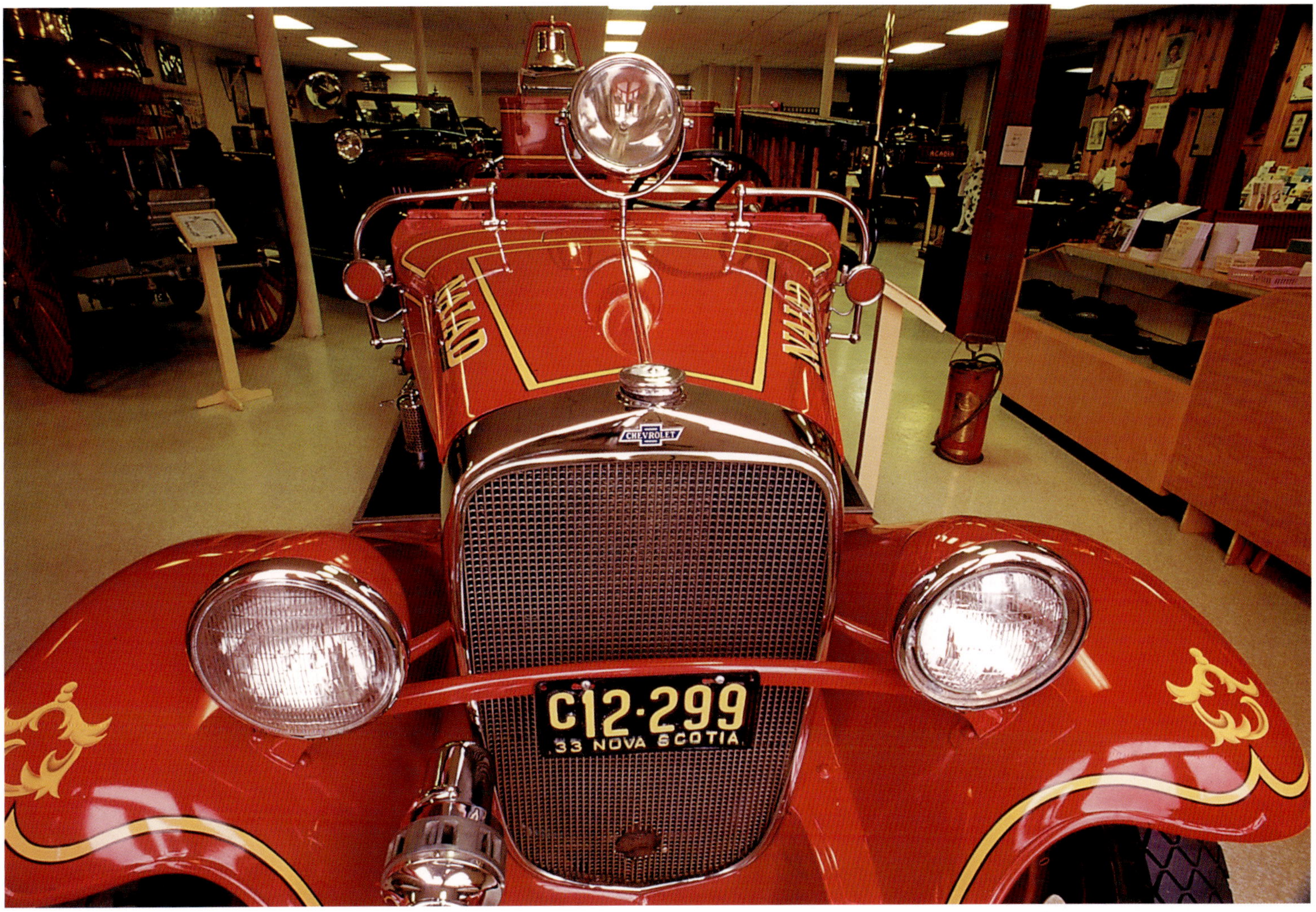

A 1933 Pumper is polished to a sheen at the Firefighters' Museum.

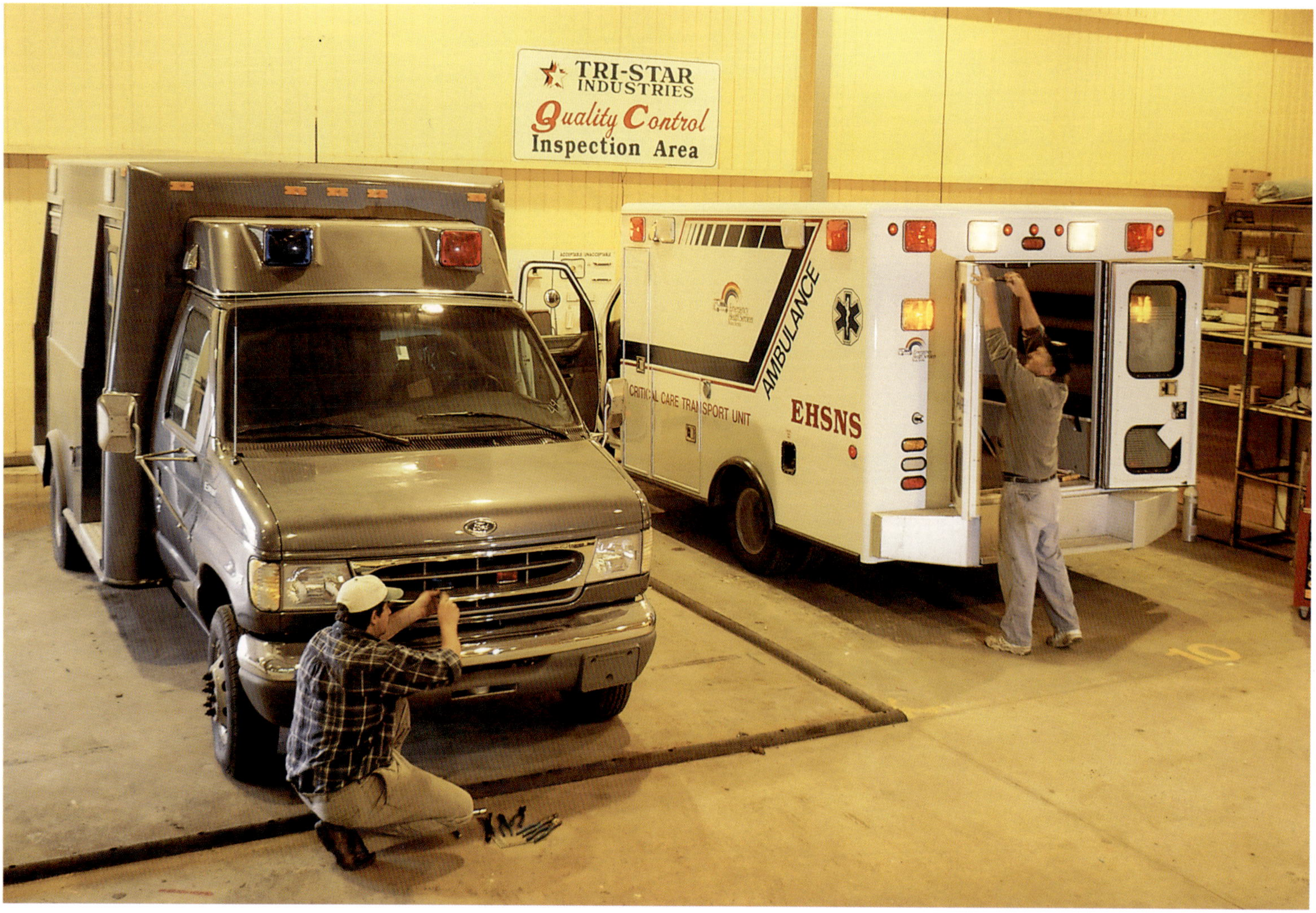

Workers at Tri-Star Industries put the final touches on an ambulance and a bomb-disposal vehicle. Tri-Star exports custom-made vehicles to the Middle East, Haiti, Cuba, and throughout North America.

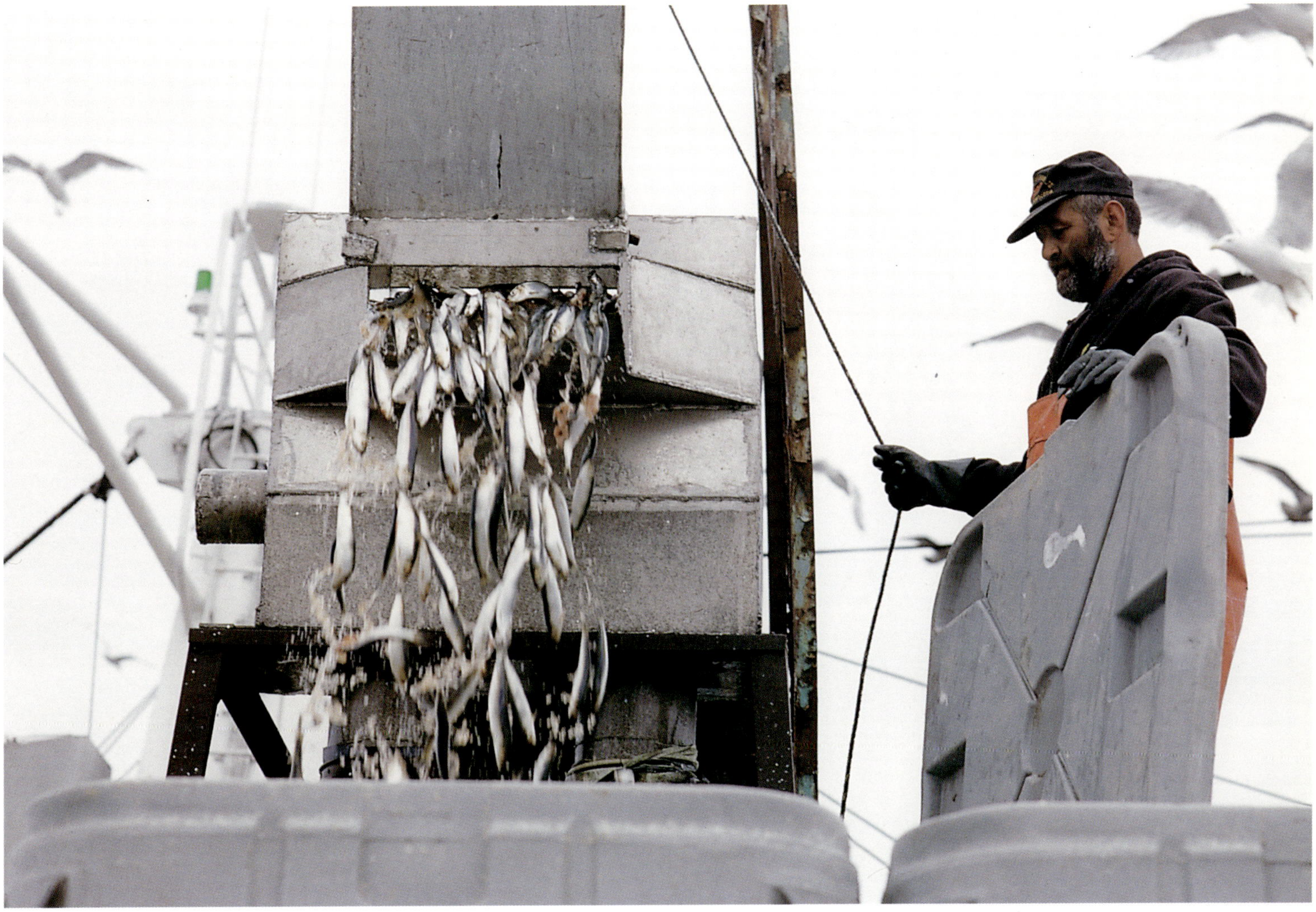

As gulls troll for a free lunch on Yarmouth's active waterfront, herring is offloaded from the seiners. The fish are sold domestically and exported as bait, fish meal, fillets and roe. The herring industry represents over $12 million per year for the county.

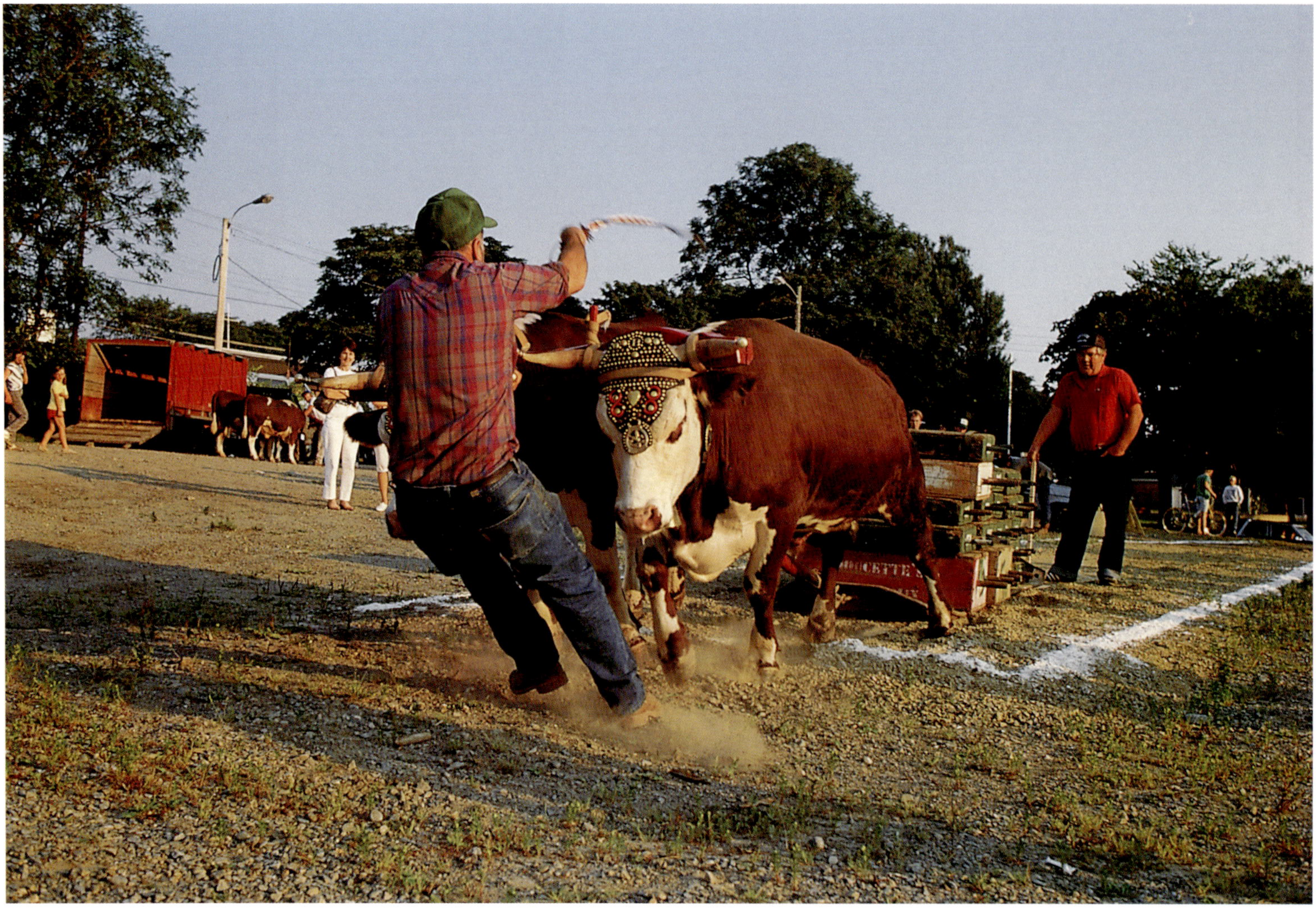

Oxen strain under a heavy load during an exciting outdoor pull. Championship ox-hauls generate standing-room only crowds at the Western Nova Scotia Exhibition held every summer in Yarmouth.

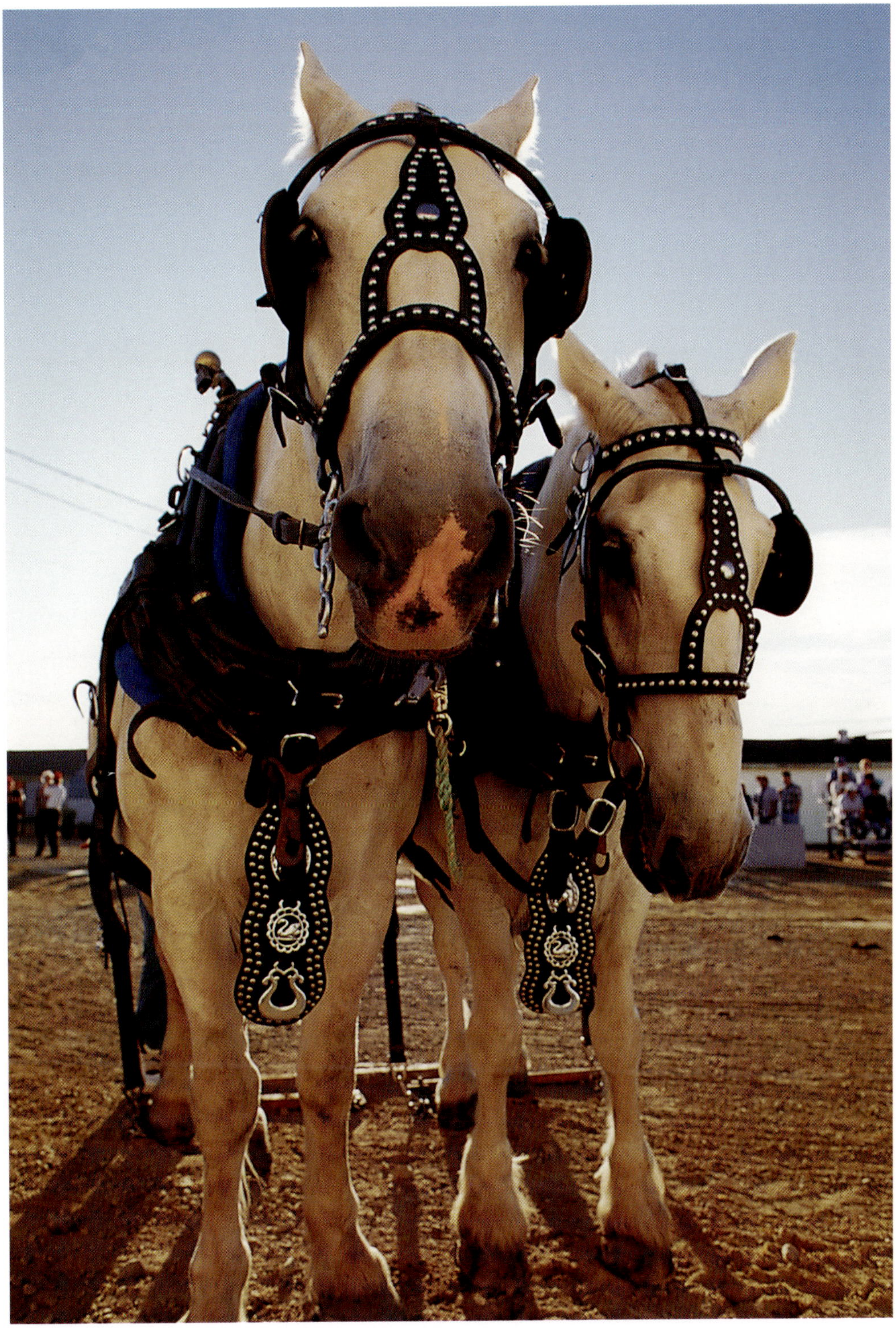

At "the Ex," two participants wait to pull a load in the outside ring.

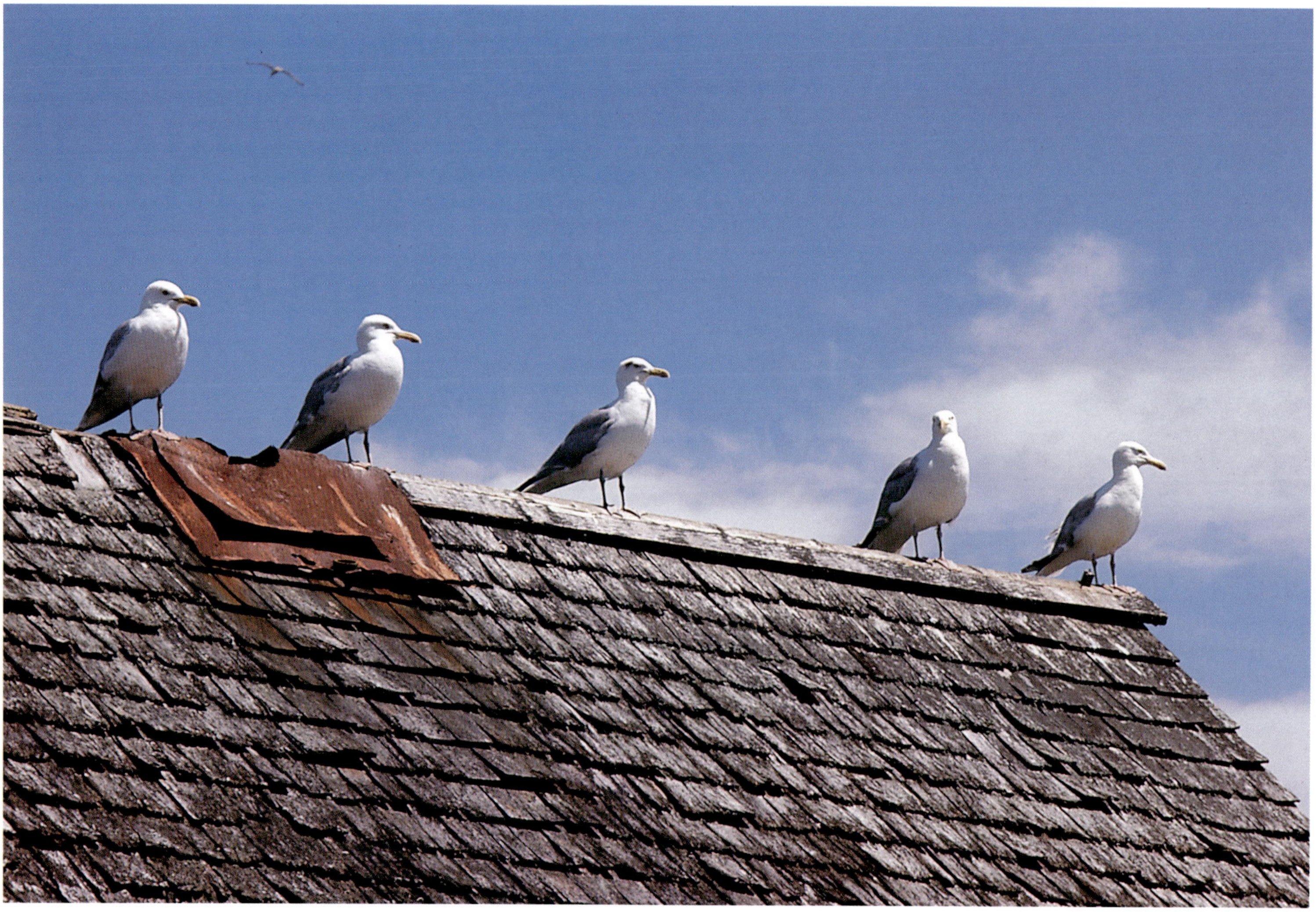

Gulls take in the action on Yarmouth's waterfront.

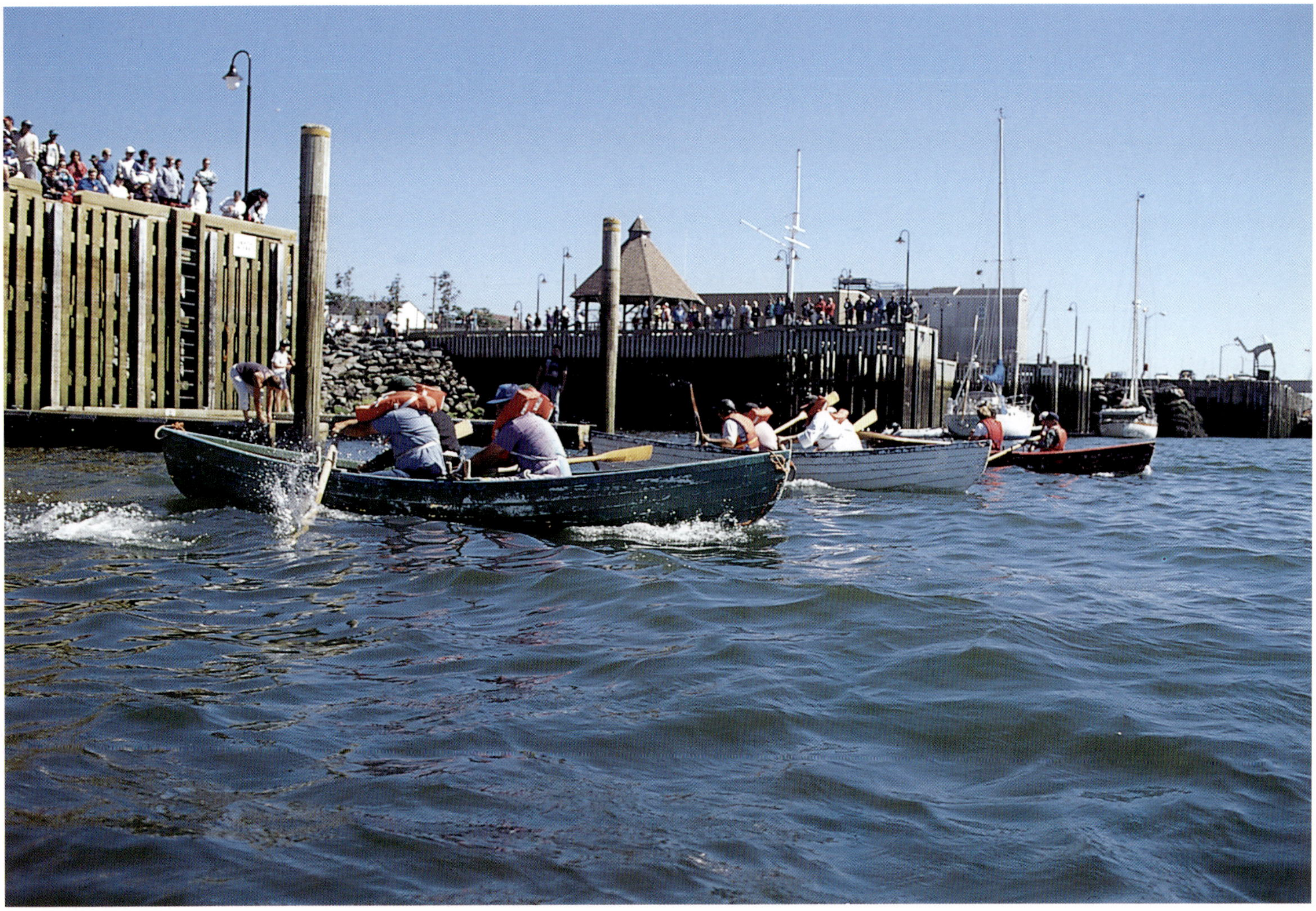

Keen competition and much hilarity occur during Yarmouth's Seafest dory races.

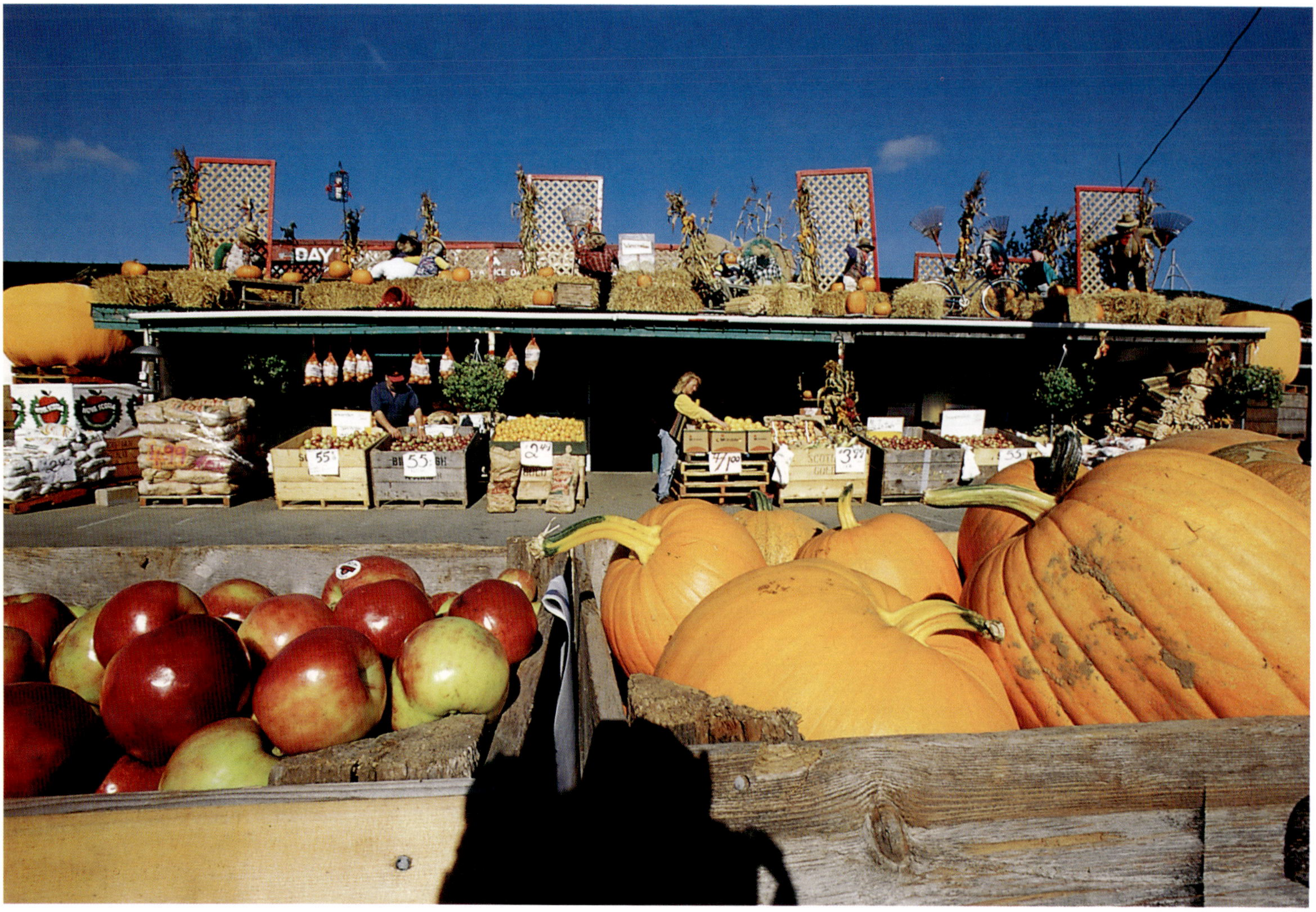

Under the watchful eyes of rooftop scarecrows, autumn's bounty overflows the bins at Dayton Fruit and Vegetable Stand.

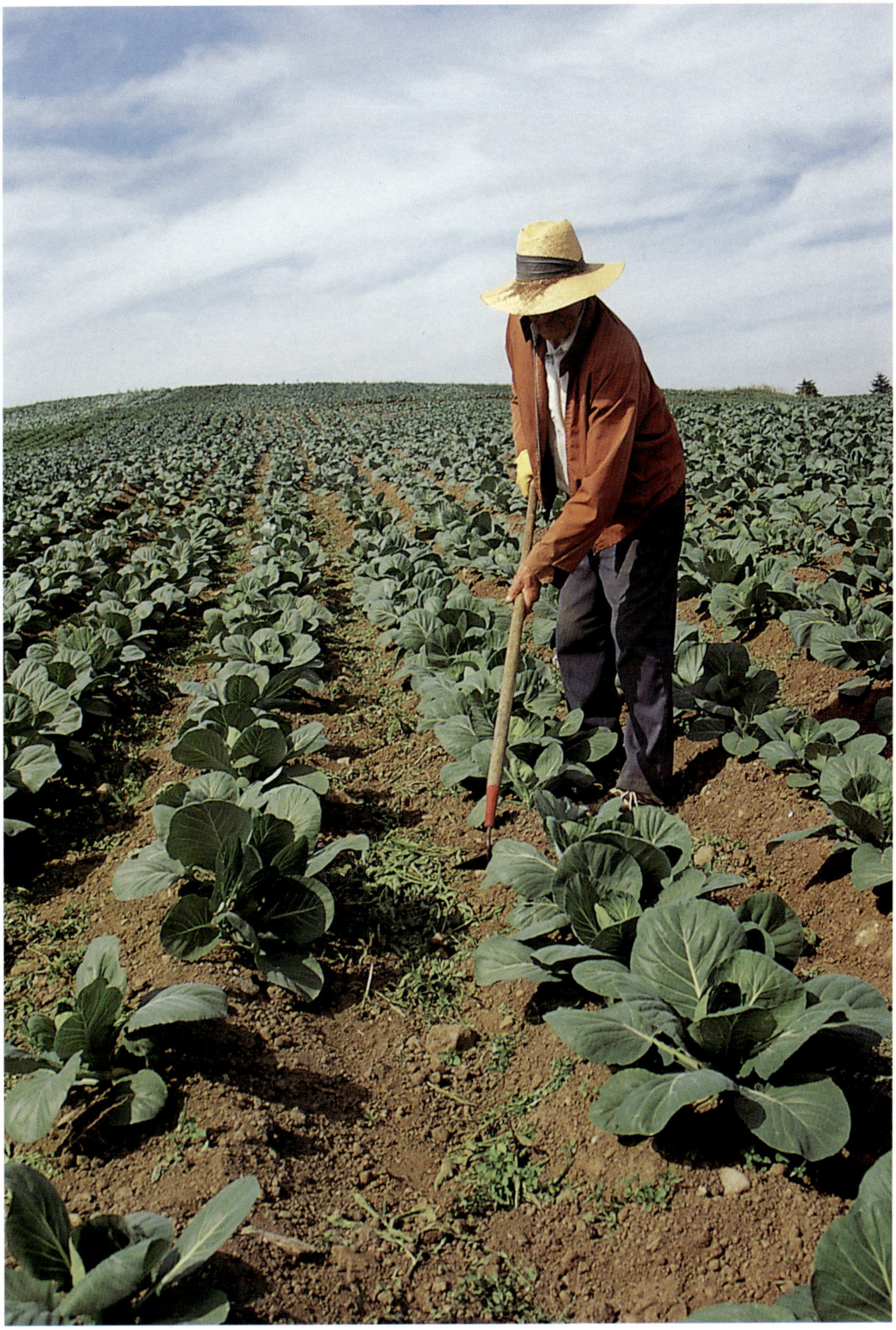

Lloyd Churchill works the cabbage field on a warm summer day in Chegoggin.

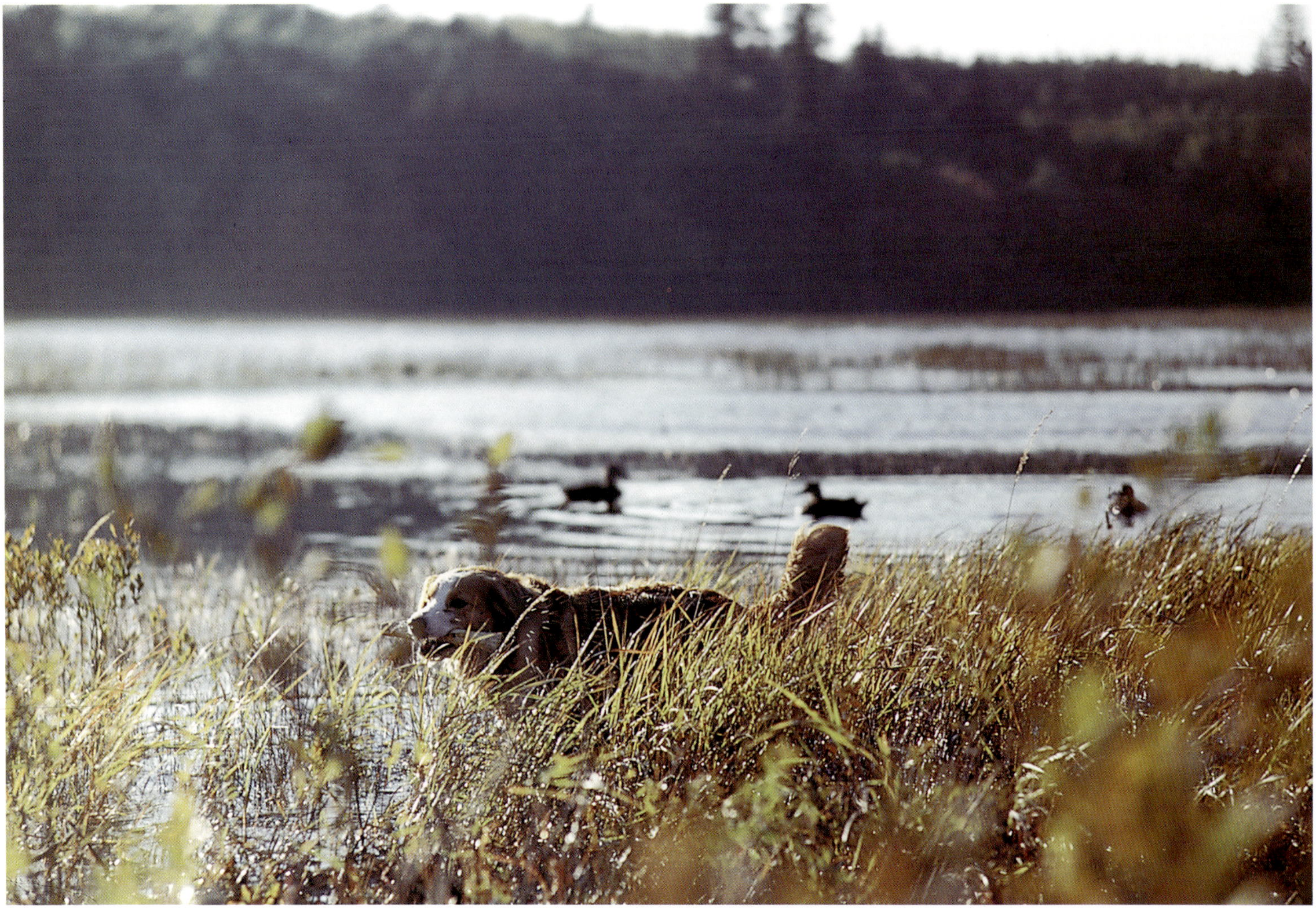

A Little River Duck Dog tolls inquisitive ducks from across a lake to a hunter's blind. Originally bred in Little River, this hearty breed has foxlike colouring and behaviour and is used to attract or "toll" ducks. (They are the only hunting dog indigenous to Nova Scotia registered with the Canadian Kennel Club.)

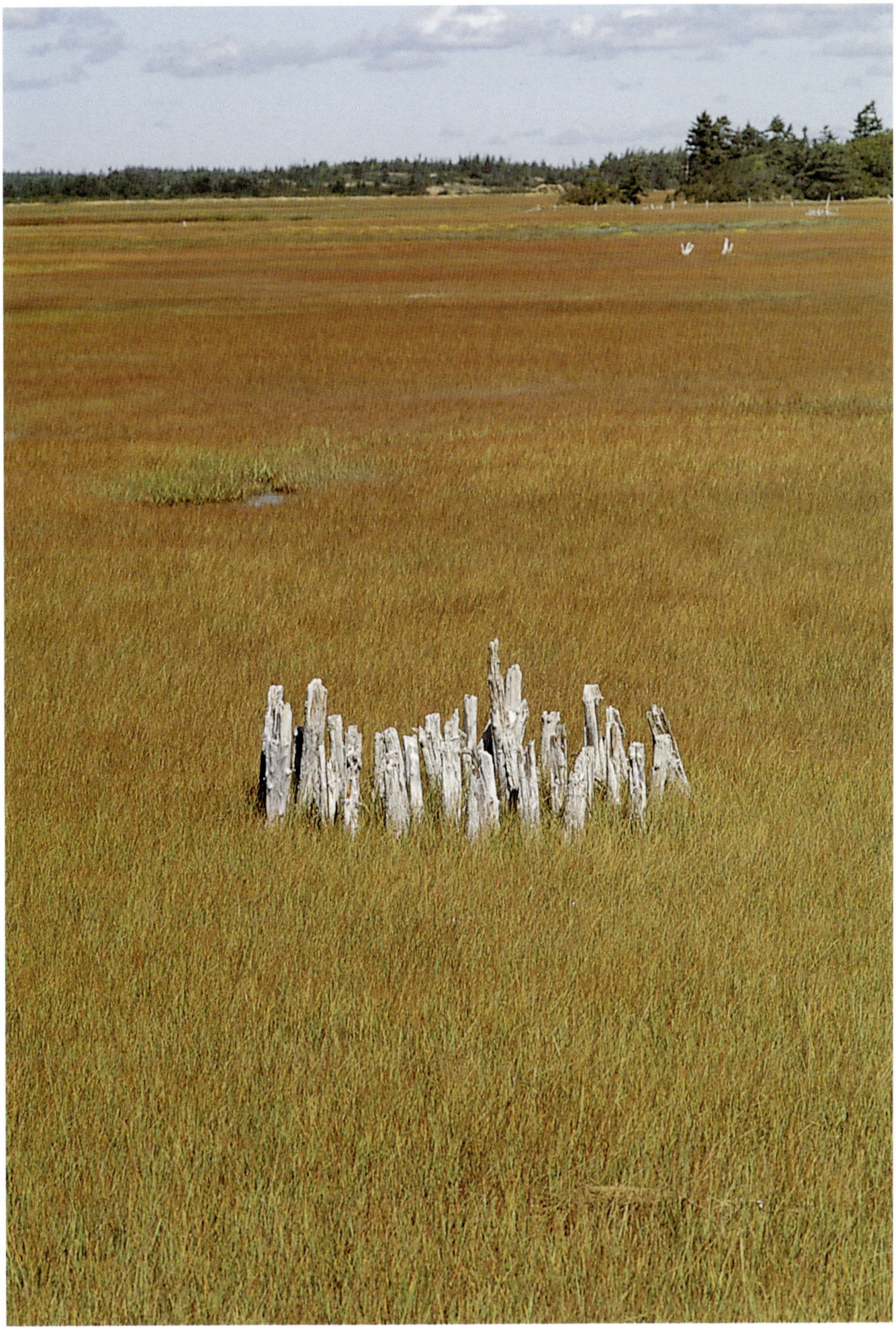

Staddles in the salt-marshes of Yarmouth County are used by farmers to keep their harvest of salt hay high and dry, safe from the Fundy tides.

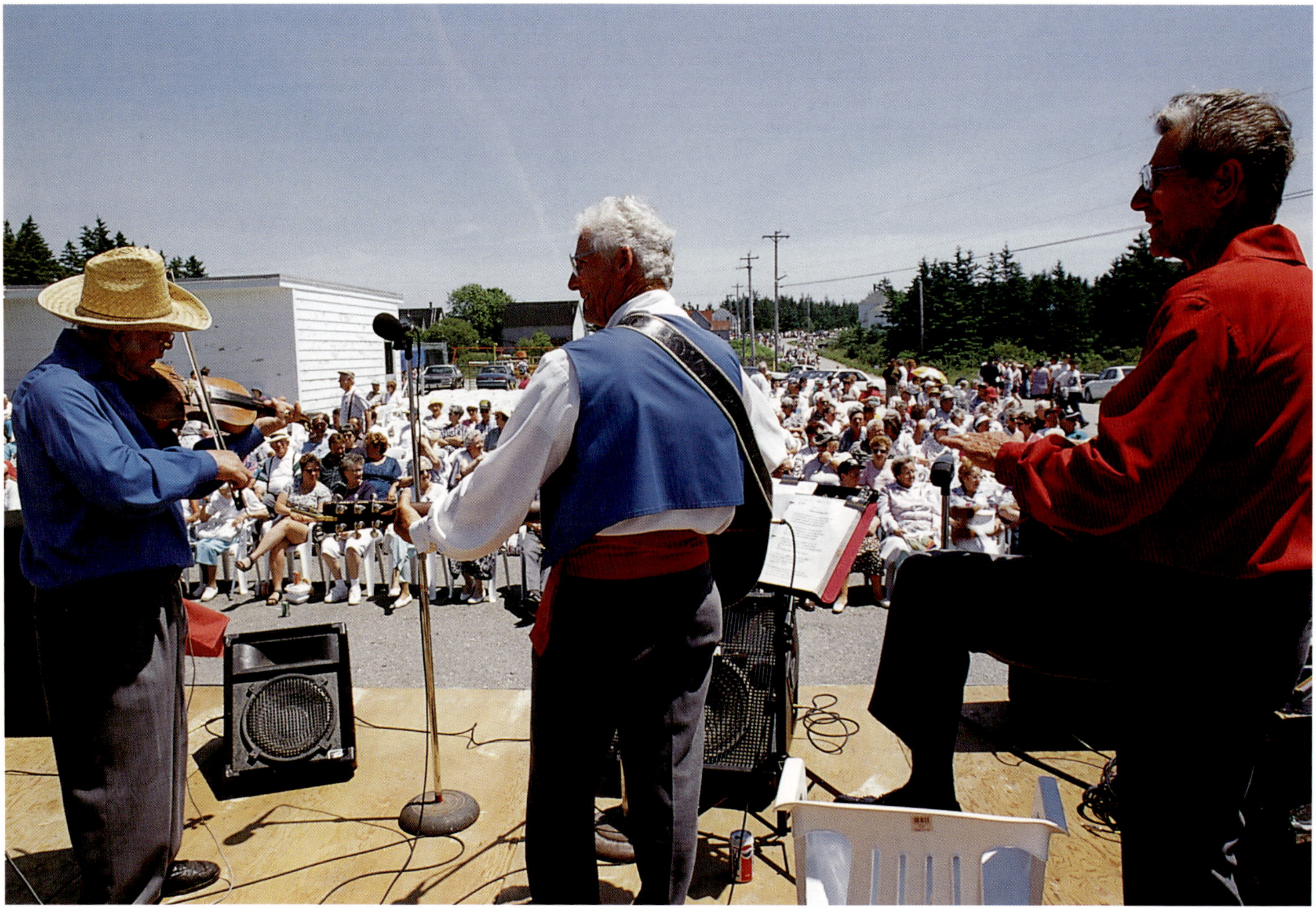

Les Tyneux De La Baie, *a popular Acadian band, performs before a huge audience during the annual* Wedgeport Acadian Festival.

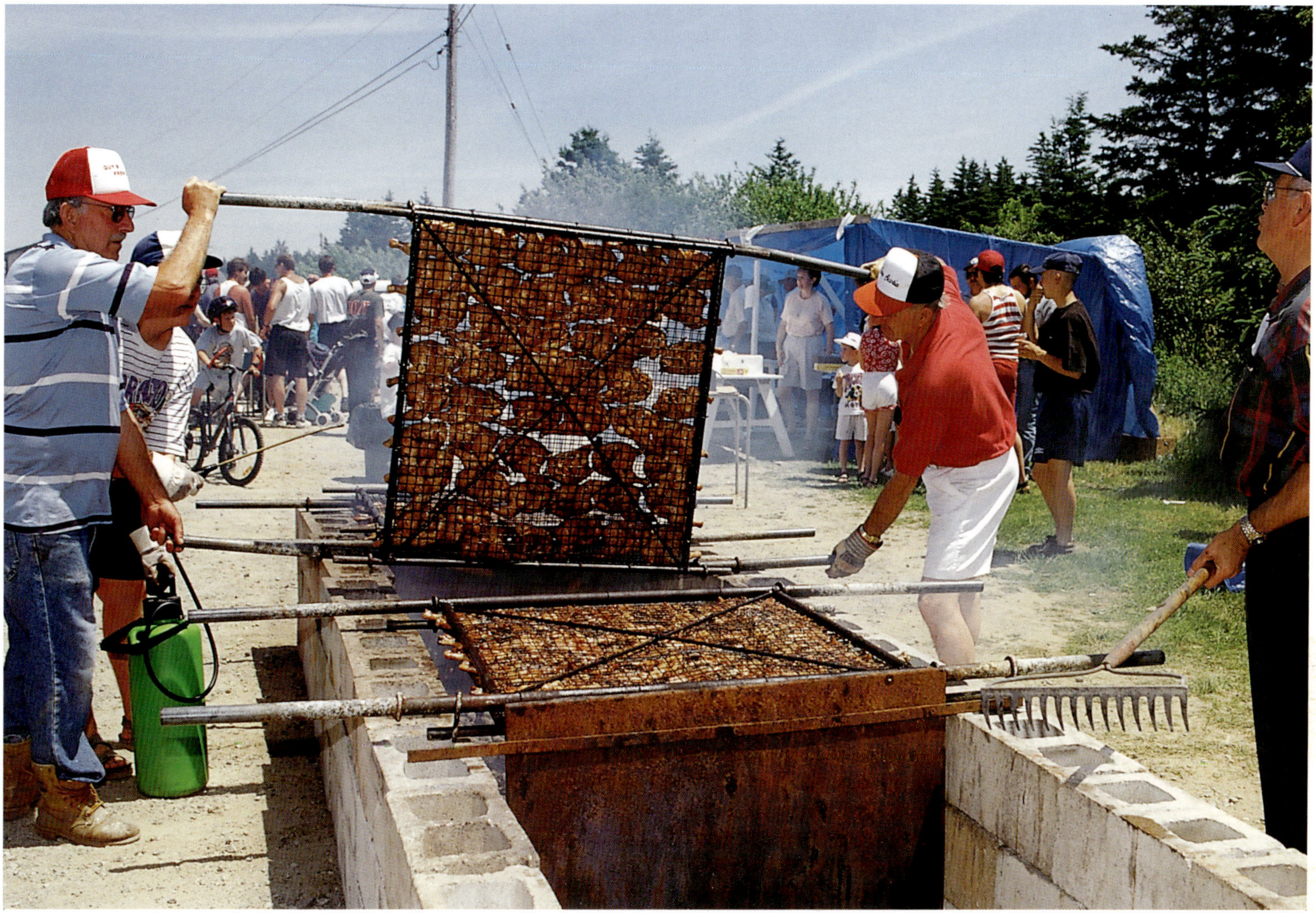

During the Wedgeport Acadian Festival, the local volunteer fire department puts on a tasty chicken barbecue.

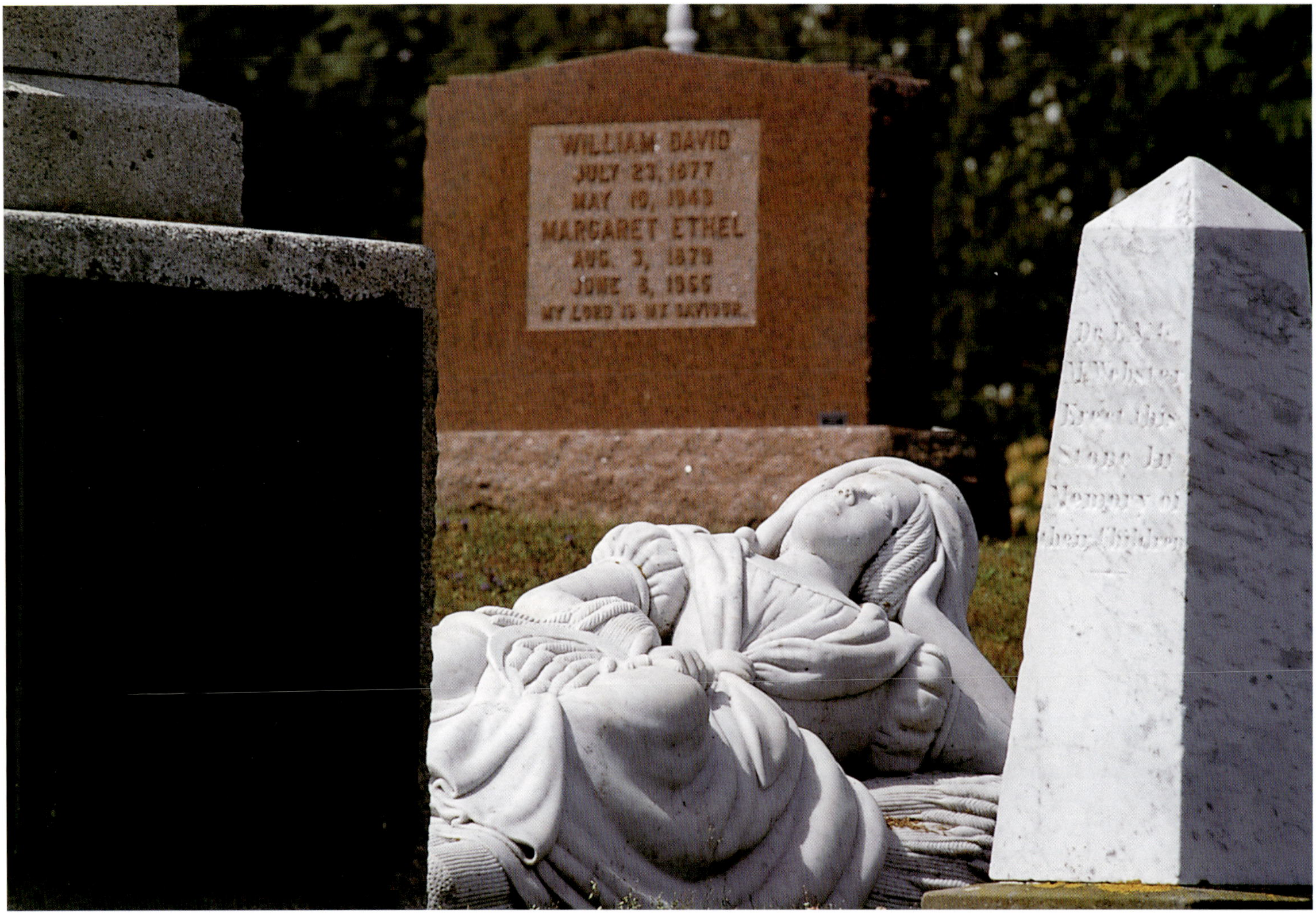

The serene beauty of the marble Webster Monument, Ruth the Gleaner, captures the peaceful atmosphere of Town Point Cemetery. The historic cemetery is the burial site of Yarmouth's first English settlers.

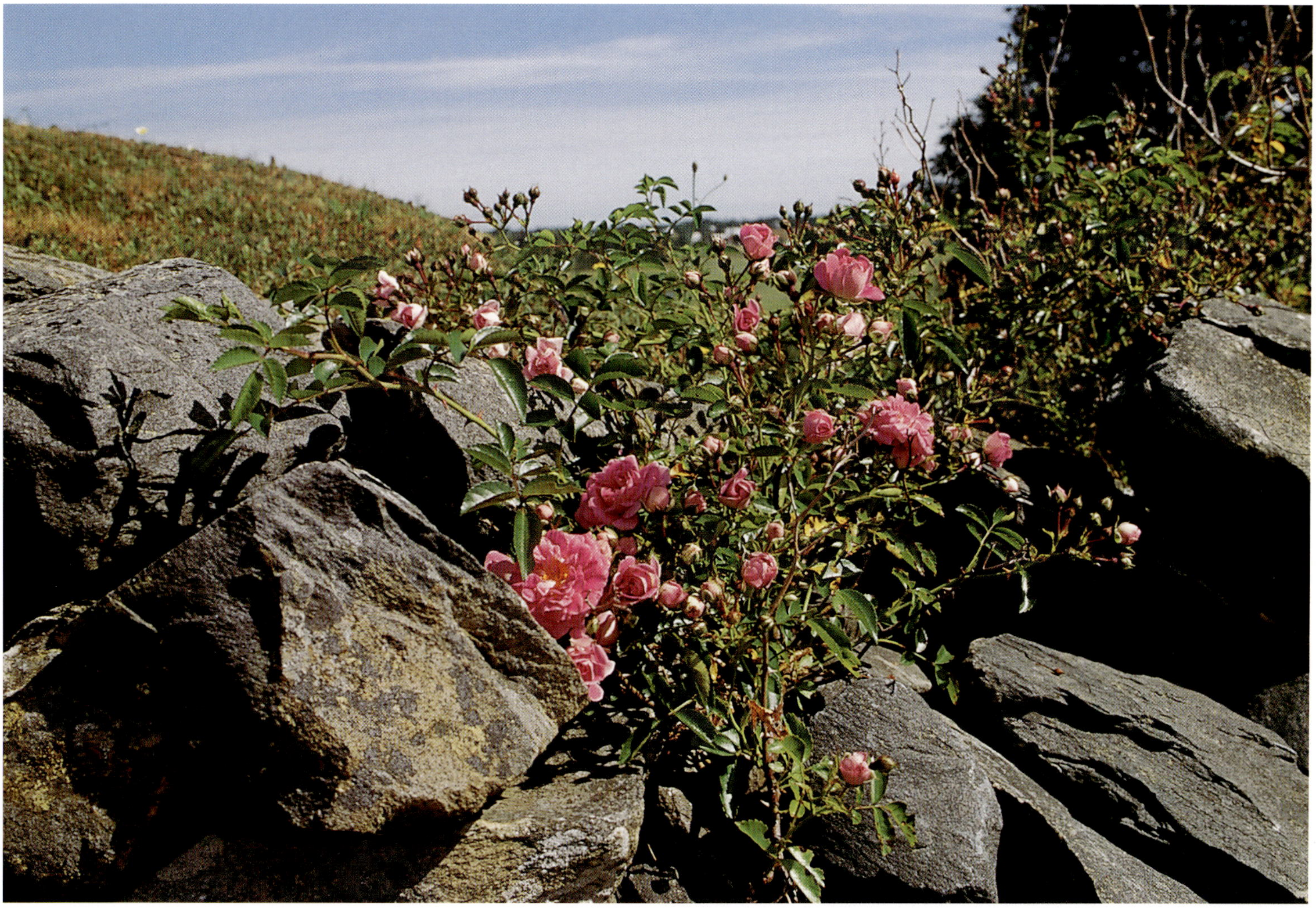

Wild roses cascade over the stone wall at Town Point Cemetery.

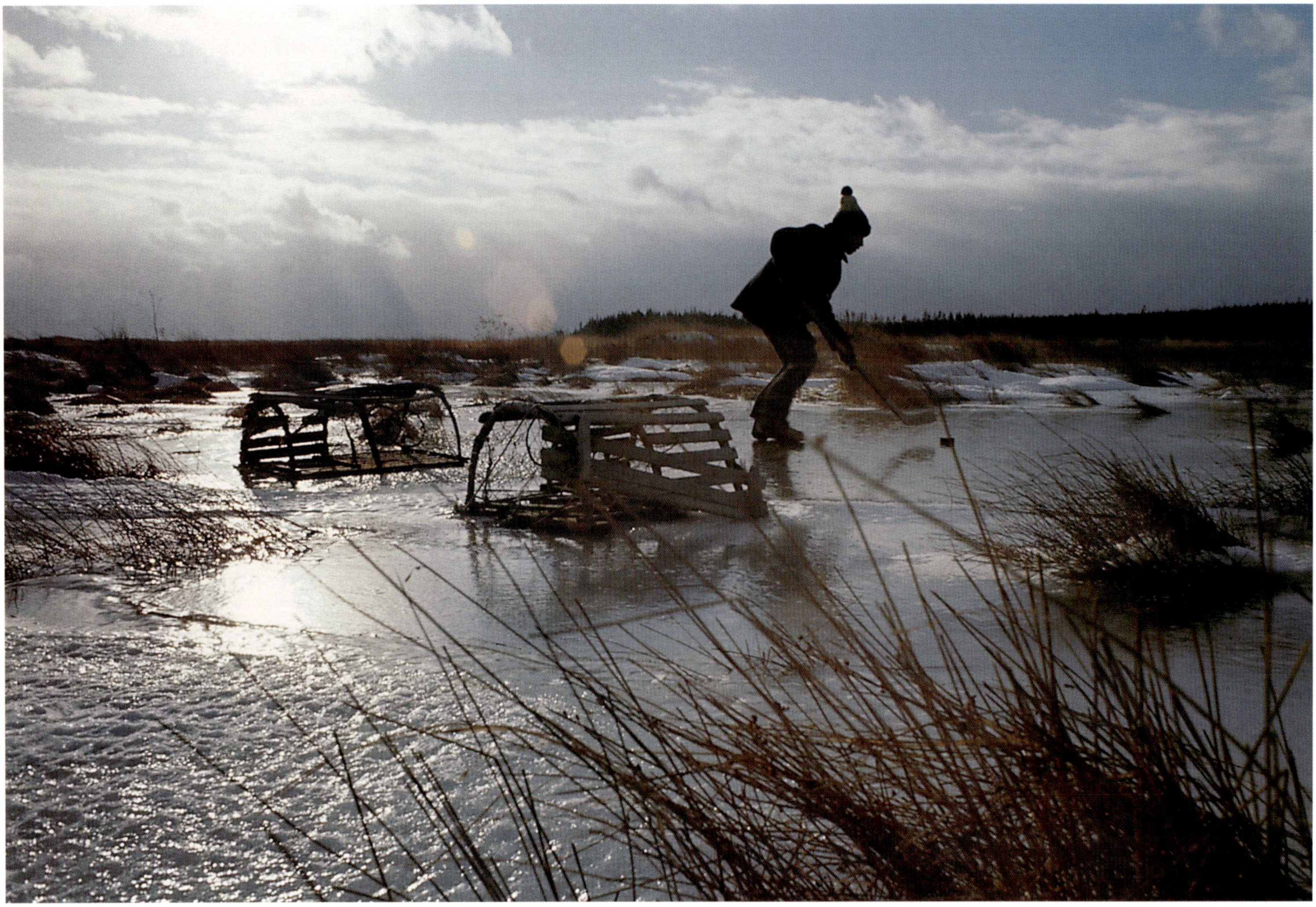

A young hockey player braves the cold on the frozen marshes of Yarmouth County.

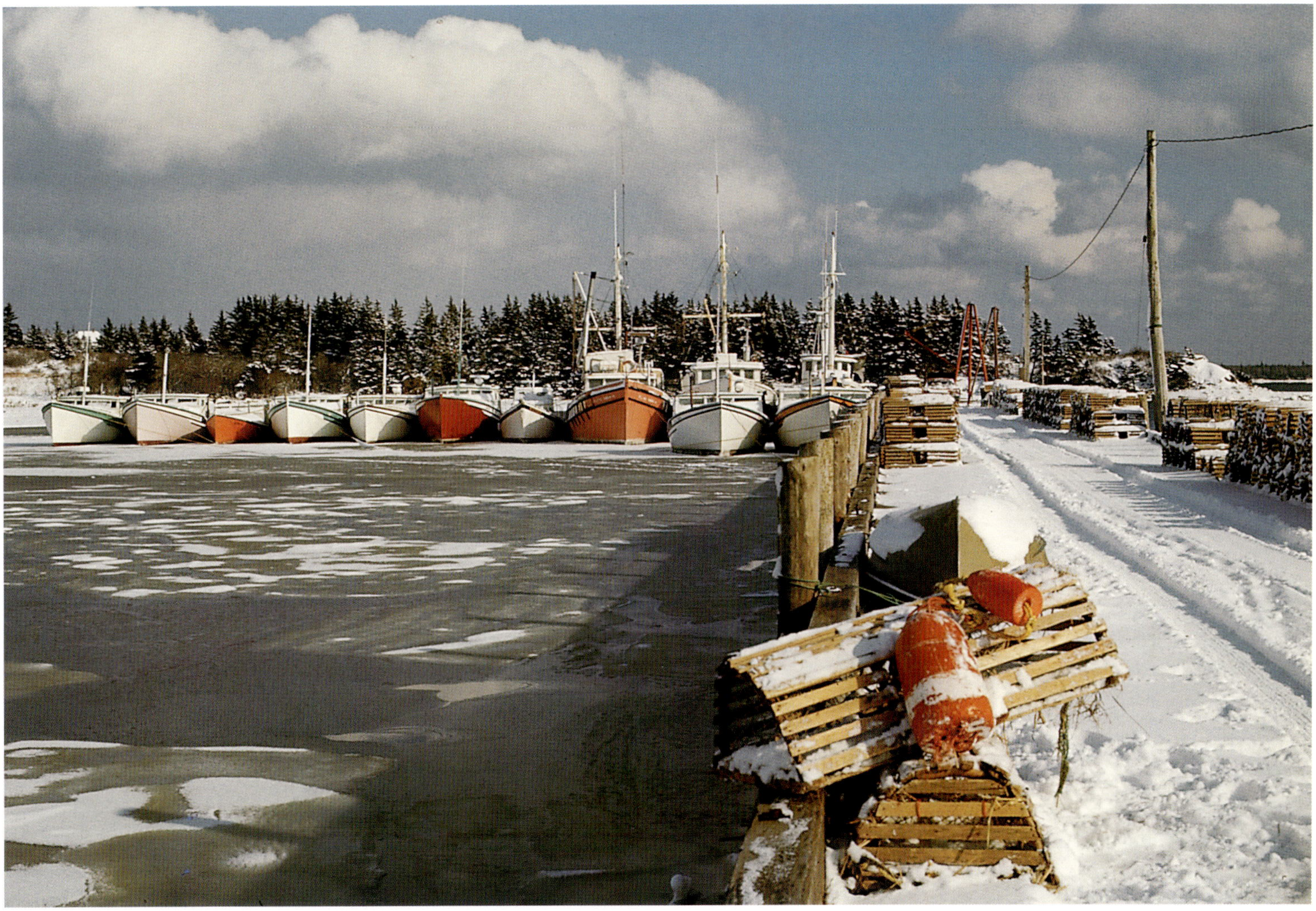

Winter brings snow and ice to Wedgeport's back harbour.

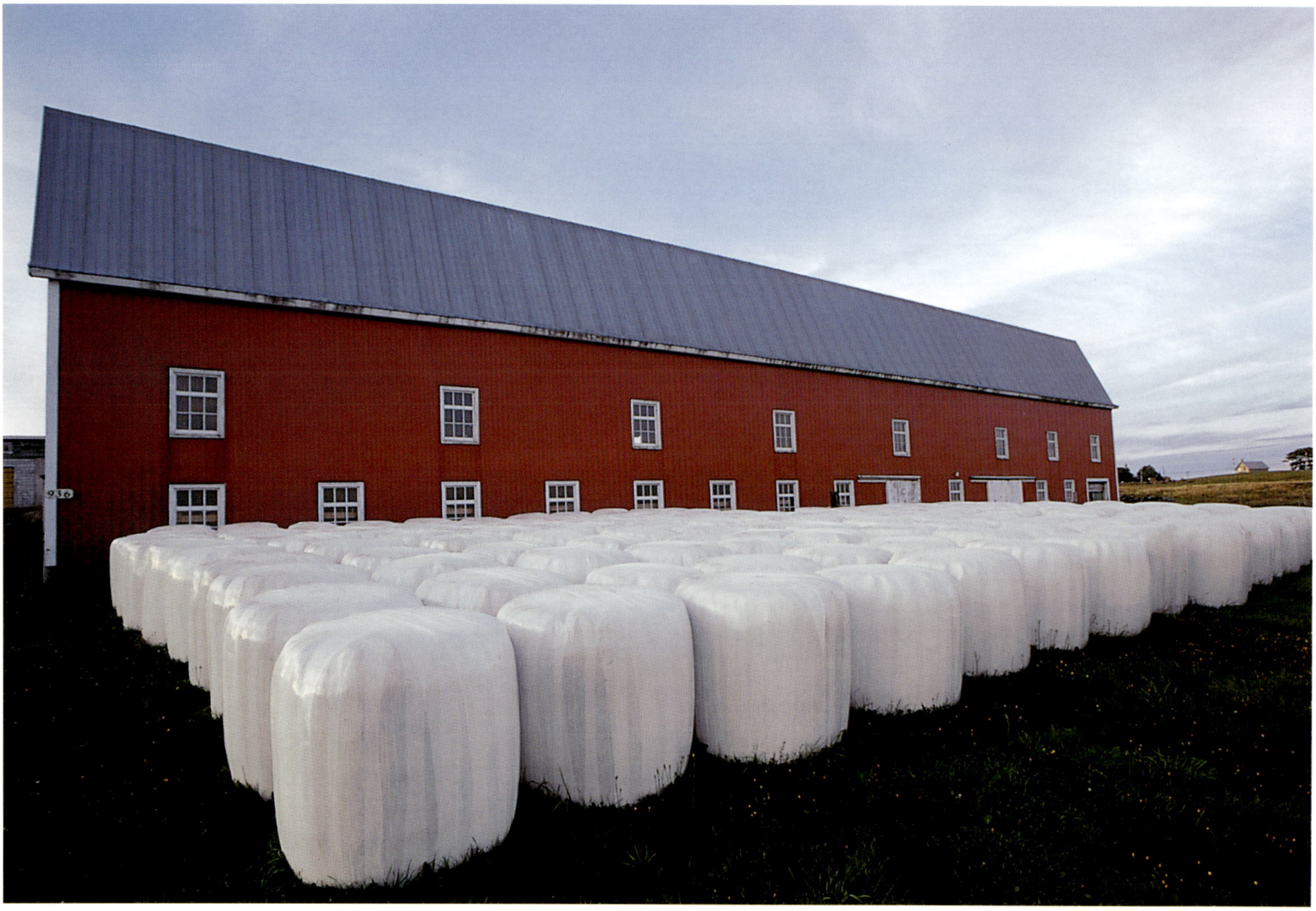

Evening light reflects off the "marshmallow" hay bales in Chebogue.

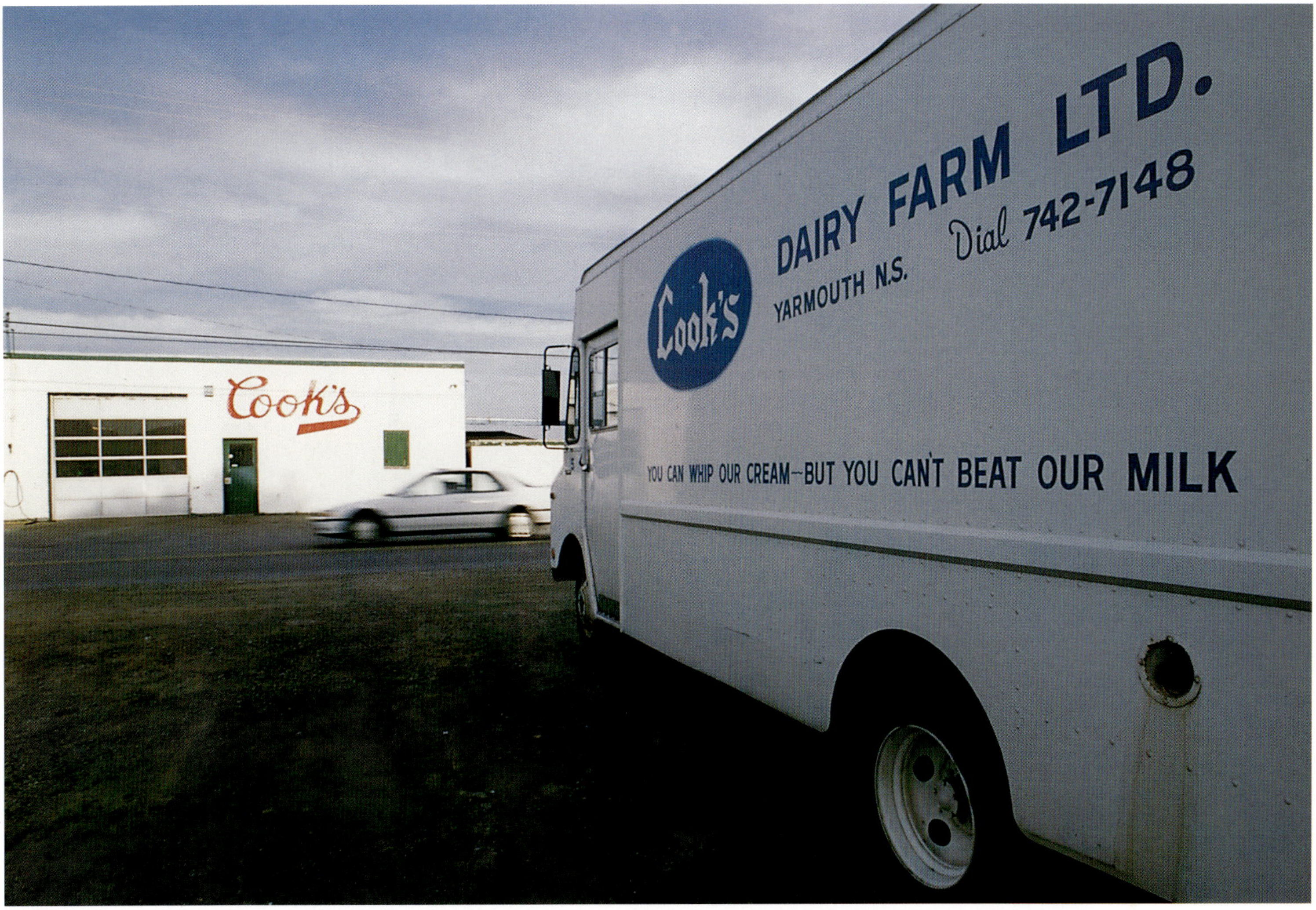

Everyone in Yarmouth County is familiar with Cook's slogan, "You can whip our cream but you can't beat our milk." Established in 1935, this family-run dairy is Nova Scotia's only surviving independent dairy. With a fleet of fourteen trucks, Cook's Dairy still delivers milk, cream, and ice cream door-to-door.

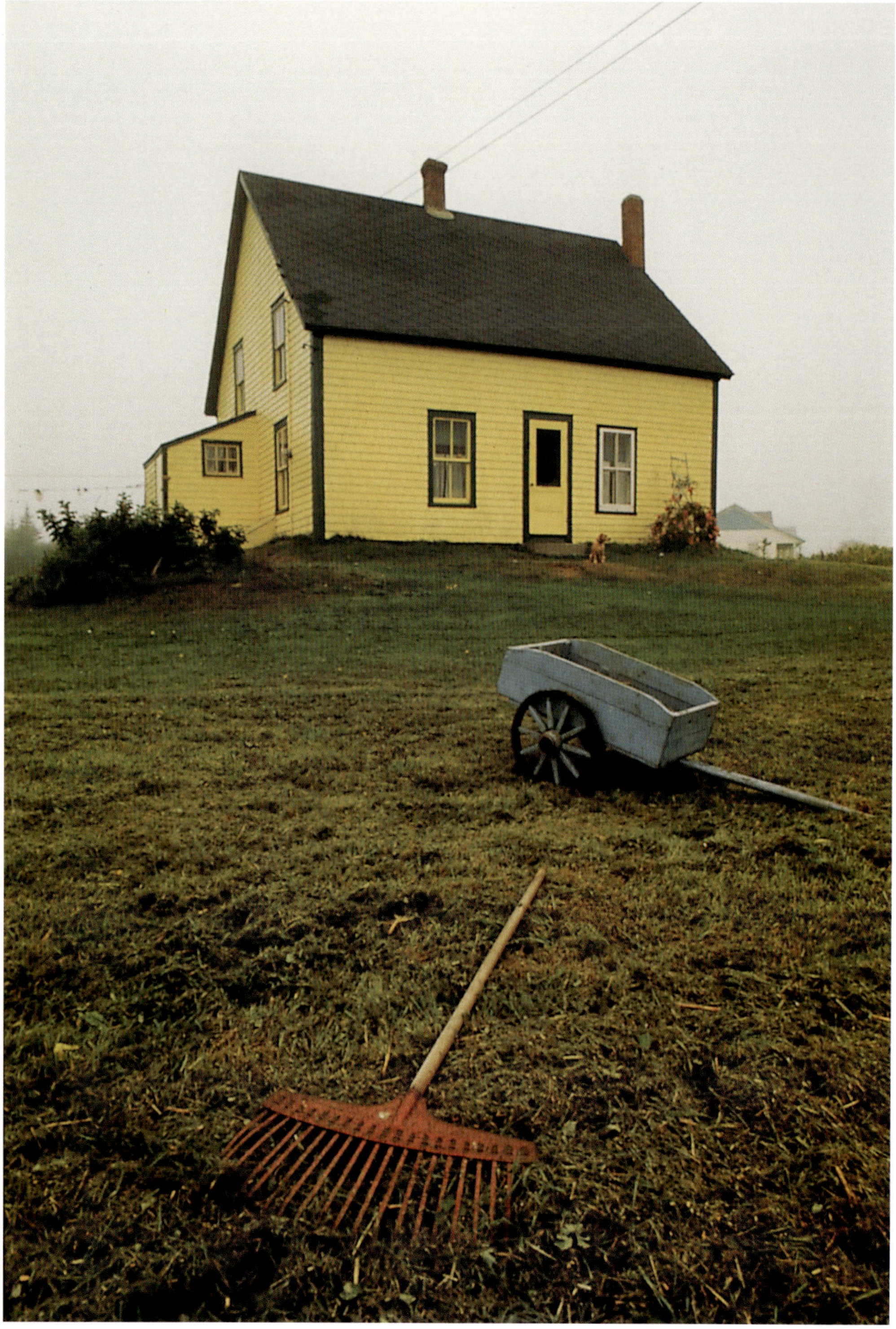

Fog drifts around an older Acadian home.

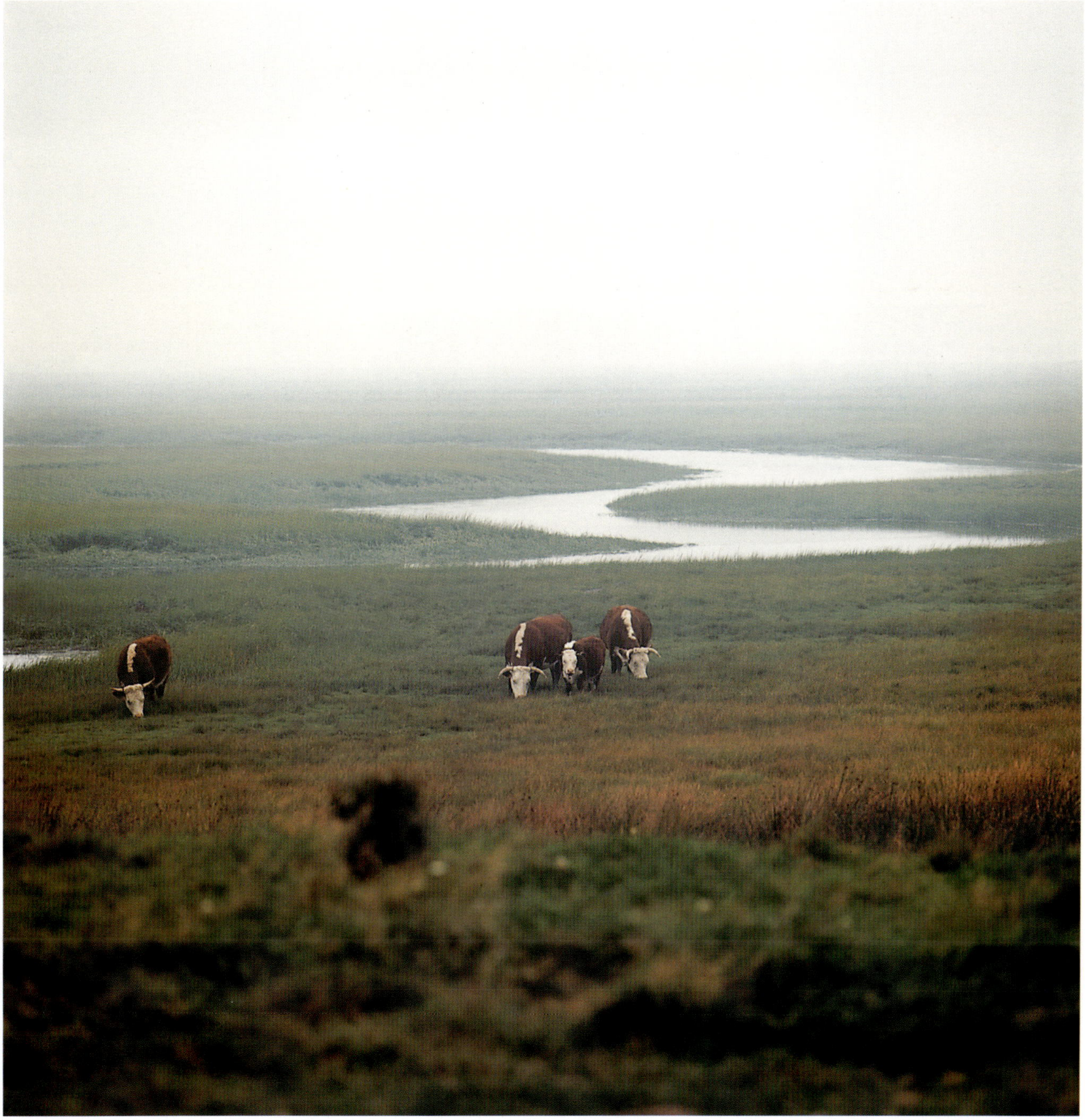

Oxen graze on the foggy tidal marshes of Arcadia.

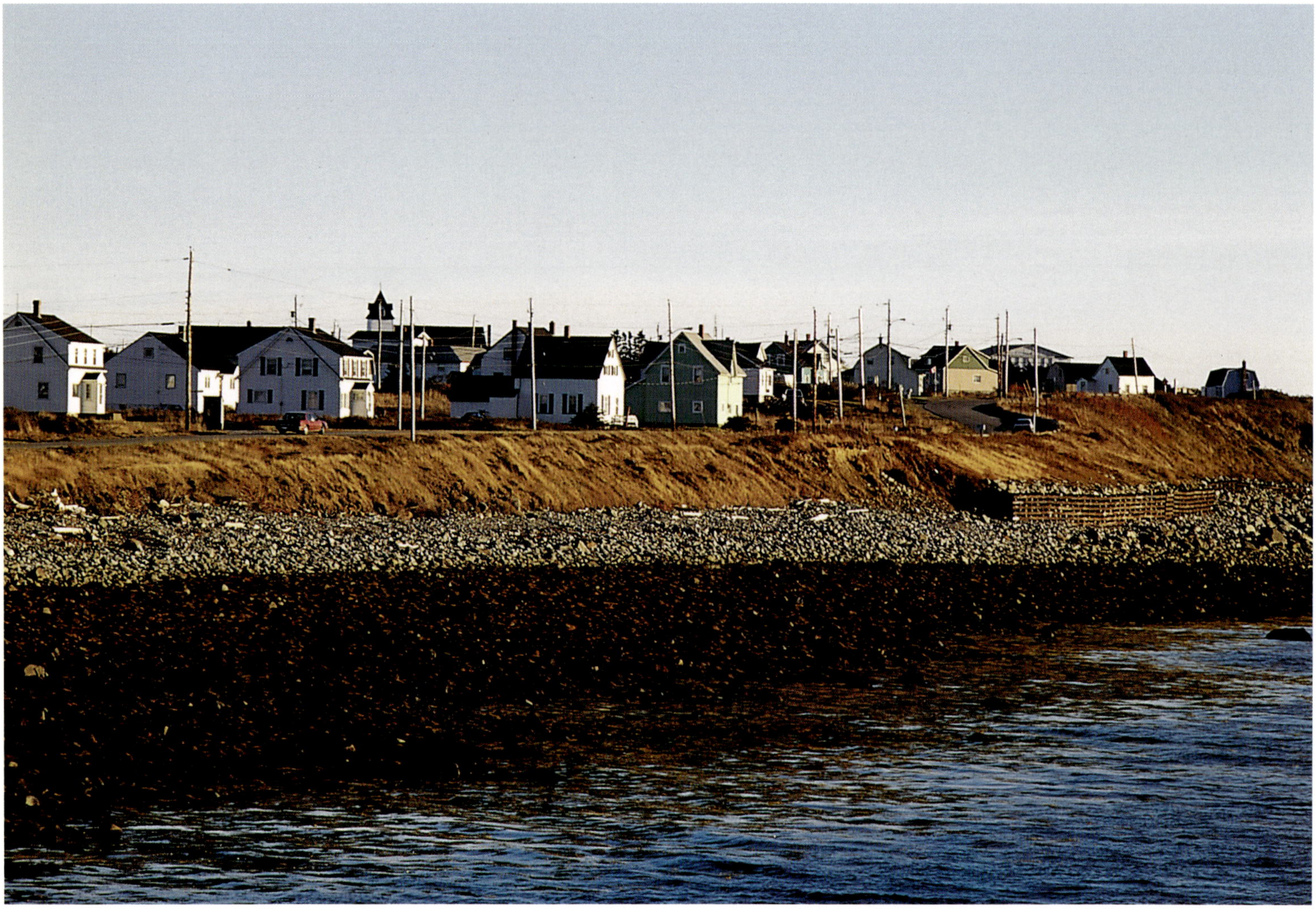

Late-day sun paints subtle layers of colour at Pinkneys Point.

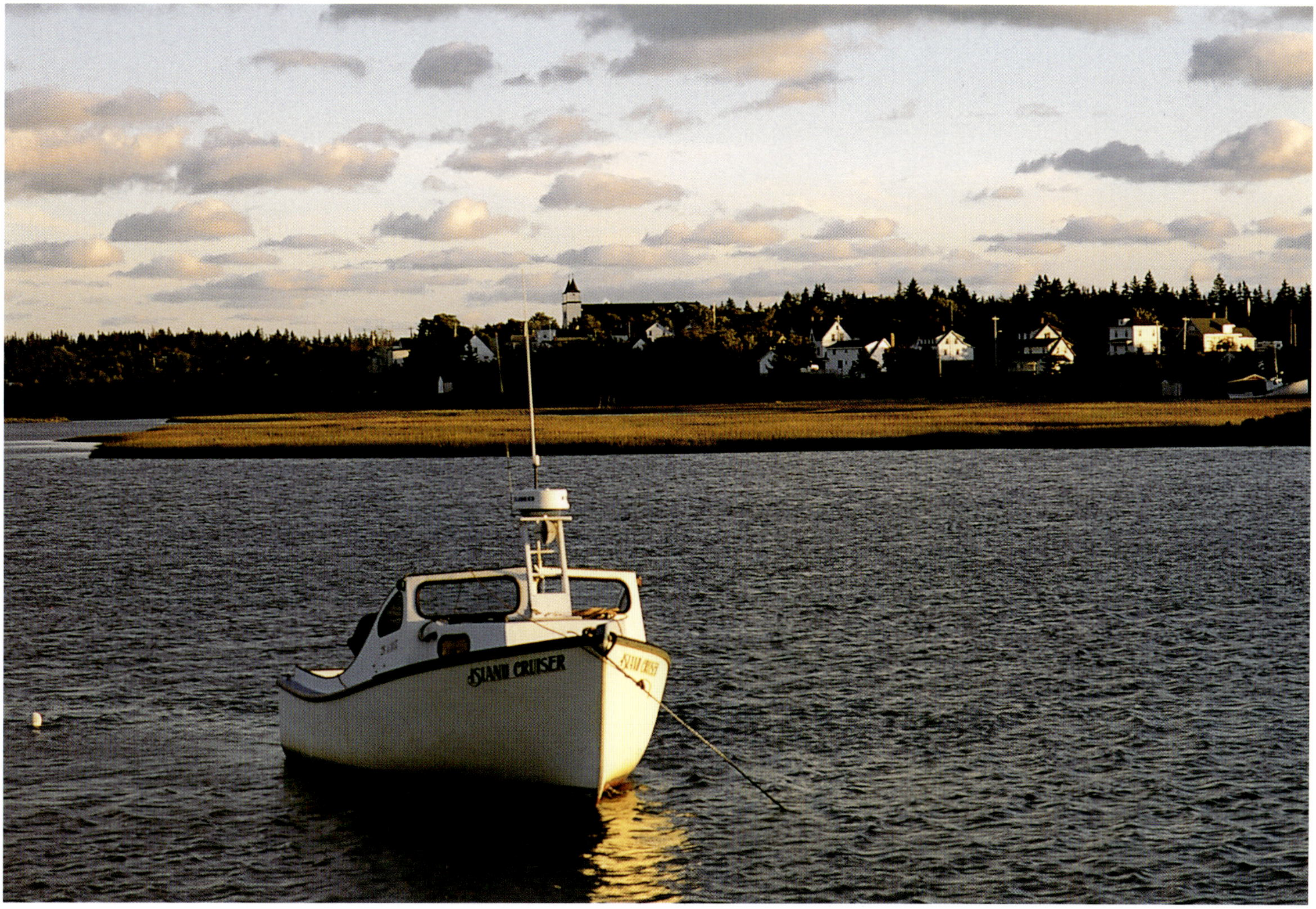

Seen from Wedgeport's back harbour, the village is bathed in the glow of the setting sun.

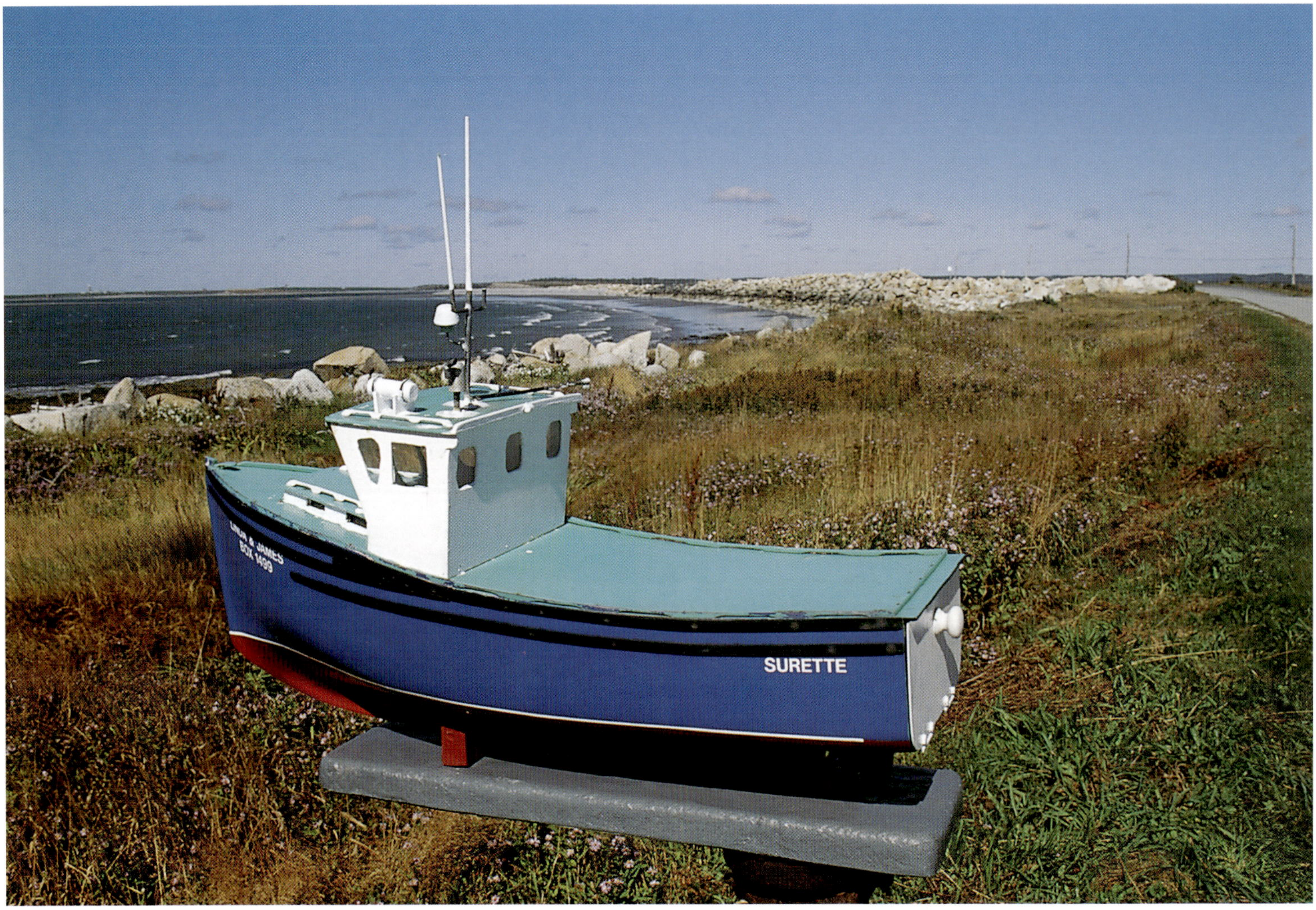

An ingenious model of a fishing boat serves as a mailbox in Pinkneys Point.

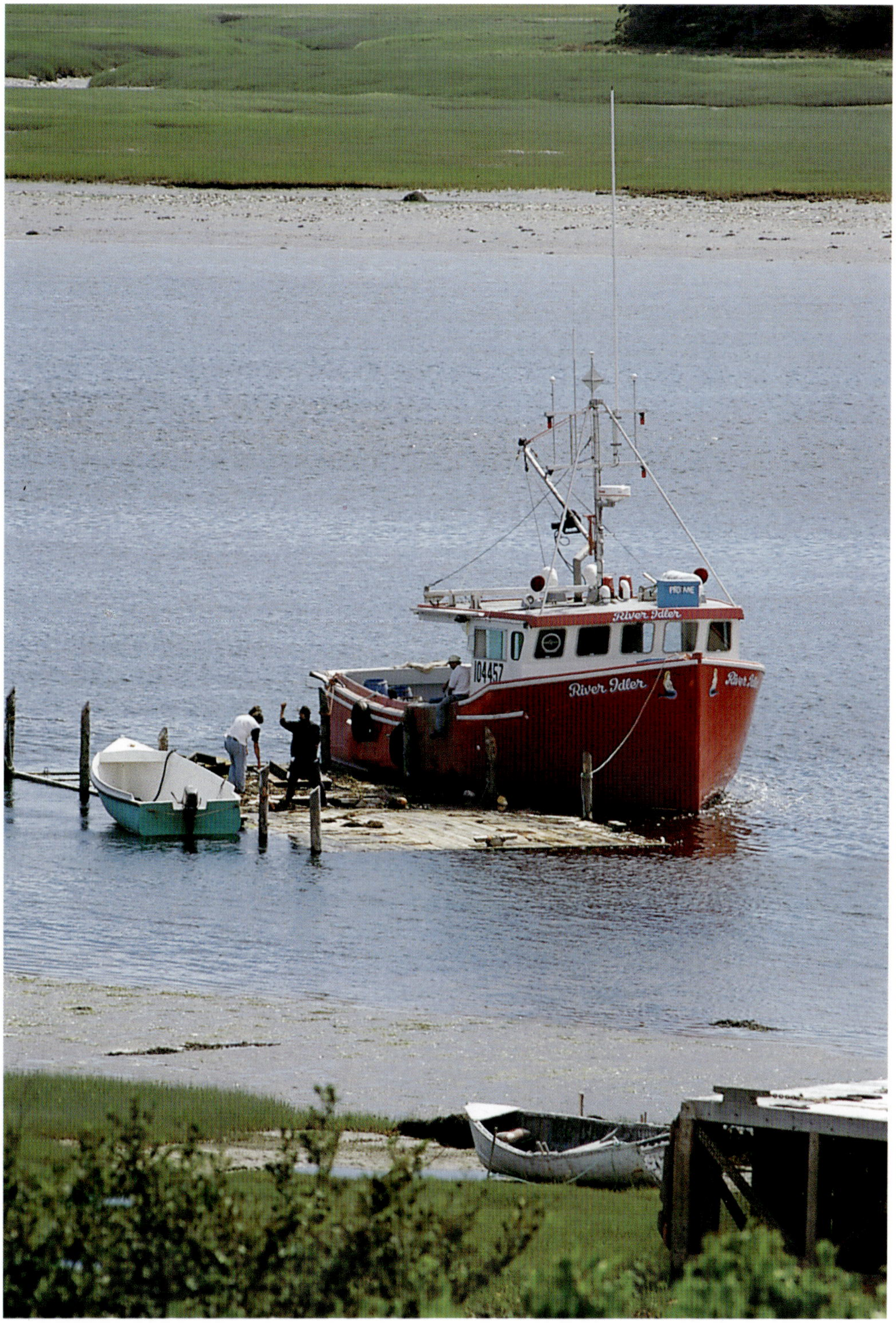

A lobster boat unloads its catch at a floating pound on the Chebogue River.

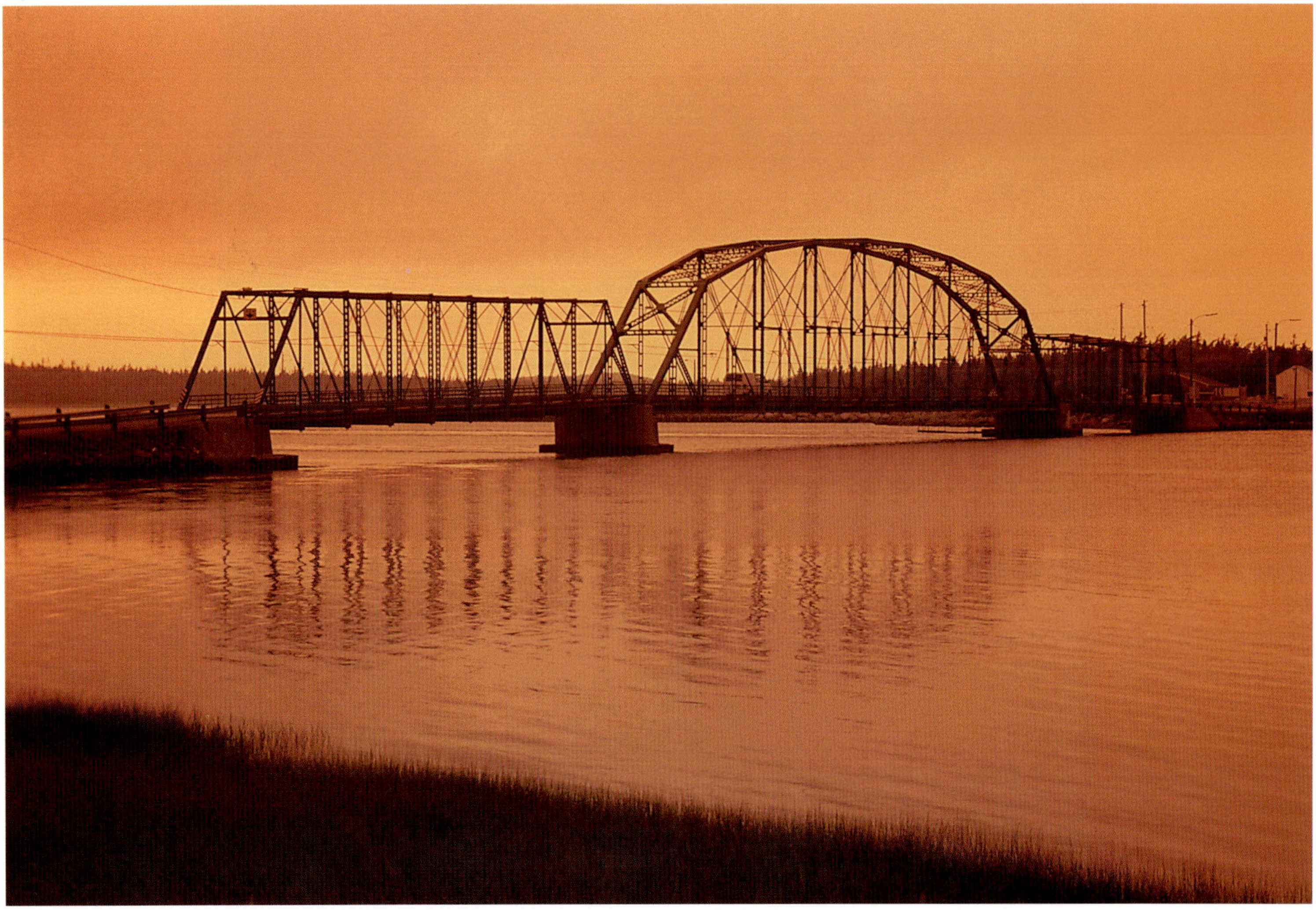

On the way to Surettes Island, this bridge casts a moody reflection.

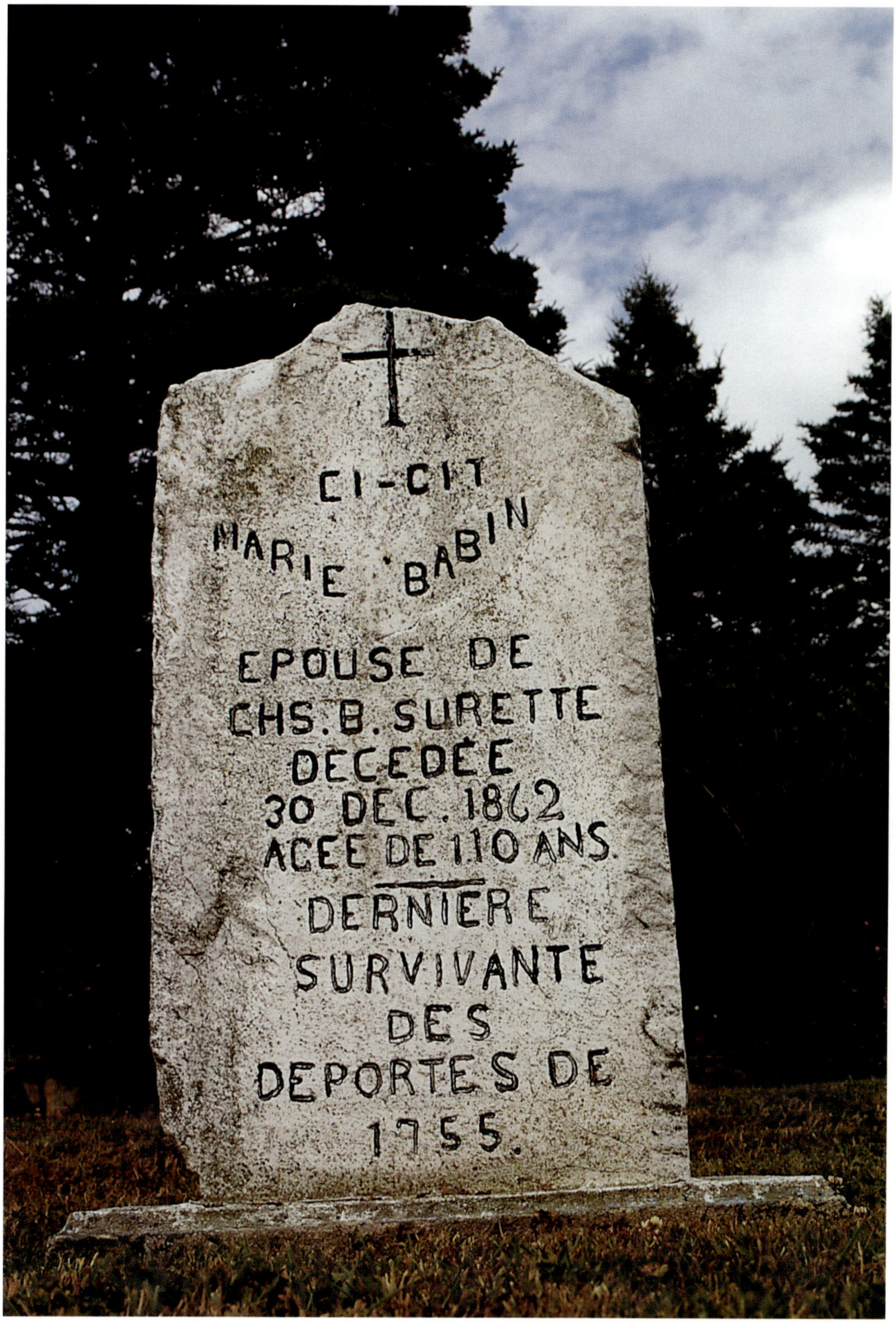

A piece of Acadian history on Surettes Island: the grave marker of Marie Babin Surette (1752–1862), the last survivor of the Acadian deportees who found their way back to Nova Scotia.

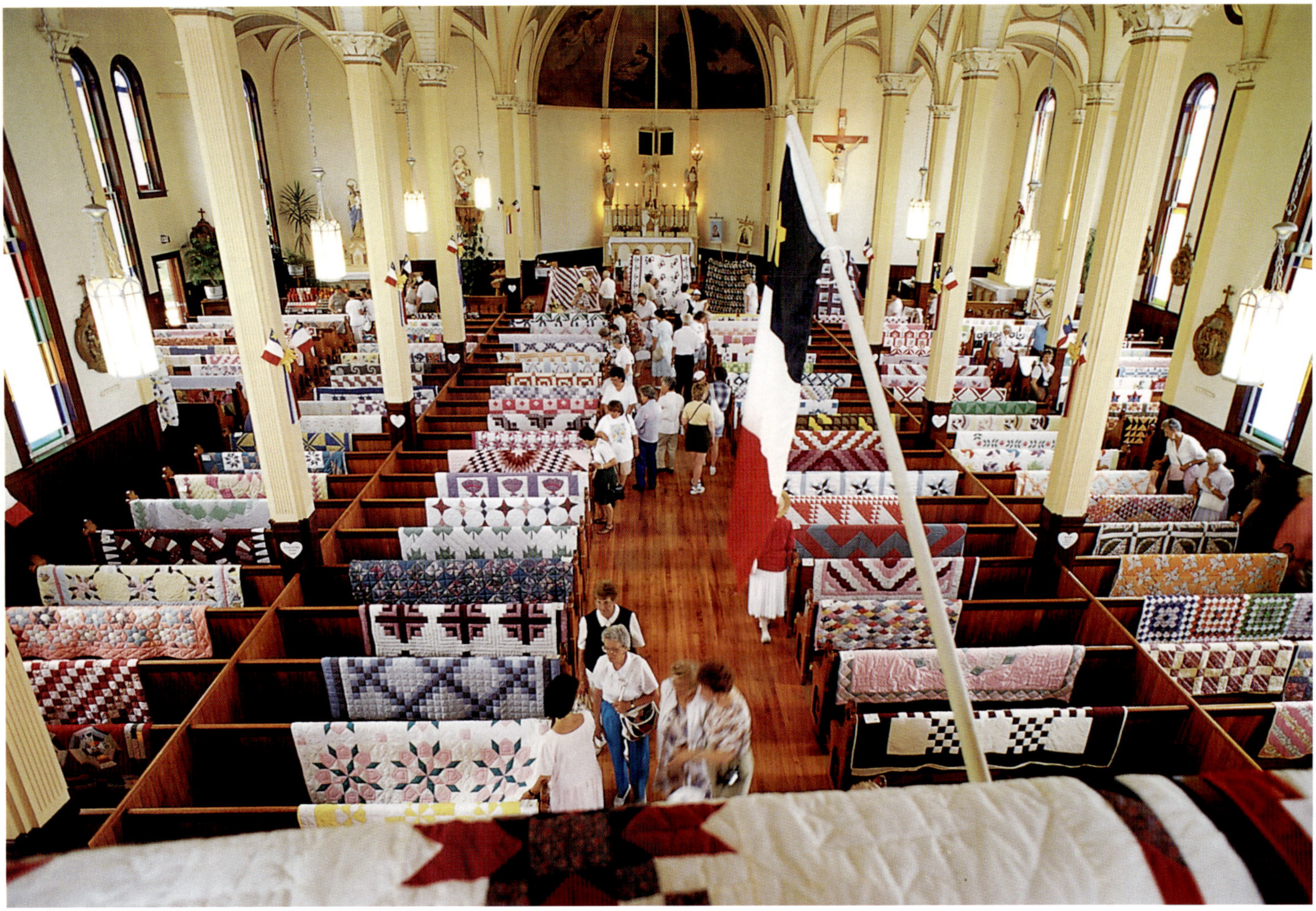

Over 175 locally made quilts on display in Sainte-Anne's Church in Ste. Anne du Ruisseau provide a kaleidoscope of colour.

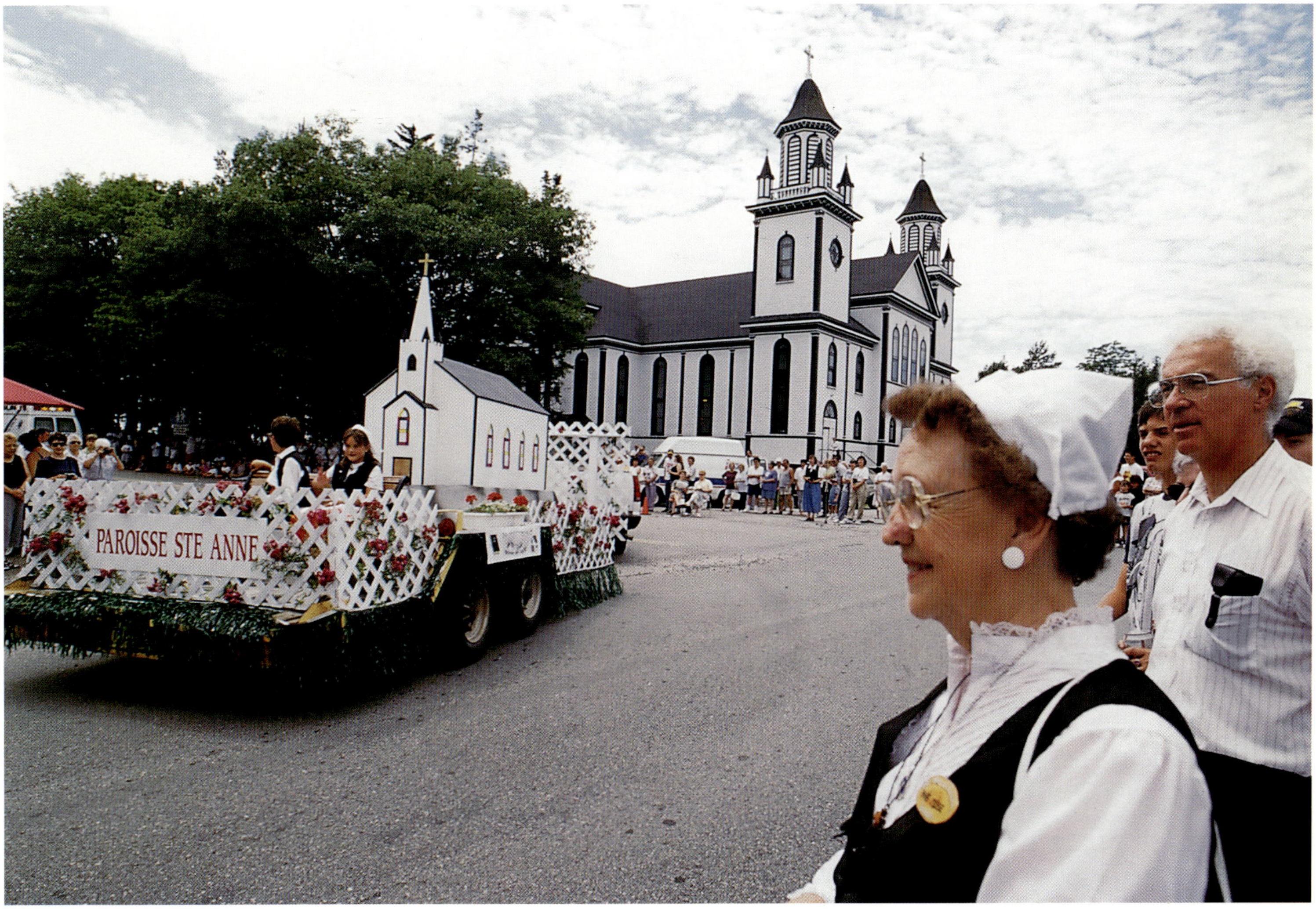

The Grand Parade draws a crowd during Ste. Anne du Ruisseau's Acadian Festival. In the background, Sainte-Anne's Church, founded in 1799, serves the oldest Roman Catholic parish in the region.

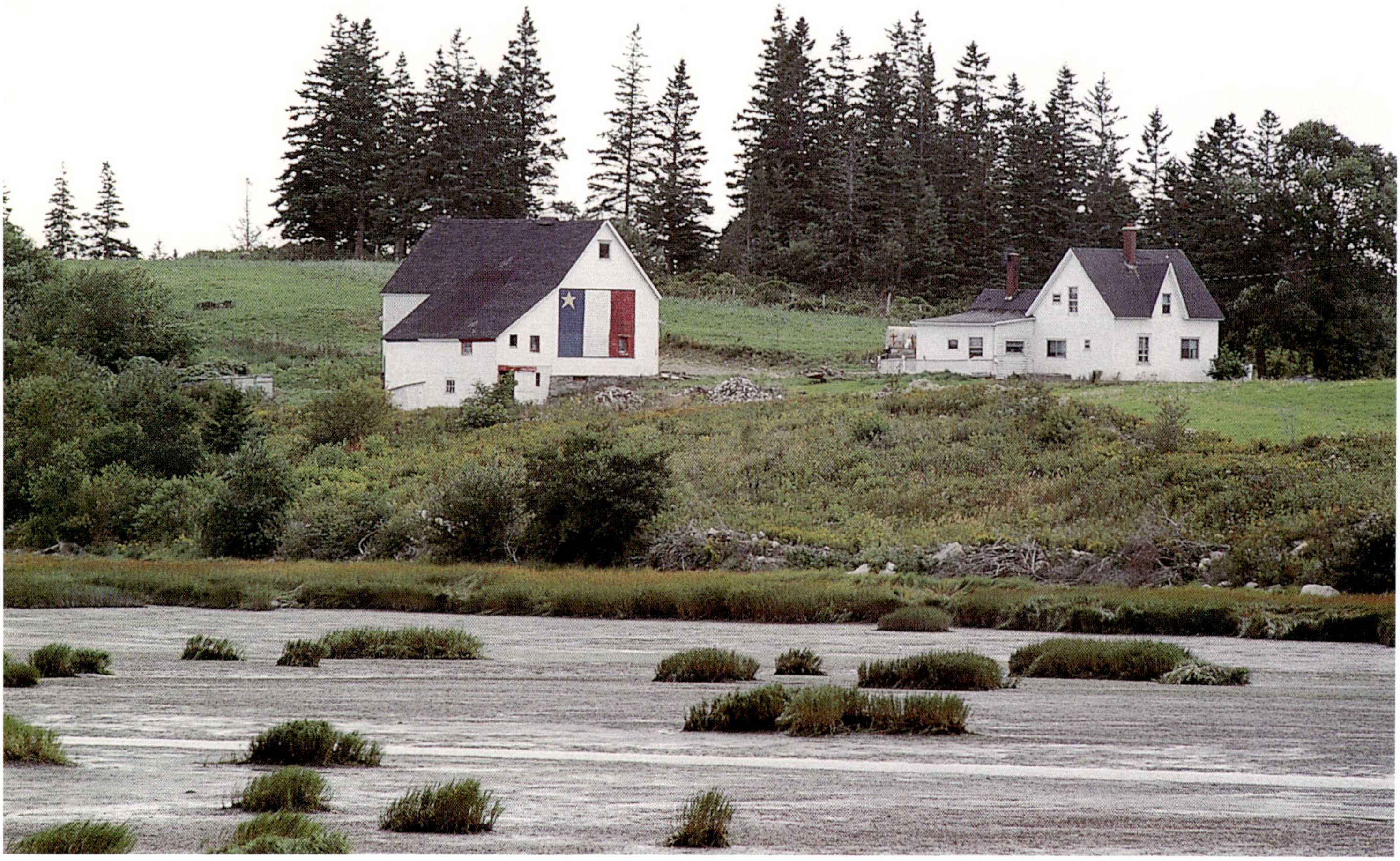

The pride of an Acadian family is on display in Ste. Anne du Ruisseau.

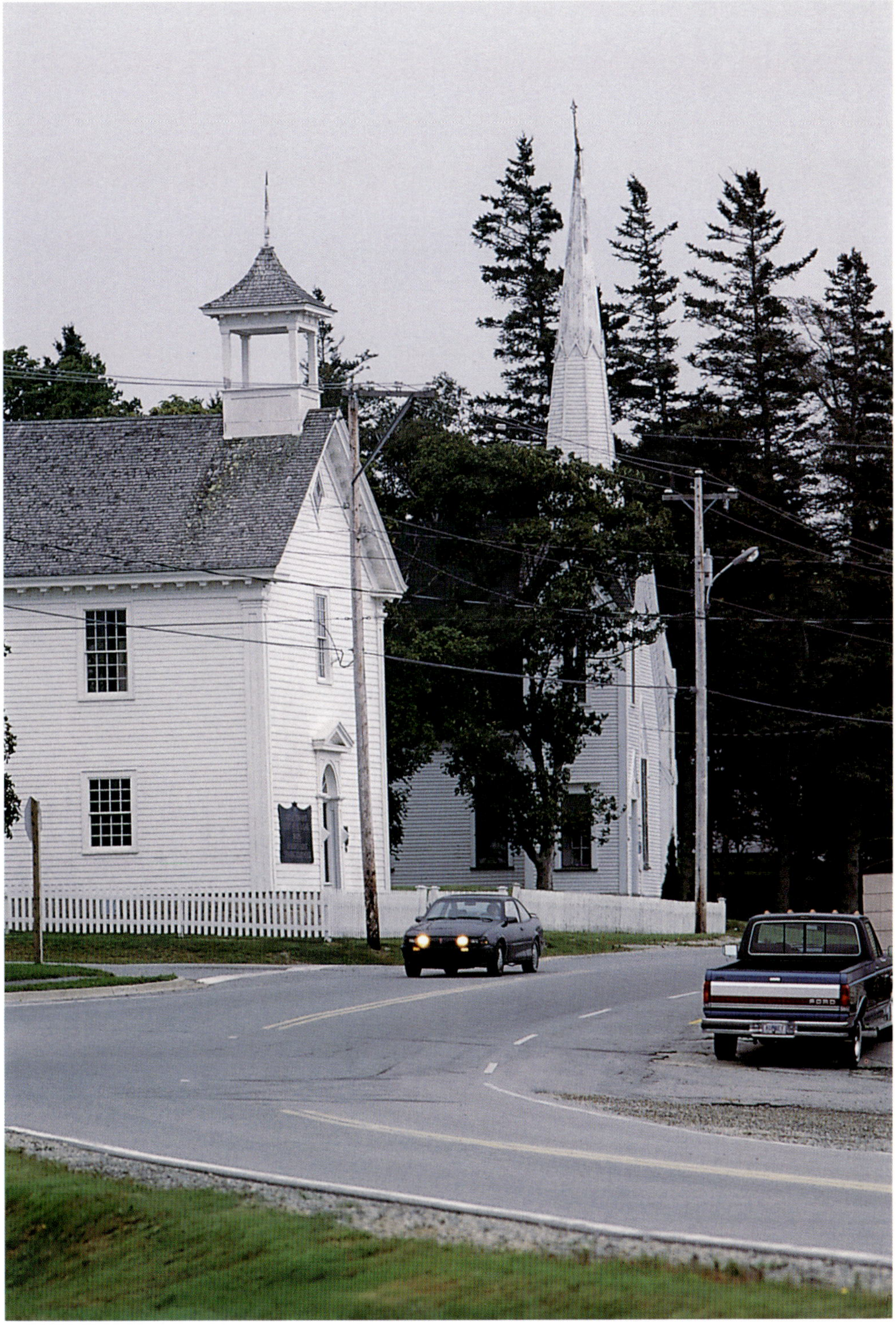

A bend in the road through the village of Tusket passes by the historic Argyle Township Court House and Gaol, the oldest standing Court House in Canada.

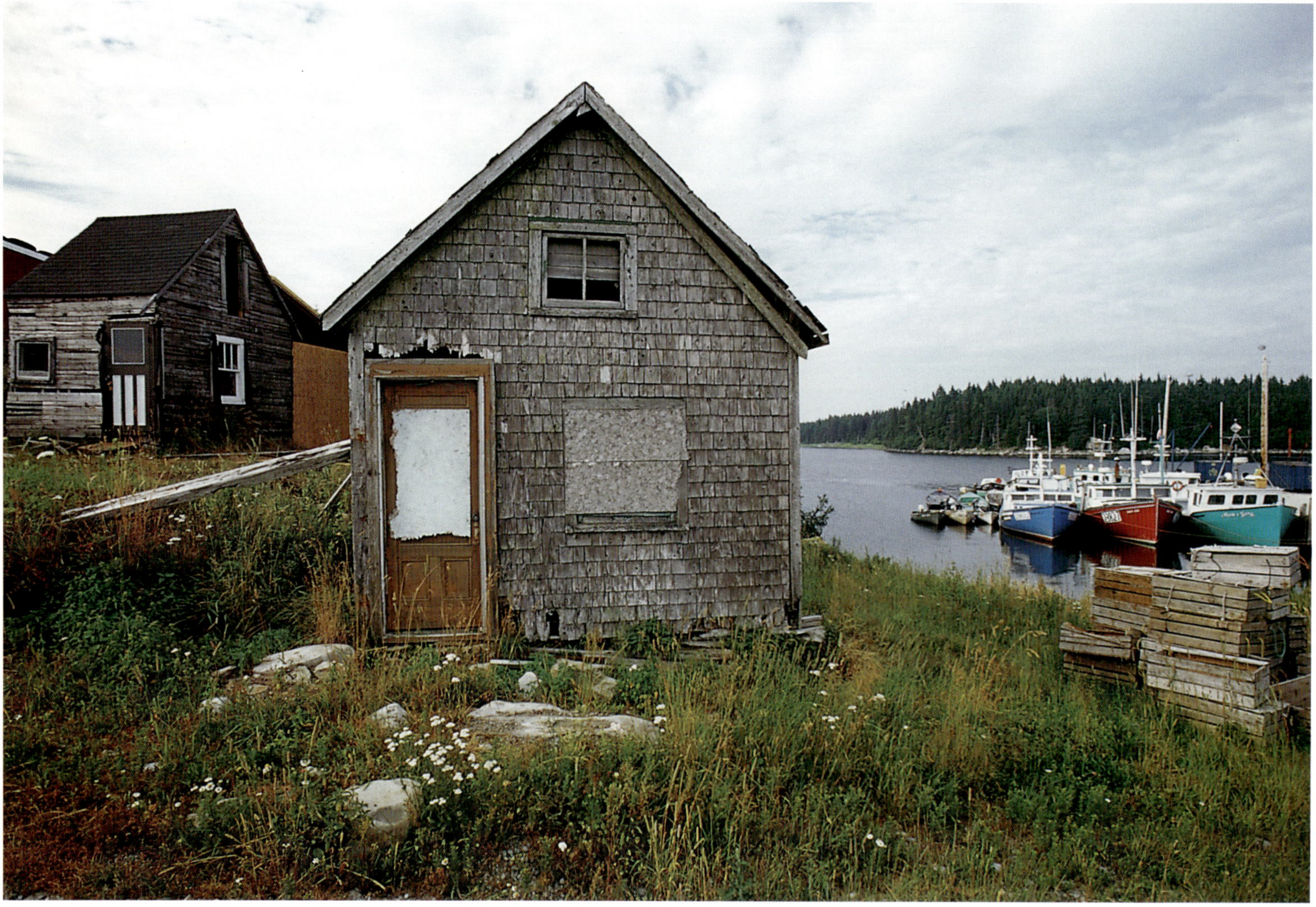

Weathered reminders of a seasonal fishing community stand near an active wharf at The Tittle, on Surettes Island. In days gone by, whole families would move here during the fishing season as poor roads and transportation prevented fishermen from making a daily commute.

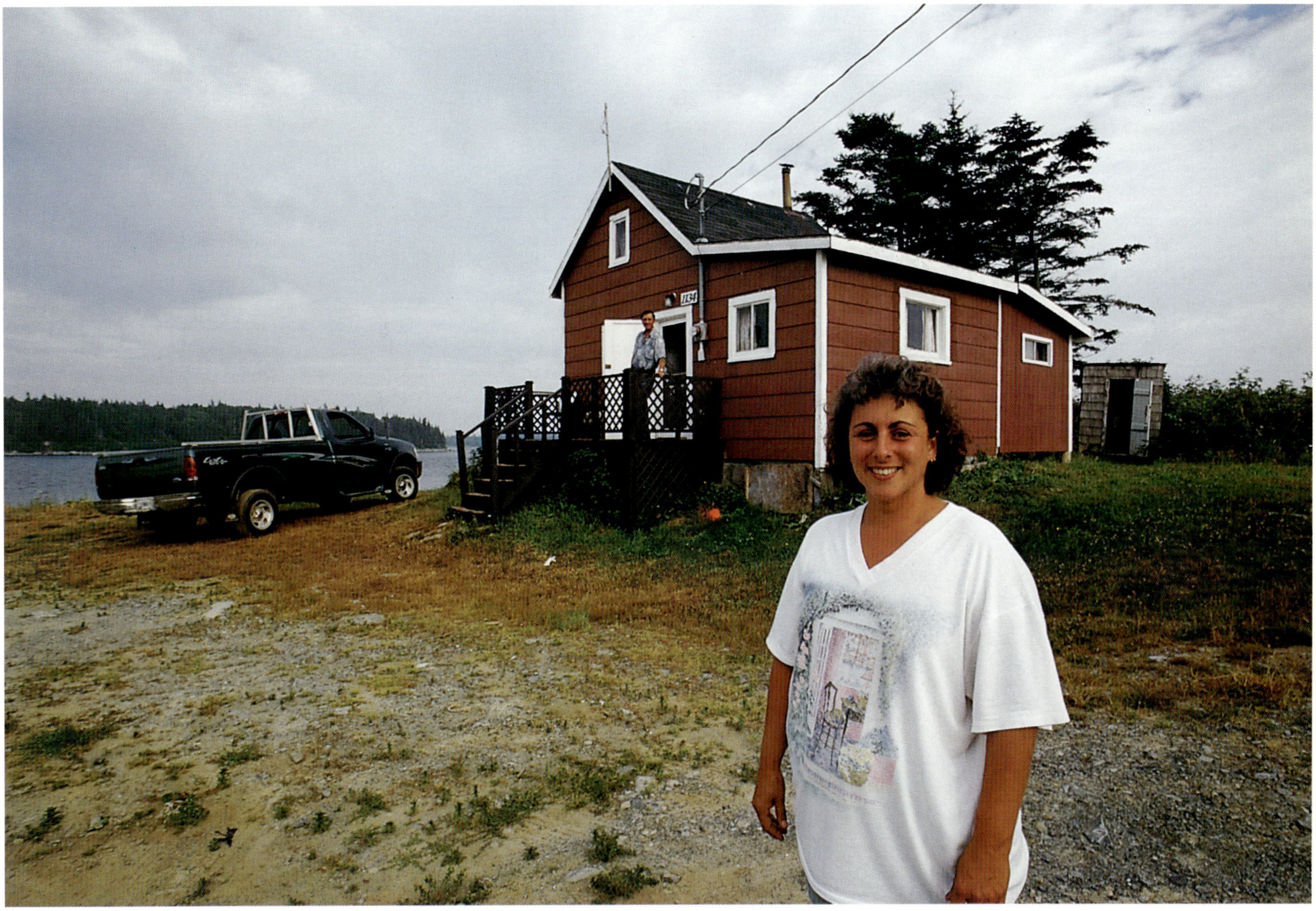

Some fishermen still prefer to take up temporary residence while they work the demanding hours of the fishing season. Della Muise has been cooking for a group of fishermen at The Tittle for over fifteen years.

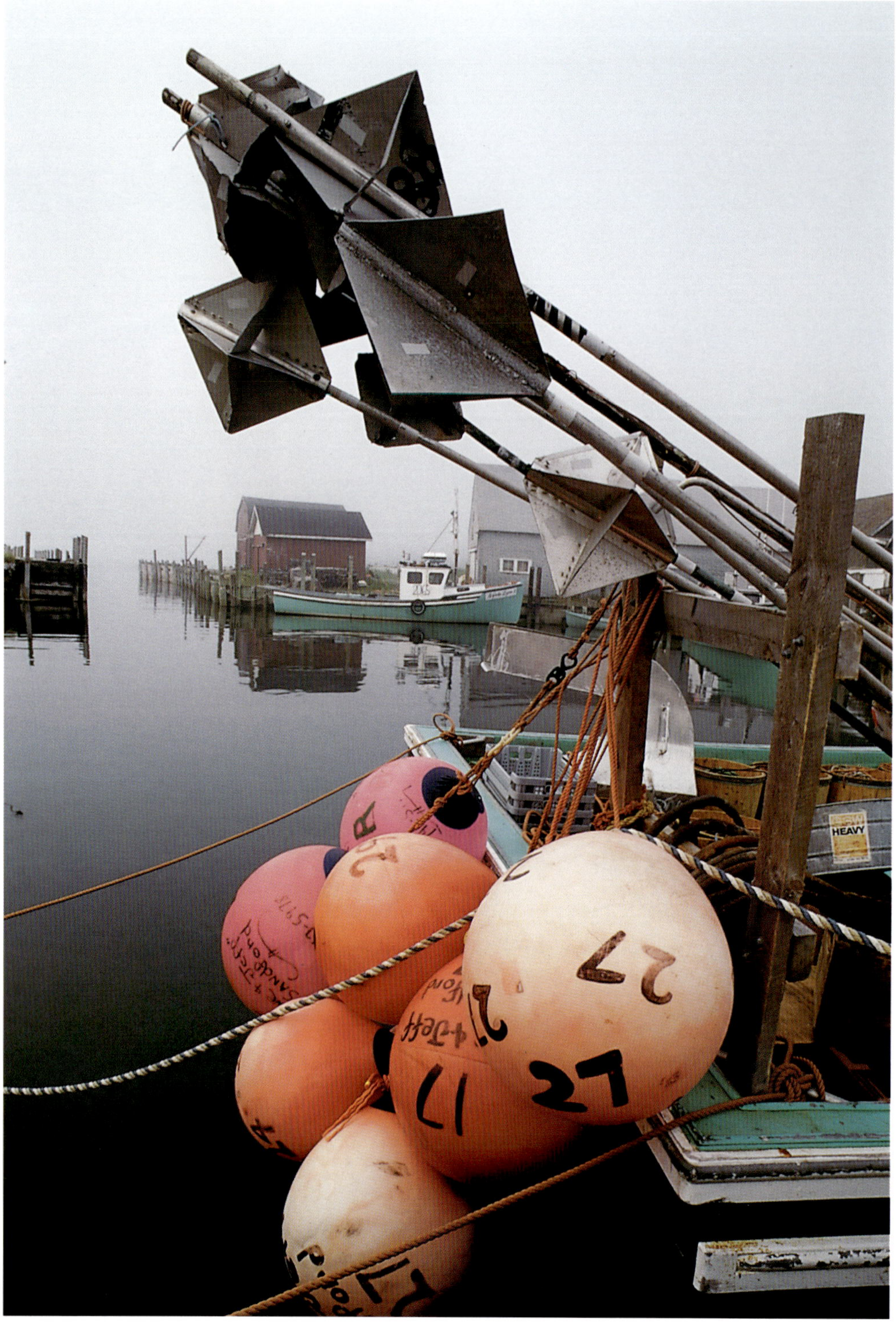

Buoys and markers stand ready at Sandford.

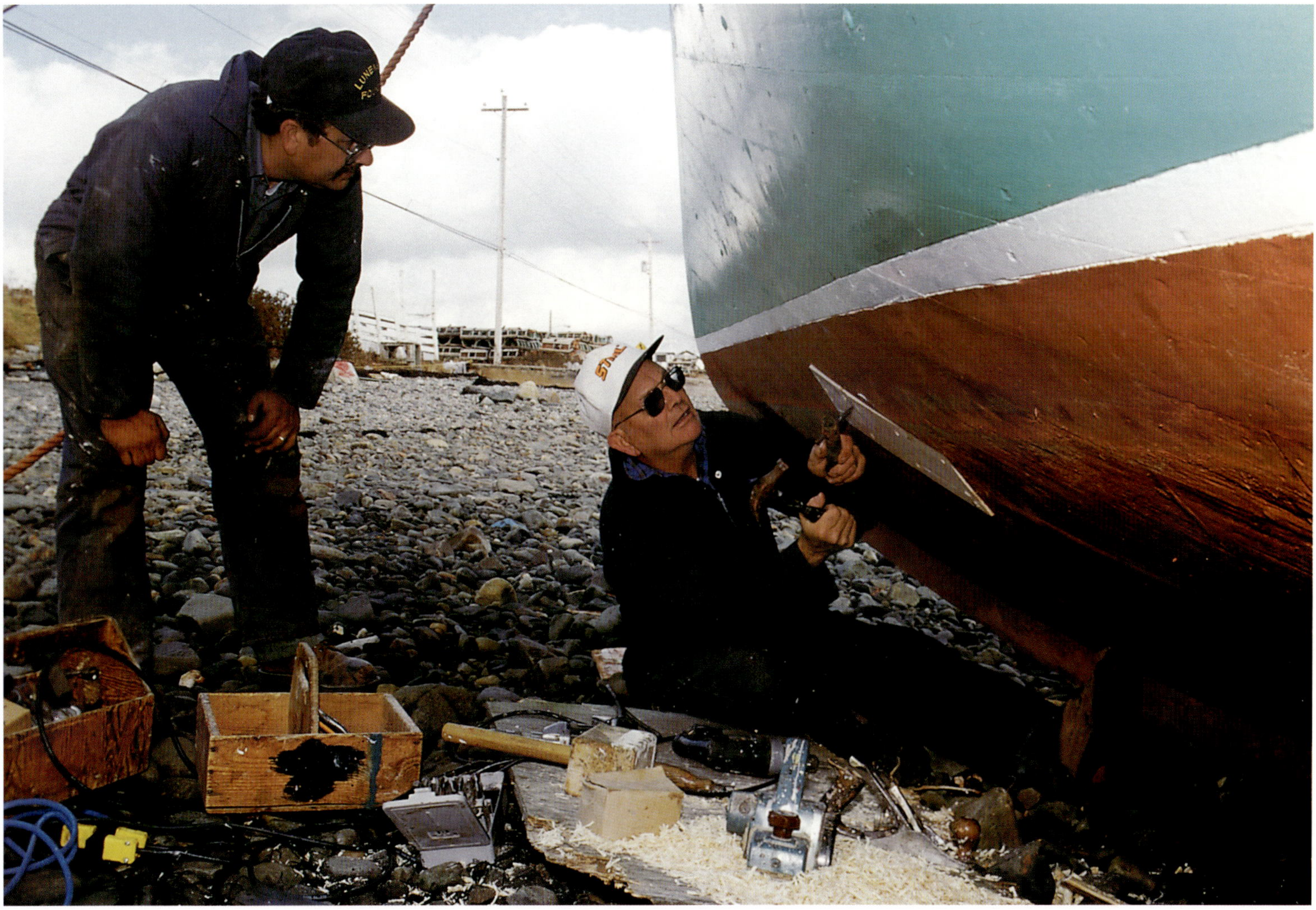

Assisted by his son, retired Cape Island boat builder Bill Newell still helps out with repairs around the Yarmouth Bar.

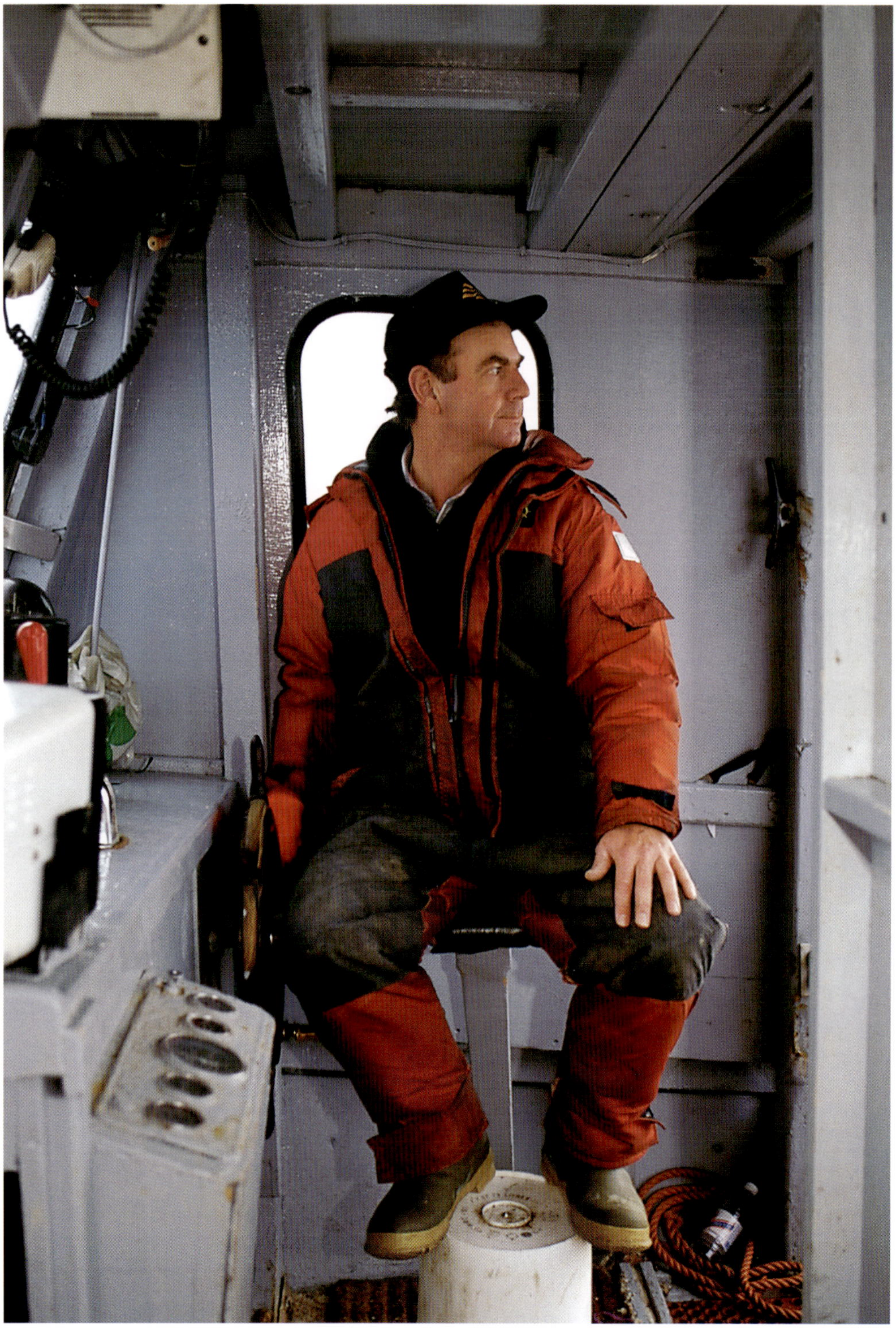

Captain Bob Rogers of Cape Forchu navigates his Cape Island boat through the choppy waters off the Yarmouth Light.

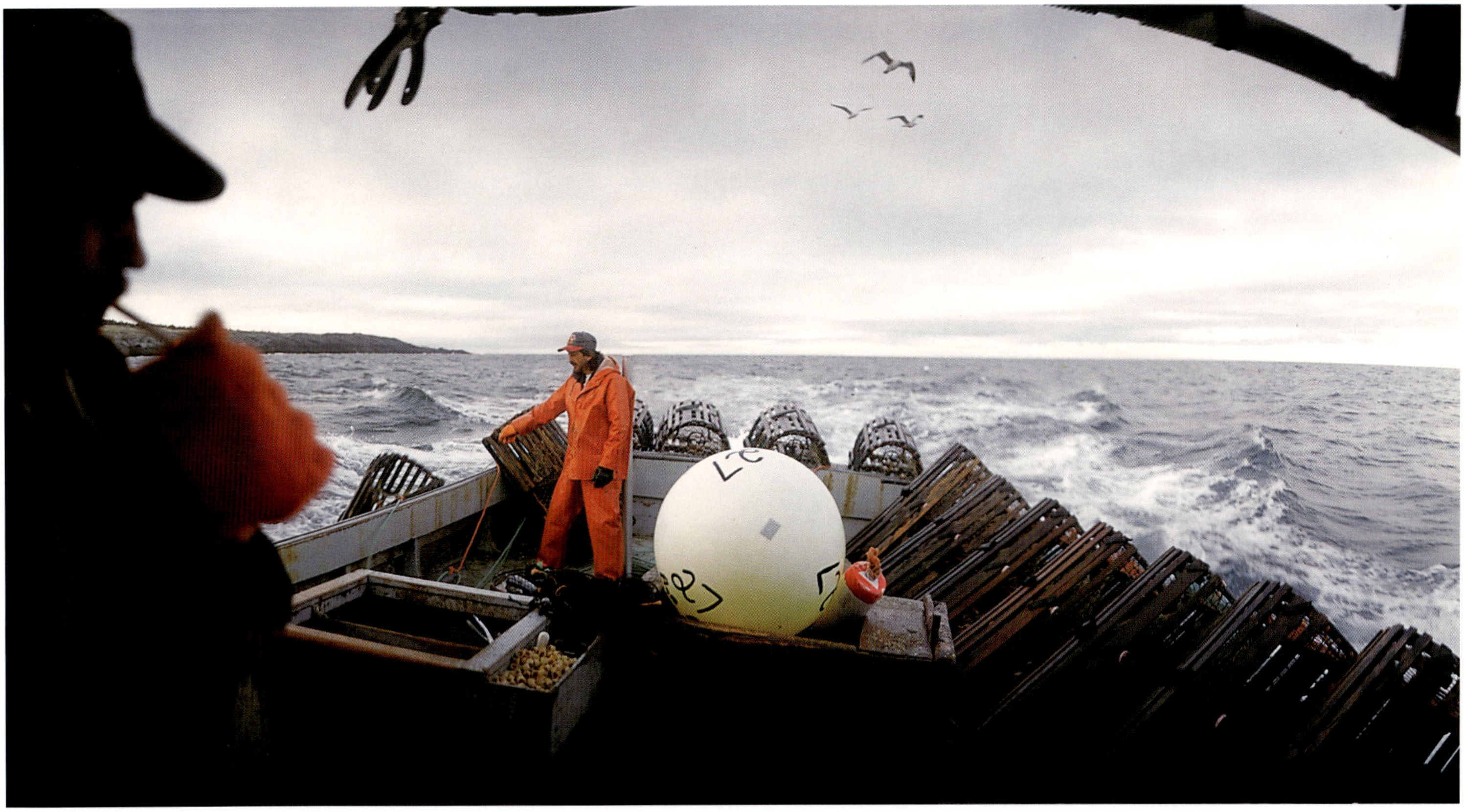

One of Roger's crew lights up while lobster traps are thrown over the side into the pitching sea. Sets of traps are tied to trawl lines, which slide off the boat in rapid succession.

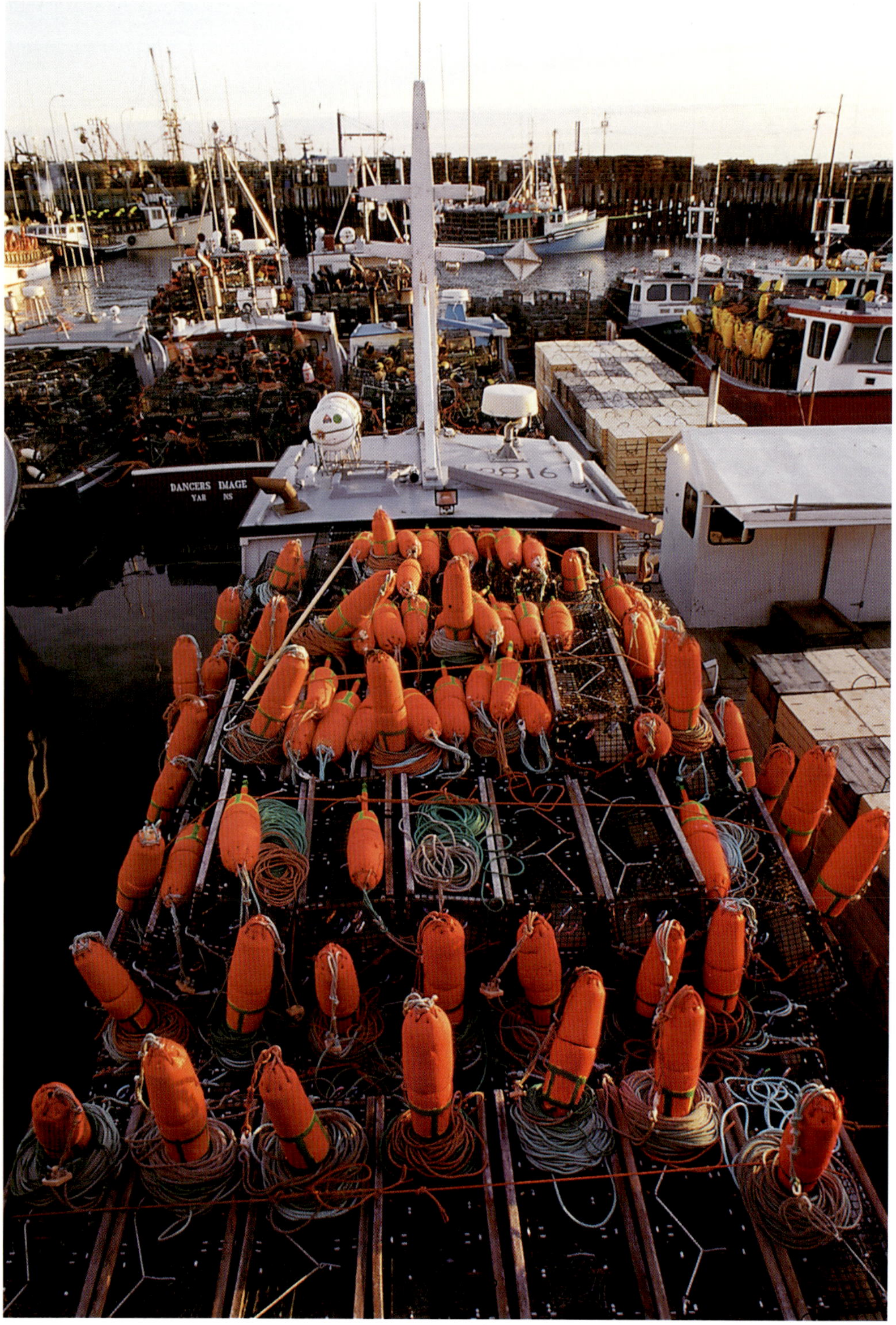

A boat laden with colourful buoys atop lobster traps waits with others for opening day of lobster season.

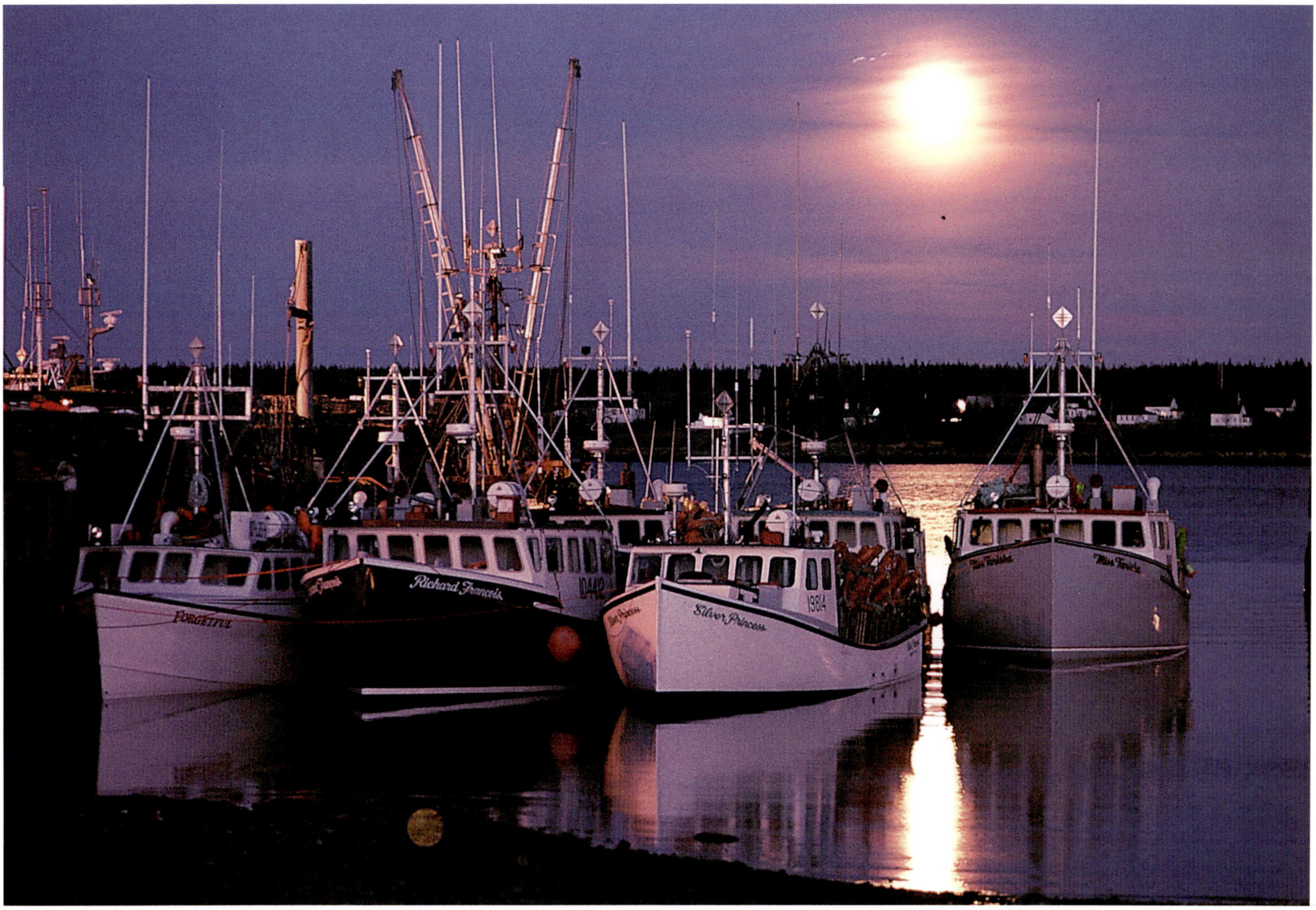

With only a few hours left until dawn and the hectic opening of a new lobster season, the moon shines quietly down on heavily loaded fishing boats in Lower West Pubnico.

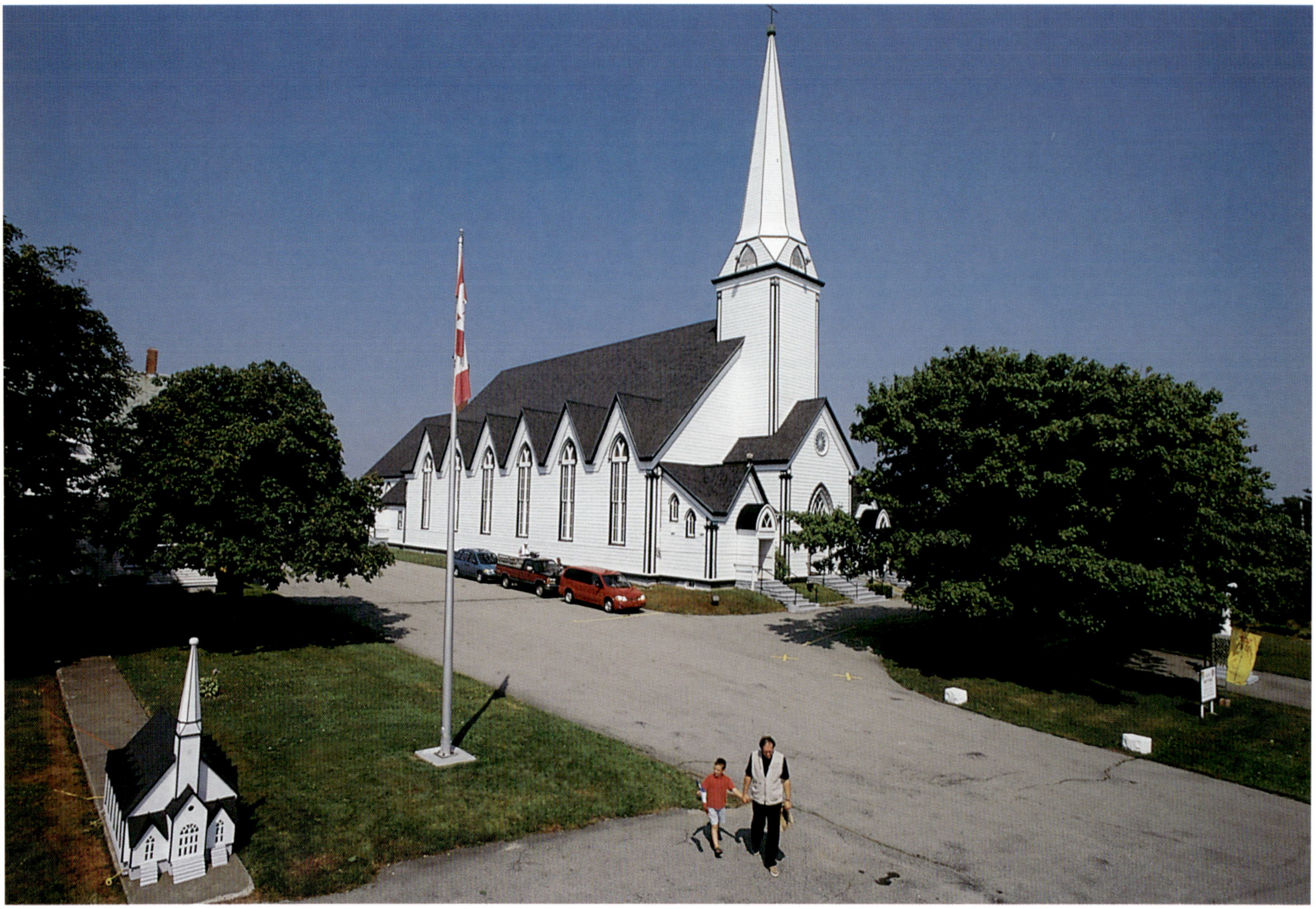

Saint Peter's Church in Middle West Pubnico, built in 1892, is the heart of this Acadian community.

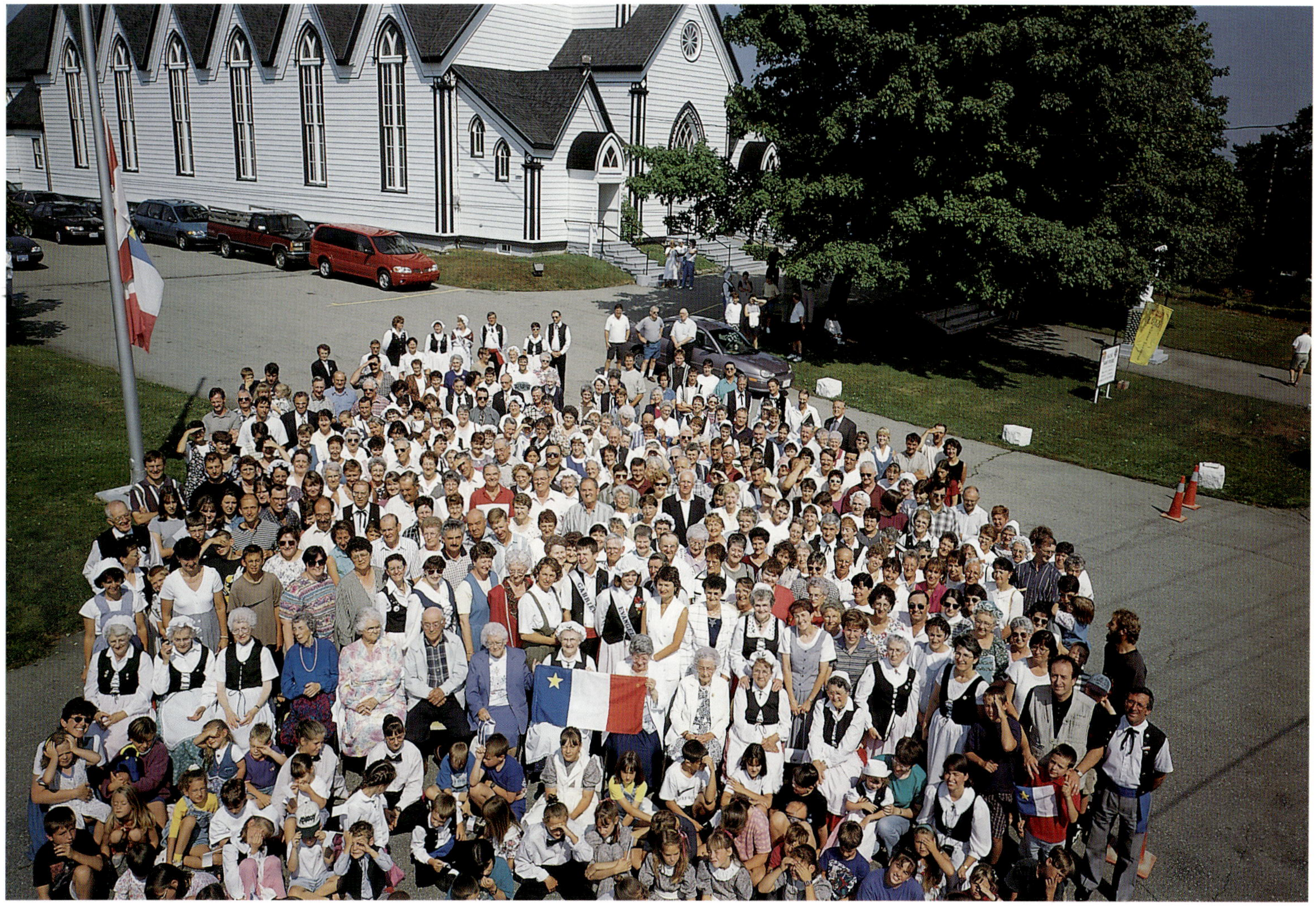

The "d'Entremont Family Portrait." Over 400 descendants of Pubnico founder, Philippe d'Entremont, gather outside St. Peter's Church following Mass during the Acadian Festival in 1997. The d'Entremont family, which includes D'Eons, Muises, and Amiraults, make up roughly 80 per cent of Pubnico's population.

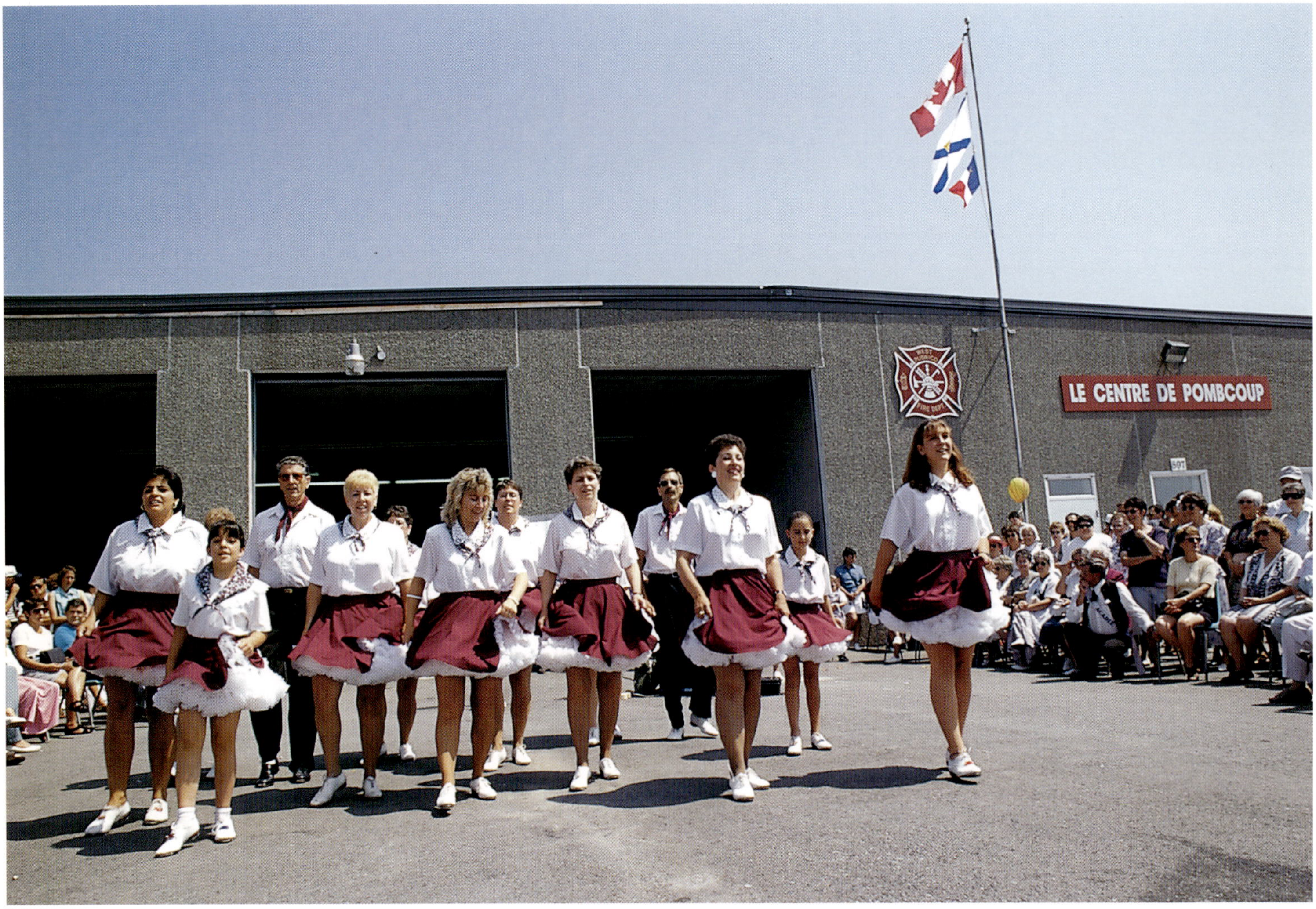

The Acadian Clickers *delight the crowd during the Acadian Festival in West Pubnico.*

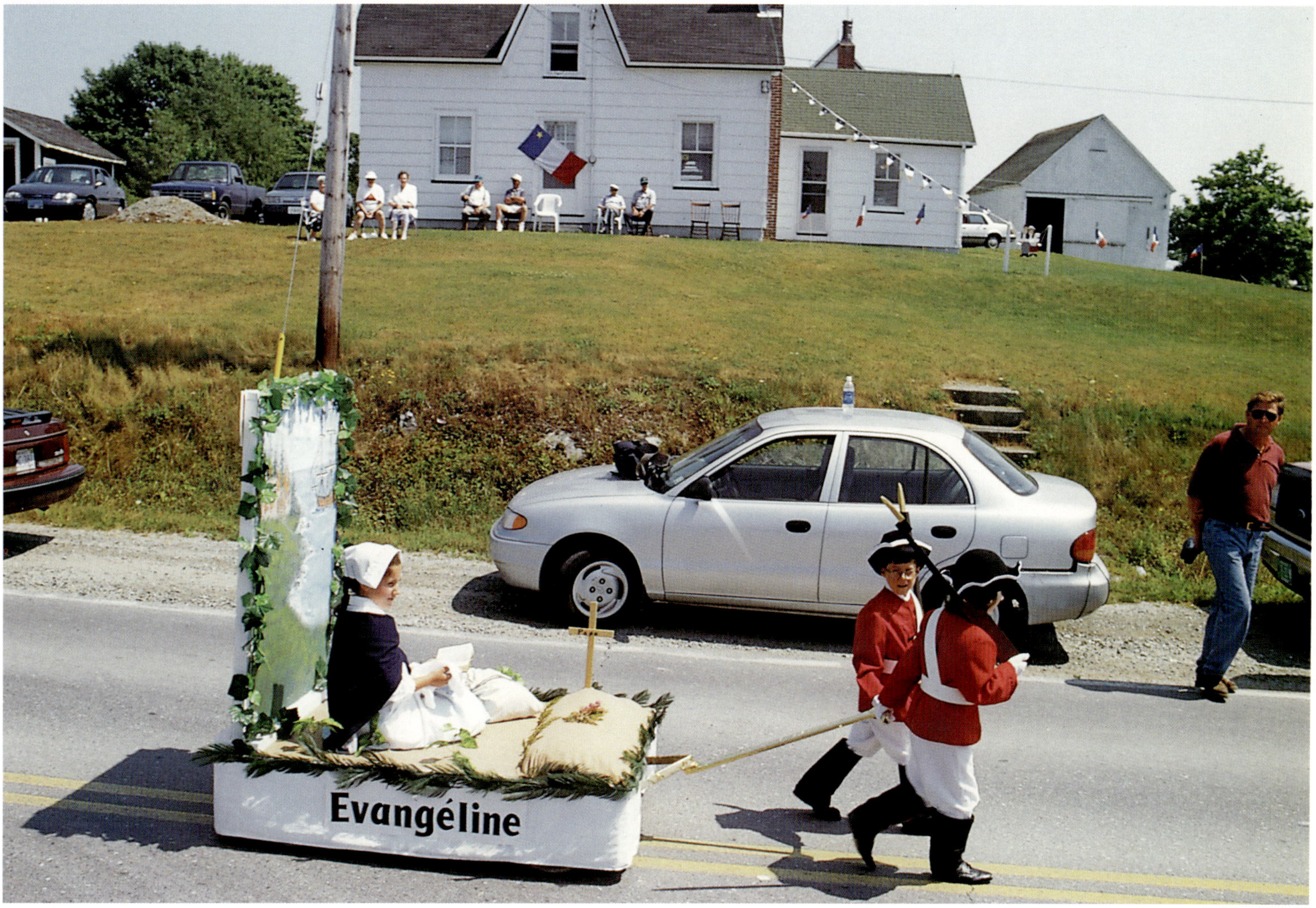

A highlight of the Acadian Festival in West Pubnico is the "people-powered" floats in the Children's Parade. Families spend days creating the elaborate entries.

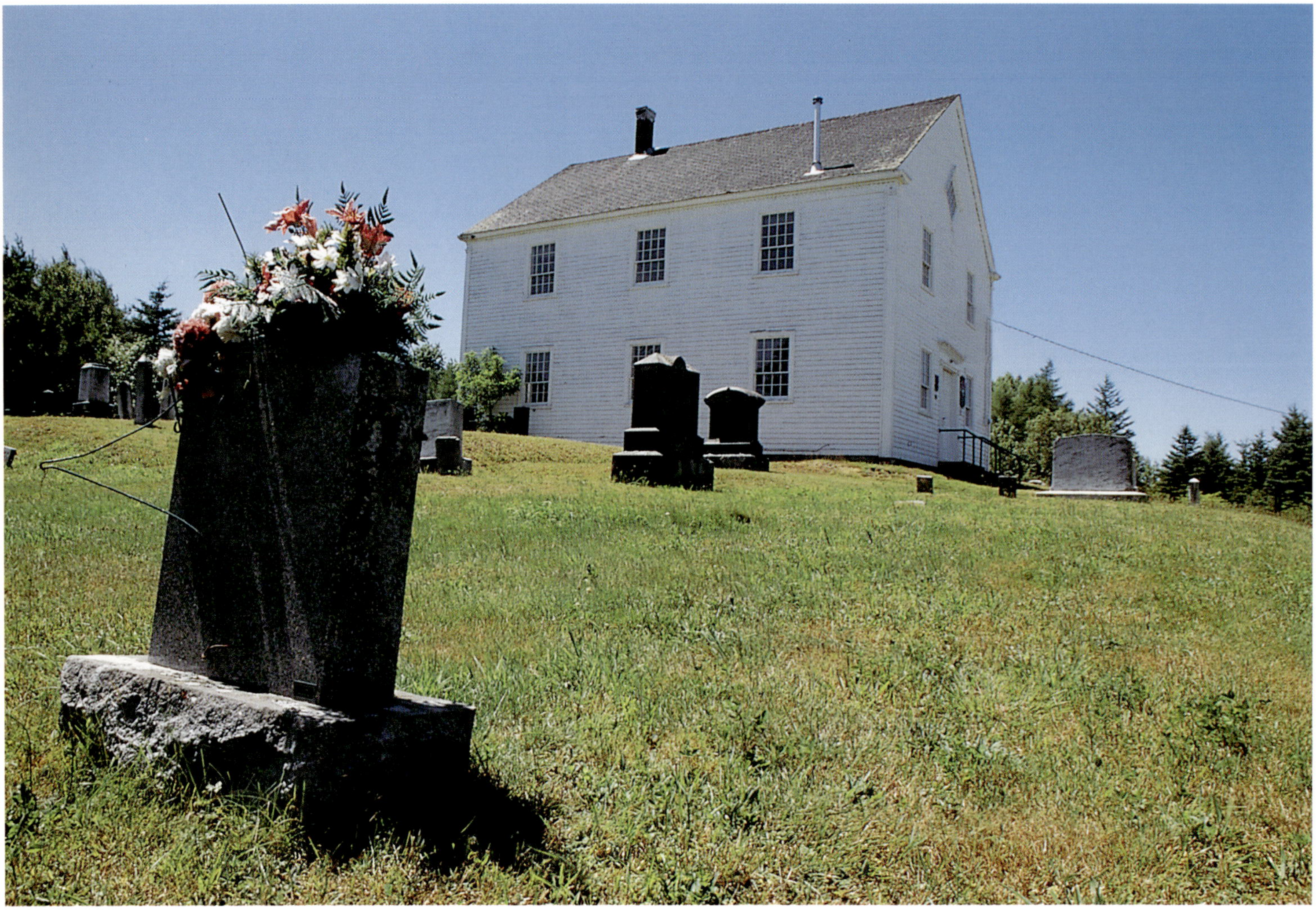

An historic Old Meeting House is found in the quiet countryside of Gavelton.

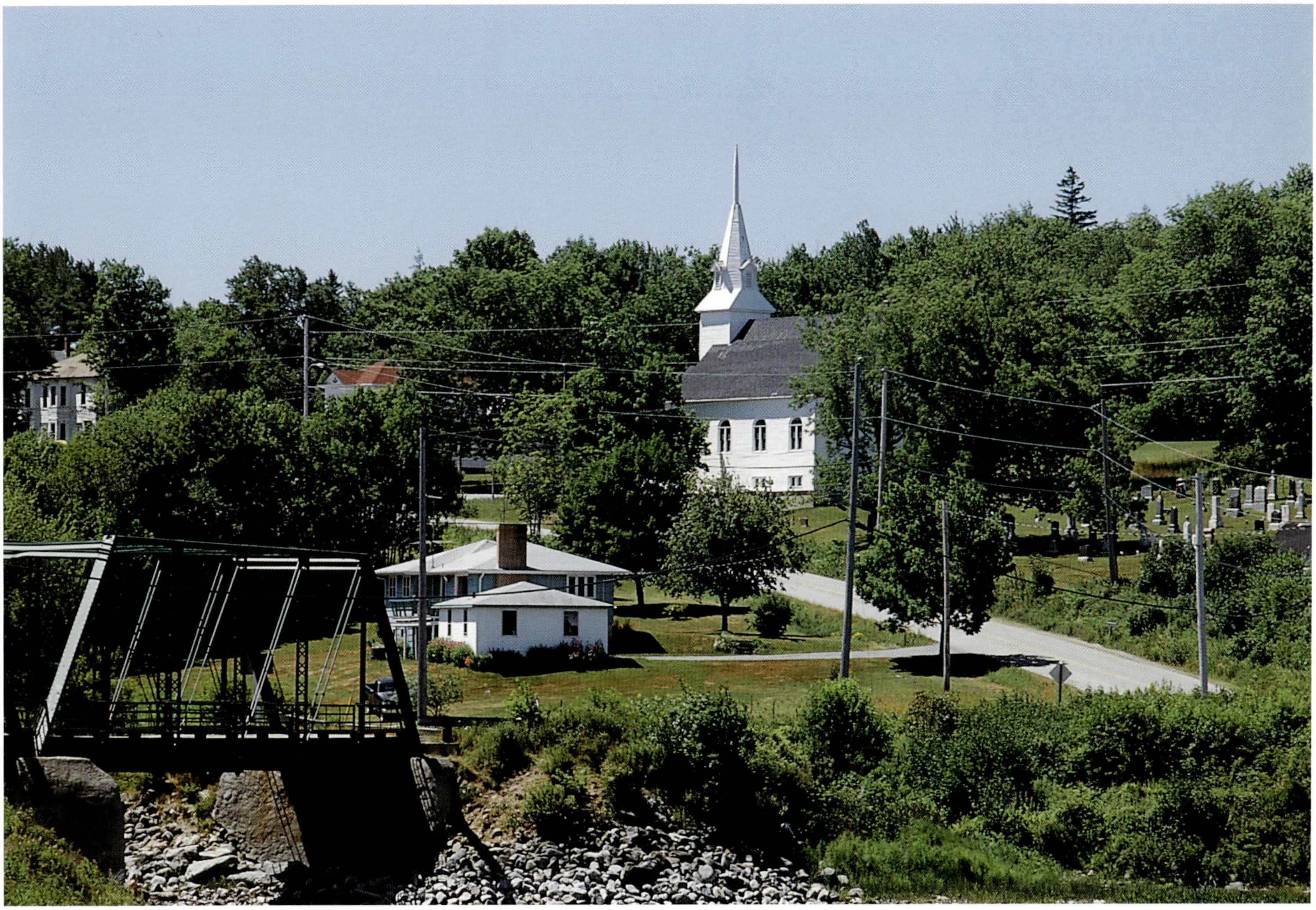

The tiny village of Kemptville with its steel bridge spanning peaceful Travis Lake.

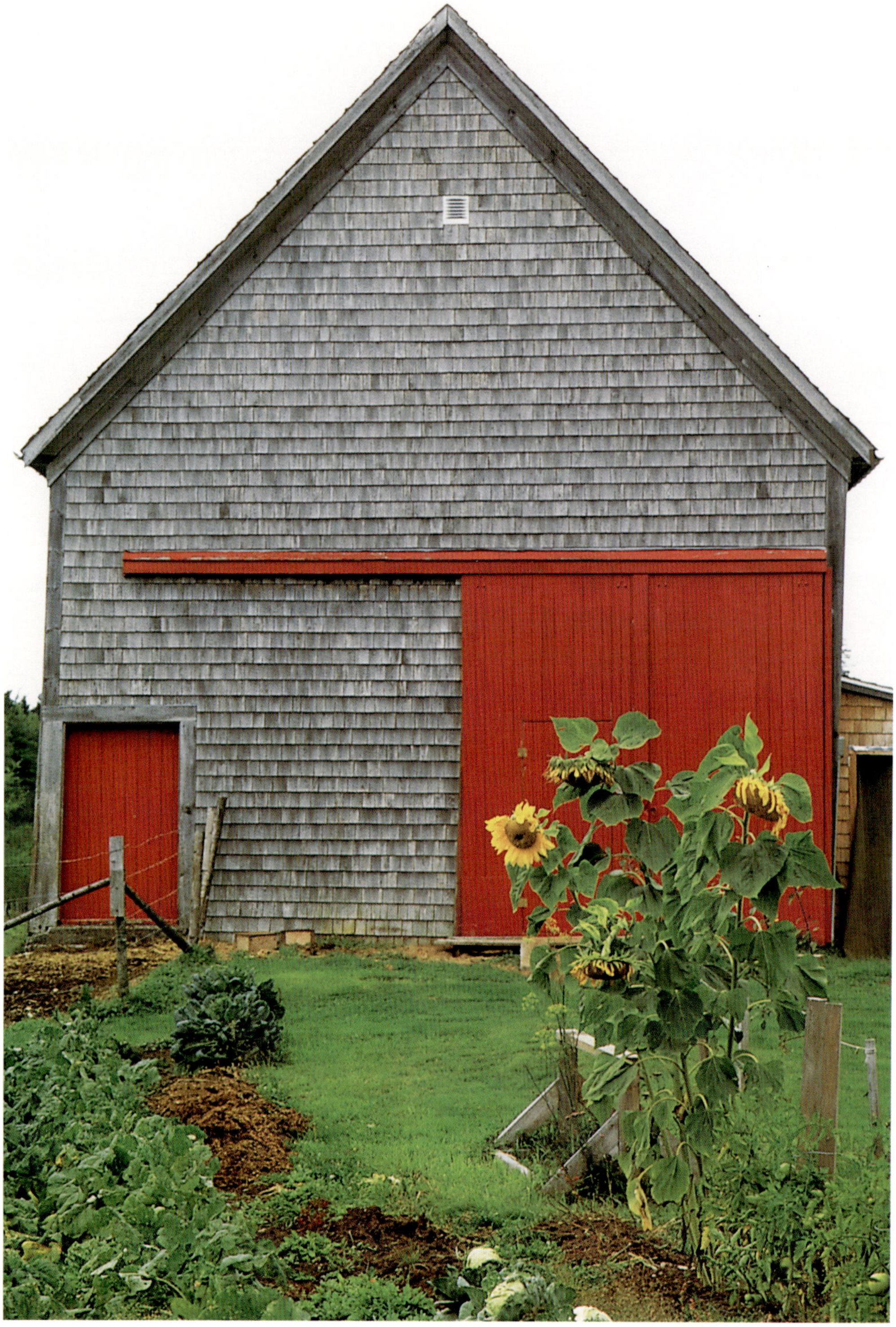

Sunflowers tower above a small farm garden in Norwood.

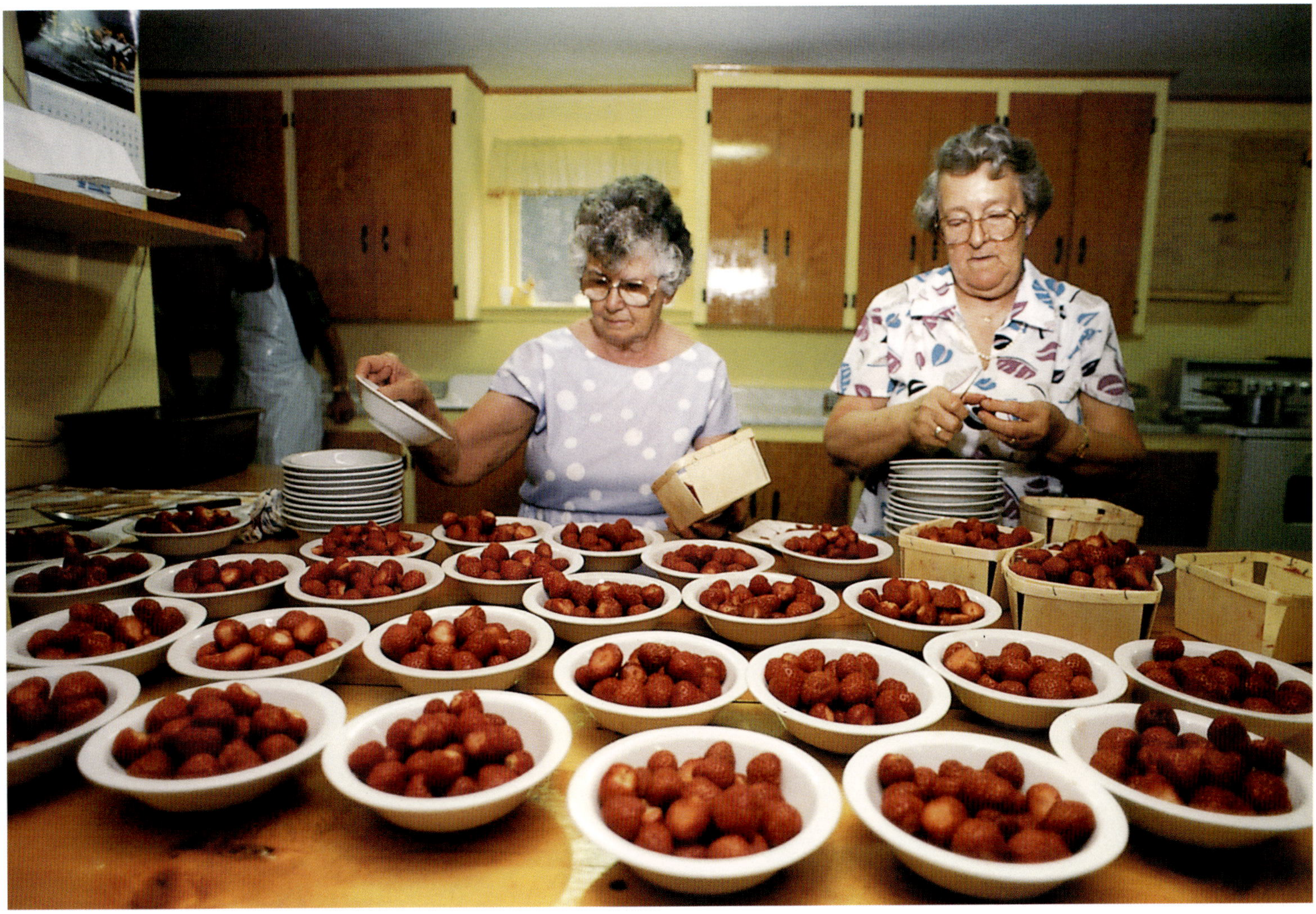

The berries are prepared at the Raynardton Fire Department's annual strawberry supper.

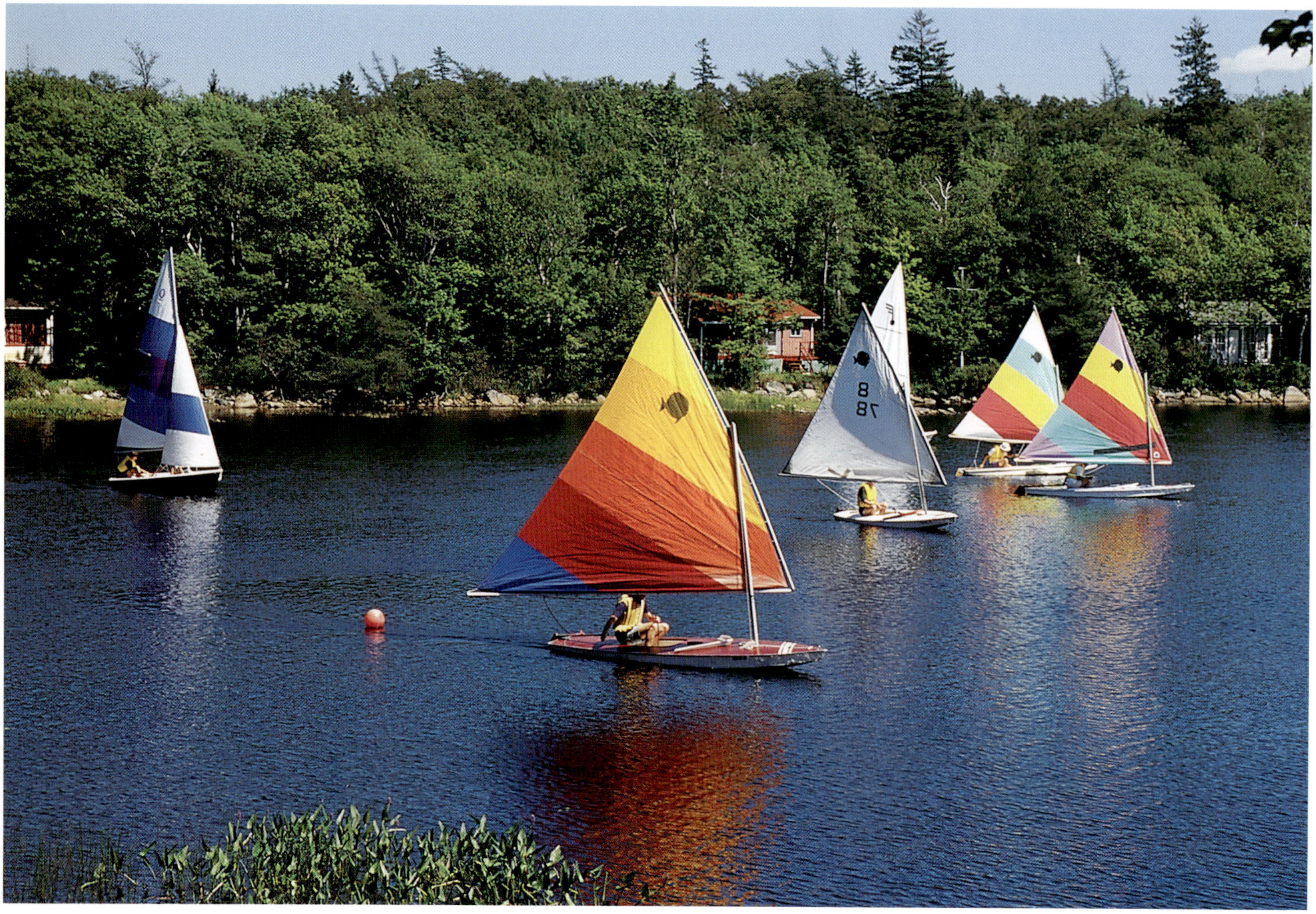

Colourful sailboats are ready to race in the Lake Annis Regatta.

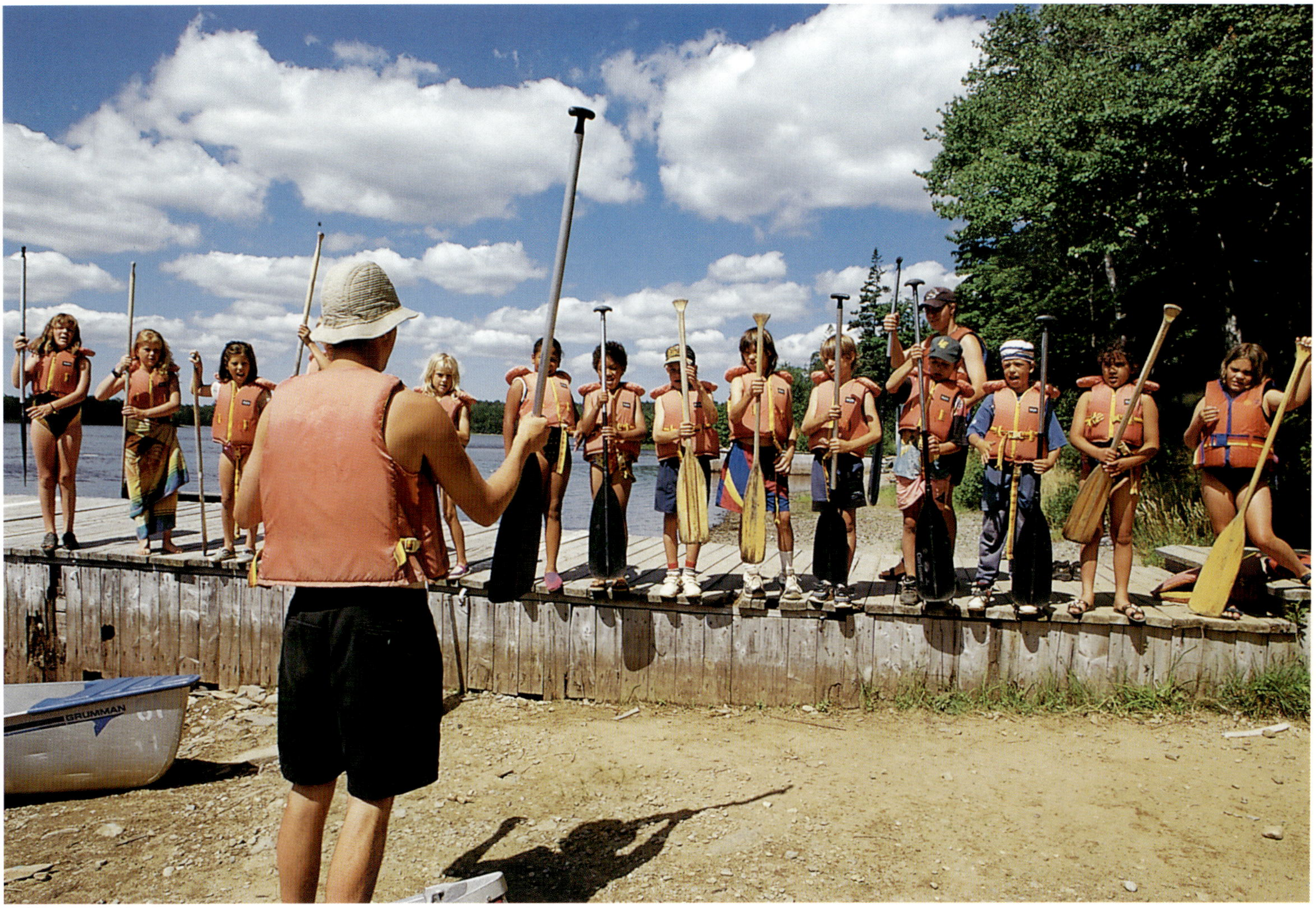

A canoe instructor at YMCA's Camp Wapomeo teaches young campers. Founded in 1921, the camp has seen over 10,000 campers from Yarmouth County and elsewhere in the Maritimes, and from as far away as Europe and Africa.

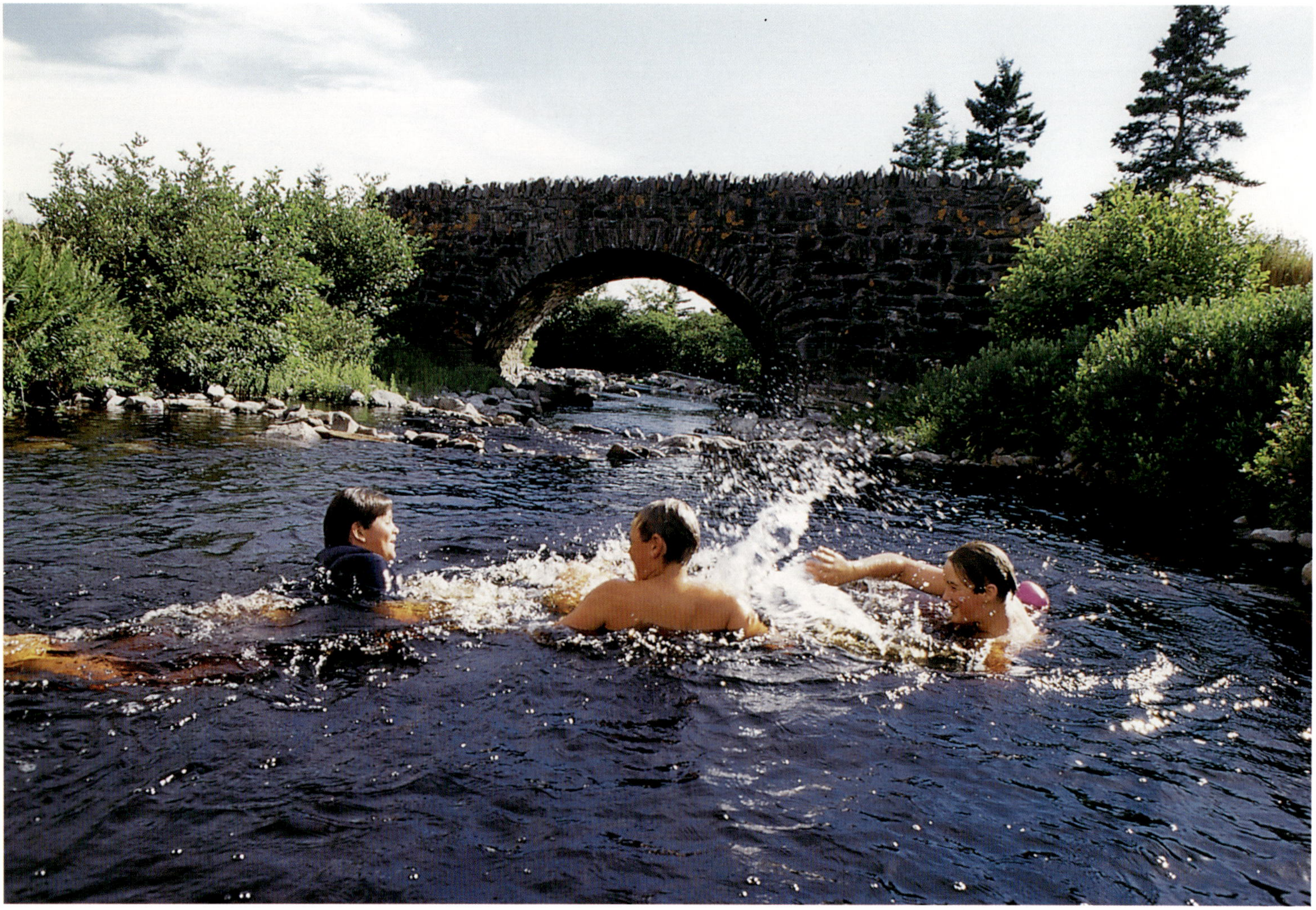

Boys frolic in a favourite East Pubnico swimming hole beneath Hipson Bridge, one of the few remaining stone bridges built in Yarmouth County between 1783 and 1889.

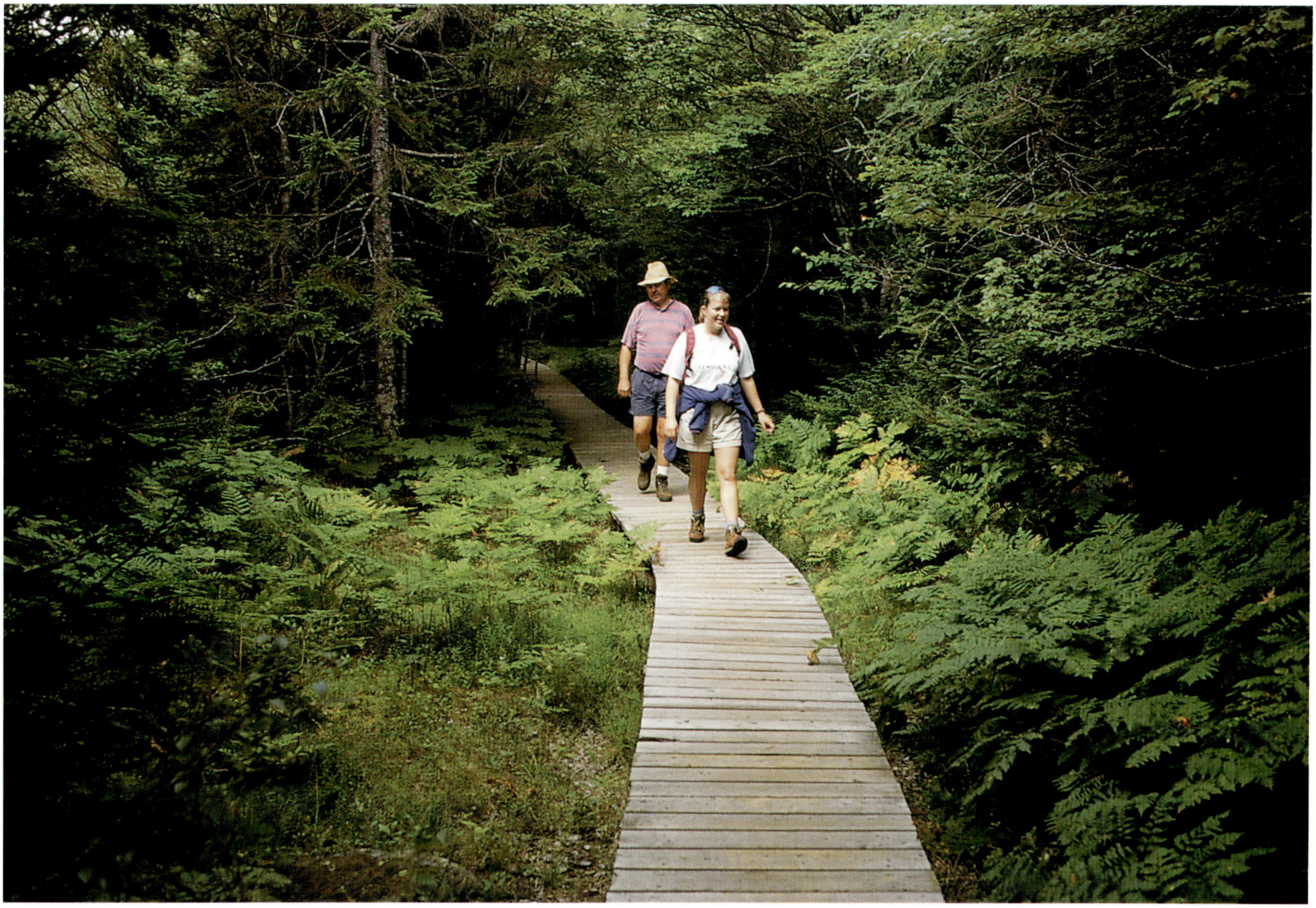

Hikers enjoy the Chebogue Meadows Interpretive Trail, a 4.5-km trail which meanders through woodland, open meadow, and along the head of the Chebogue River.

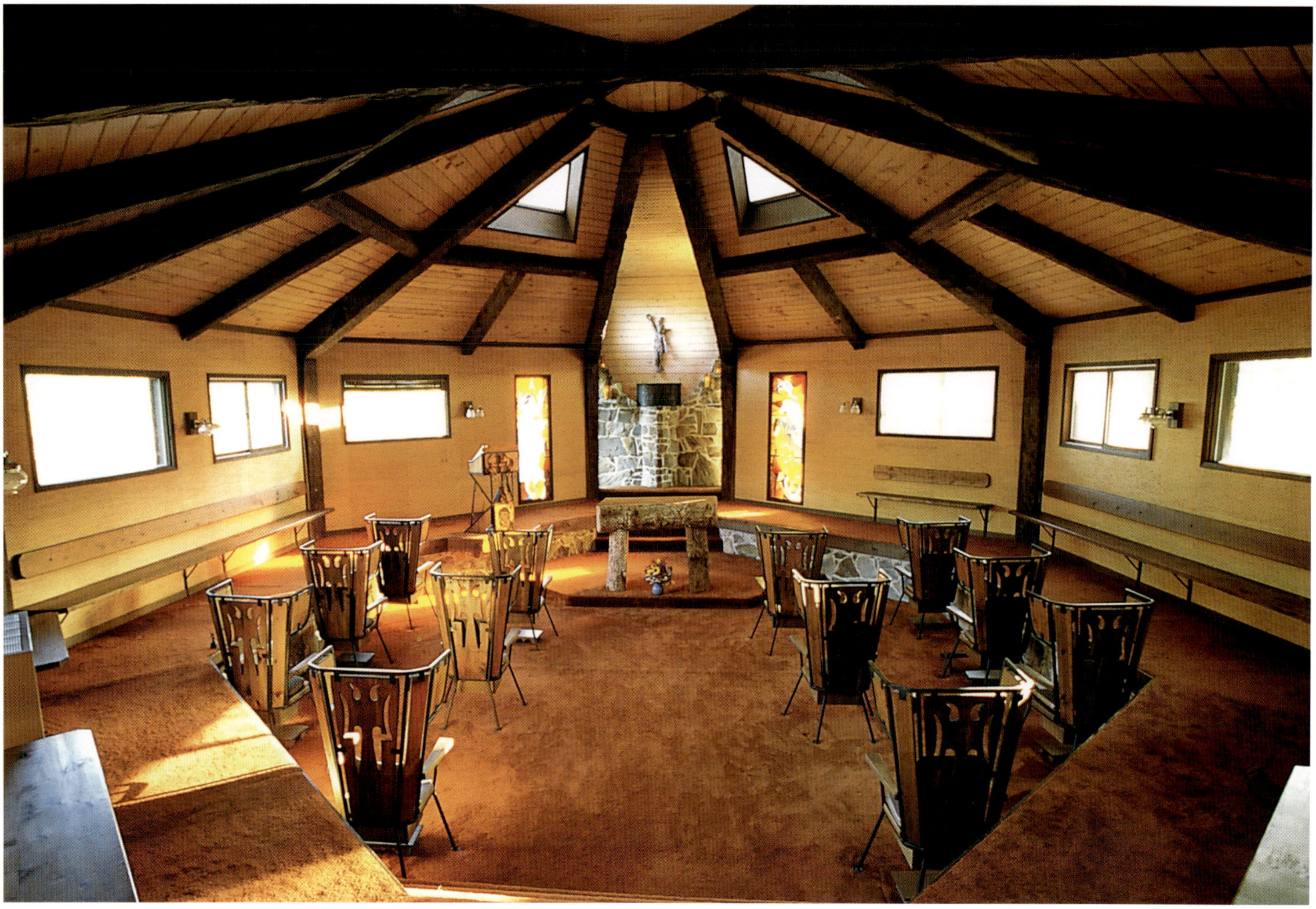

The sun streams into the beautiful hand-hewn chapel of Nova Nada, a monastery located on the former site of a hunting and fishing lodge north of Kemptville. The stately pine and birch forest provides an ideal setting for this silent order.

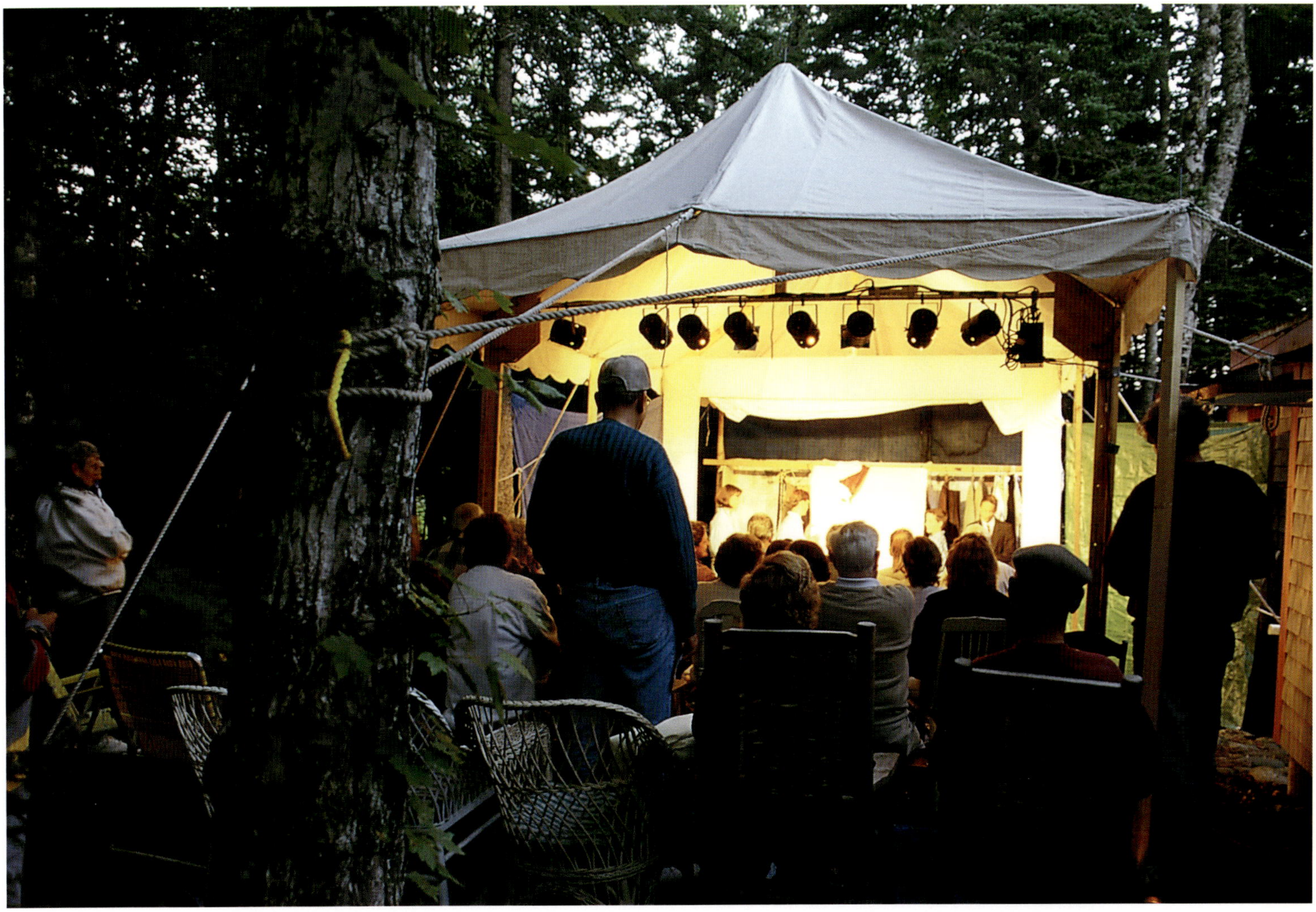

Summertime theatrical pursuits are enjoyed in a woodsy backyard at Lake Annis.

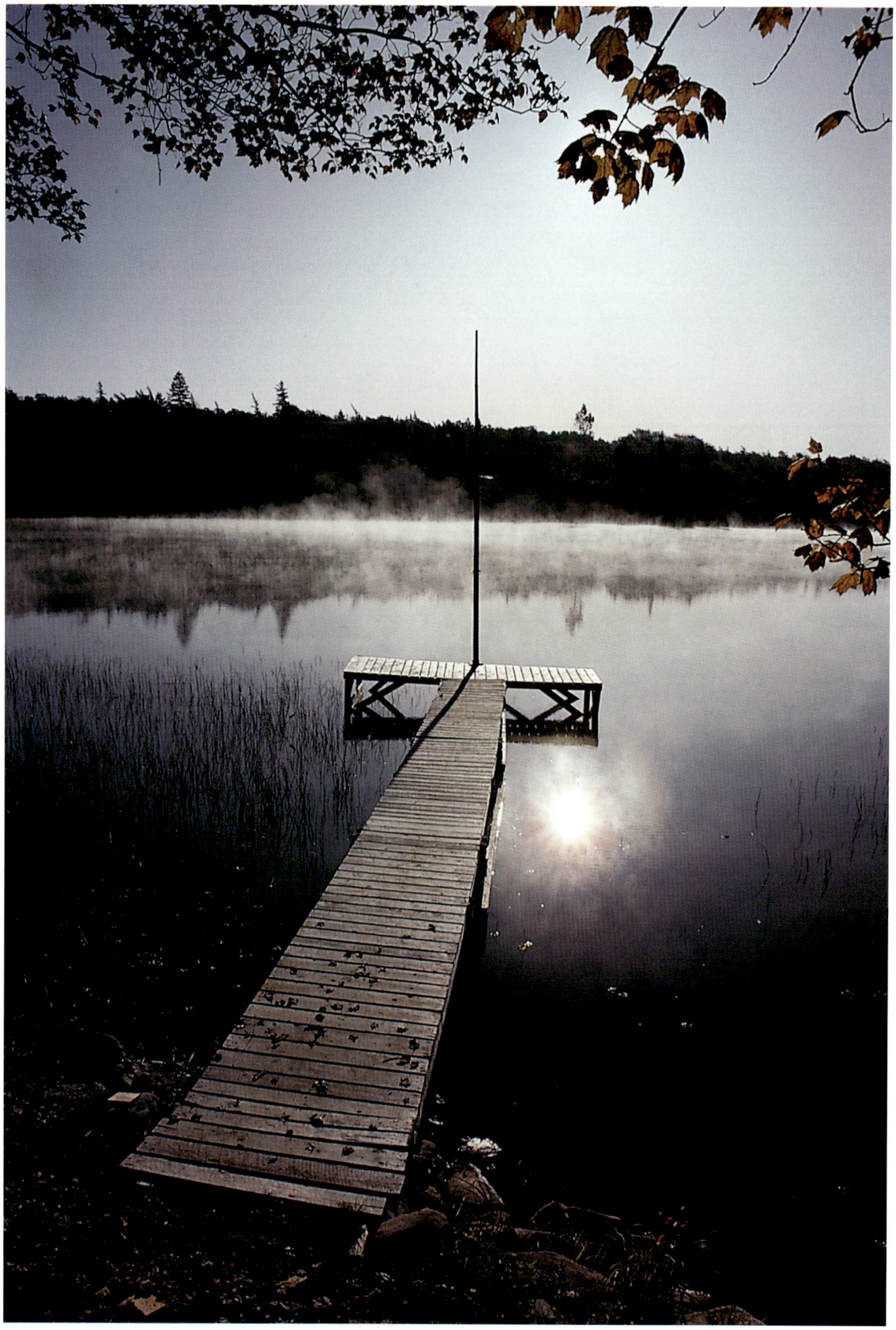

The early morning sun peeks over a rustic dock.

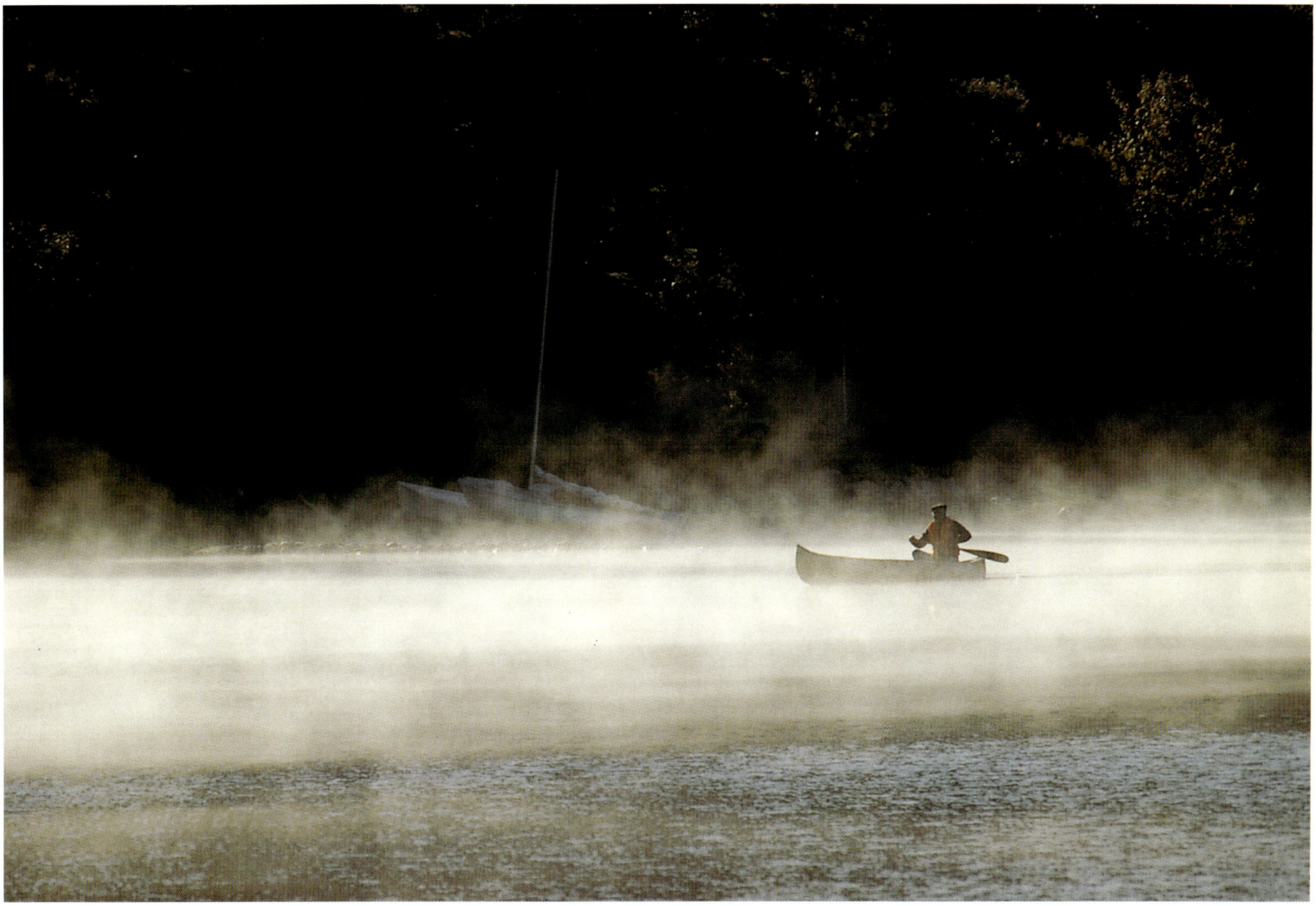

A gentle mist engulfs a canoeist as he glides silently along in the early morning.

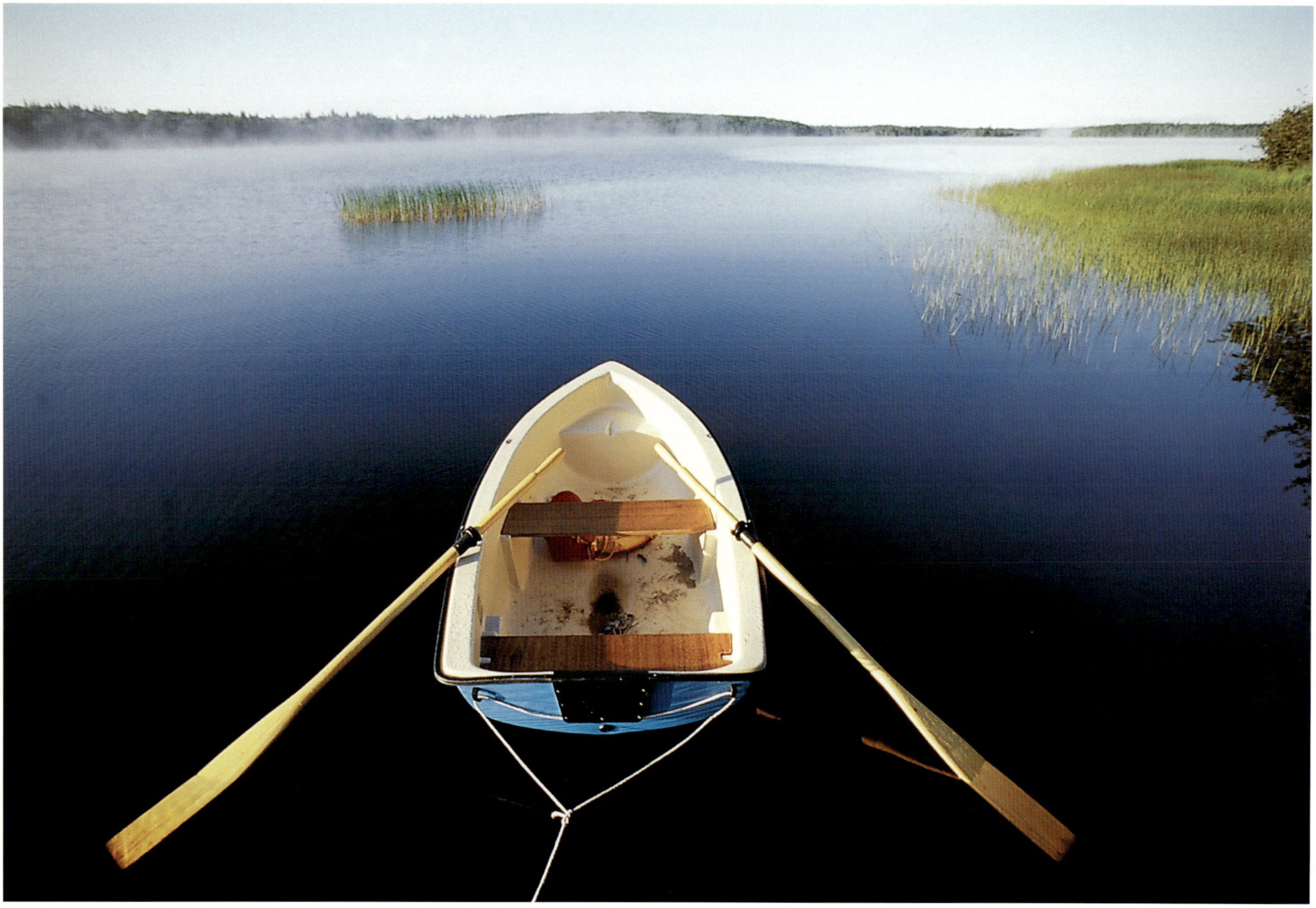

A tiny boat, moored to a lakeside dock, greets a new day in Yarmouth County.